Employment Relations and the Health Service

Employment relations within the health sector have undergone radical reform over recent years. This book is an important new study that examines the responses of managers and workers to these different reforms, at both national and local level.

Bringing together analyses of both employment relations and public sector management, the book focuses on understanding why certain initiatives have been adopted, how managers have responded to them and the consequences of the HR modernisation agenda. Topics covered include:

- HR strategy and structure at the workplace
- employee involvement and union influence
- pay modernisation
- management of work.

Featuring detailed case study research in three NHS trusts, the book illustrates precisely how government policies are implemented in the workplace and in doing so offers a unique insight into the sector's changing work environment. *Employment Relations and the Health Service* is a comprehensive study of this topical area, and will be of interest to students and academics in health service management, human resource management and employment relations.

Stephen Bach is Reader in Employment Relations and Management at King's College, London.

Employment and Work Relations in Context Series

Series Editors

Tony Elger
Centre for Comparative Labour Studies
Department of Sociology
University of Warwick

Peter Fairbrother
Centre for Research on Economic and Social
  Transformation
Cardiff School of Social Sciences
Cardiff University

The aim of the *Employment and Work Relations in Context Series* is to address questions relating to the evolving patterns and politics of work, employment, management and industrial relations. There is a concern to trace out the ways in which wider policy-making, especially by national governments and transnational corporations, impinges upon specific workplaces, occupations, labour markets, localities and religions. This invites attention to developments at an international level, marking out patterns of globalization, state policy and practice in the context of globalization and the impact of these processes on labour. A particular feature of the series is the consideration of forms of worker and citizen organization and mobilization. Thus the studies address major analytical and policy issues through case study and comparative research.

EMPLOYMENT RELATIONS AND THE HEALTH SERVICE

THE MANAGEMENT OF REFORMS

Stephen Bach

Routledge
Taylor & Francis Group

LONDON AND NEW YORK

In Memory of Vernon Stephen Bach, 1925–2000

First published 2004
by Routledge
2 Park Square, Milton Park, Abingdon, Oxfordshire OX14 4RN

Simultaneously published in the USA and Canada
by Routledge
270 Madison Ave, New York, NY 10016

Routledge is an imprint of the Taylor & Francis Group

© 2004 Stephen Bach

Typeset by YHT Ltd., London
Printed and bound in Great Britain by MPG Books Ltd, Bodmin

British Library Cataloguing in Publication Data
A catalogue record for this book is available from the British Library

Library of Congress Cataloging in Publication Data
A catalog record for this book has been requested

ISBN 0-415-36299-7

CONTENTS

List of Tables

PREFACE

This book has a lengthy history, reflecting my long-standing interest in health service employment relations. This involvement stems from my initial employment after graduation as a health service management trainee. I worked in one of the London Regions during the mid–1980s, and this allowed me to witness the implementation of general management during periods spent at hospital, district and regional levels. I subsequently returned to one of the hospitals that I worked at to conduct research on the contracting-out of support services. This was followed by a research post at the Centre for Health Planning and Management at Keele University researching the impact of the Griffiths reforms on a series of workplace issues including hospital closures and waiting list management. During my time at the Warwick University Business School I researched health service employment relations, examining the impact of the internal market reforms on employment relations. Since my move to King's College, I have continued to research health service employment relations, including work on a Department of Health funded research project on establishing an evidence base in human resource management. Over this period I have benefited from discussions that I have had with health service managers, nurse leaders and general management trainees on programmes that I taught at Keele, Warwick and King's. My understanding of health service employment relations has also been developed by my participation in trade union research seminars and staff conferences organized by the BMA, MSF and the RCN.

As Roger Seifert (1992) highlighted a decade ago there are very few accounts of NHS employment relations. This is surprising considering the centrality of NHS employment relations for the reform of the health service and the prominence of the health service within British public policy debates. This should probably have alerted me to some of the difficulties of researching and writing a book about a highly contested and rapidly evolving area of public policy.

This book would not have been completed without the help of many people. I am very grateful to all the directors of human resources and other managers, union representatives and employees, associated with the workplace studies and the national fieldwork. Without their willingness to answer my questions, provide documentation and in some cases comment on draft material, the book would not have been possible. I would like to thank the Leverhulme Trust for enabling me to develop further research on public service unionism as part of the 'Future of Trade Unions in Modern Britain' programme.

I am thankful to my colleagues within the employment relations community at King's College and at Warwick University for their interest in the research and for helping me refine my ideas. I am particularly grateful to my colleague Stephen Deery for his continuous encouragement over the last eighteen months. I also benefited from very helpful discussions with John Humphries, Roger Kline, Richard Darch and Ian Kessler. Richard provided me with helpful comments on the concluding chapter of the book and Ian read many of the chapters, providing numerous suggestions for improvement. Peter Fairbrother gave me invaluable comments on the manuscript of this book that helped to improve the final version.

David Winchester supervised the doctoral research that formed the initial material for some of this book. He was an unfailing source of good advice, was generous with his time, and provided invaluable comments on successive drafts. Caroline Hyde-Price commented on my drafts more often than I had a right to expect and helped me retain my enthusiasm for the project. Richard and Alexandra provided, in their different ways, constant support, diversion and disruption throughout the researching and writing of this book.

As I was starting to write this book my father died. He had an enormous intellectual curiosity about issues and people that has provided me with an example that I have tried to emulate in my own working life and research activities. He always took a great interest in my work and encouraged me to pursue an academic career. This book is dedicated to his memory.

King's College
October 2002

ABBREVIATIONS

ACAS	Advisory, Conciliation and Arbitration Service
BMA	British Medical Association
CHI	Commission for Health Improvement
COHSE	Confederation of Health Service Employees
CPHVA	Community Practitioners' and Health Visitors' Association
CSU	clinical service unit
CSW	clinical support worker
DHA	district health authority
DoH	Department of Health
DPM	divisional personnel manager
ECG	electro-cardiogram
EFL	external financing limit
GDP	gross domestic product
GM	general manager
GMB	General and Municipal Boilermakers' Union
GP	general practitioner
HCA	health care assistant
HMO	health maintenance organisation
HR	human resources
HRM	human resource management
HSW	hotel support worker
IPP	Investors in People
IWP	Improving Working Lives
JCC	joint consultative committee
JCNC	joint consultative and negotiating committee
JCSC	joint consultative staff committee
JNC	joint negotiating committee
KSF	Knowledge and Skills Framework
MSF	Manufacturing, Science, Finance Union
NAHA	National Association of Health Authorities
NAHAT	National Association of Health Authorities and Trusts
NALGO	National and Local Government Officers' Association
NBPI	National Board for Prices and Incomes

NHS	National Health Service
NHSE	National Health Service Executive
NHSME	National Health Service Management Executive
NICE	National Institute for Clinical Excellence
NISCM	Nursing Information System for Change Management
NPM	new public management
NSF	National Service Framework
NUPE	National Union of Public Employees
NVQ	National Vocational Qualification
OECD	Organisation for Economic Cooperation and Development
PAMs	professions allied to medicine
PCG	Primary Care Group
PCT	primary care trust
PFC	patient focused care
PFI	Private Finance Initiative
RAWP	resource allocation working party
RCN	Royal College of Nursing
SaFF	Service and Financial Framework
SHRINE	Strategic Human Resources Intelligence Network
SLA	service level agreement
TERF	Trust Employee Relations Forum
TGWU	Transport and General Workers' Union
TUC	Trades Union Congress
TUPE	Transfer of Undertakings Protection of Employment
UKCC	United Kingdom Central Council for Nursing, Midwifery and Health Visiting
WTE	whole time equivalent

1 INTRODUCTION

In the last two decades there has been a great deal of interest in how the management of employees has changed. Traditional institutions of employment relations have been eroded with reductions in trade union membership and declining coverage of collective bargaining. Management has been in the driving seat with greater scope unilaterally to decide employment relations matters (see Millward *et al.* 2000). Other commentators have highlighted a process of work intensification and more direct scrutiny of the work of professions (Burchell *et al.* 2002; Dent and Whitehead 2002). In the public sector, traditional institutions of employment relations remain intact, nevertheless, analysis of the public sector has been dominated by debate about the extent of change in organizational structures, management practices and the decline of the model employer tradition (Carter and Fairbrother 1999; Corby 2000; Winchester and Bach 1999). These trends indicate a variety of changes in employment relations, raising questions about the type of organizational change being introduced, the process used to implement employment relations initiatives and who the dominant actors are in shaping the reform agenda.

Under successive Conservative and Labour governments, the restructuring of the organization and management of public services moved centre stage. In the health service, the impact on employment relations of the market-style reforms of Conservative governments and the modernization agenda of the Labour government has been a source of controversy. Conservative government ministers suggested that their reforms were leading to higher performance standards; managers had acquired the autonomy and influence to establish their own organizational employment practices, without hindrance from trade unions or interventionist governments. Labour government ministers have emphasized the centrality of employment relations issues to their modernization agenda; developing a human resources (HR) strategy

1

for the health service, incorporating HR targets into the National Health Service (NHS) performance management framework, and embarking on a fundamental reform of the system of pay determination.

The scope and significance of these changes have been disputed. During 1979–97 many studies emphasized the radical nature of health service reform and suggested transformation was under way in organizational structures and employment practices (Burchill and Casey 1996: 63; Ferlie *et al.* 1996: 236). Nonetheless, there were plenty of dissenting voices that were struck by the limited impact of the internal market (Le Grand, Mays and Dixon 1998: 129; West 1997: 145). By 2002, neo-liberal commentators had revised their assumption about the radical nature of Conservative reforms and stressed the problems of the 'triple nationalization' of the NHS in terms of state owned provision, state defined demand (i.e. cash limits) and state defined resource allocation (i.e. no patient choice) (Blackwell and Kruger 2002: 5; Lea 2002: 42–3). These criticisms were almost identical to the Prime Minister's critique of monolithic, state-managed public services (Blair 2002). What is clear is that continuing debate about the direction and pace of health service restructuring has prompted unprecedented interest in health service employment relations.

This chapter starts by outlining the overall aims of the book and goes on to identify its research focus. The central premise of this study is that workplace behaviour at trust level reflects the interaction of national policy developments and local decision-making shaped by the idiosyncrasies of the political economy of the health service. This research approach is developed in relation to management strategy and structure, the management of employment relations, and pay determination and work organization. The research methods and forms of data collection are then outlined before the structure of the book is explained.

Purpose of the study

The aim of this book is to examine the responses of managers and workers to the reform of employment relations in the health service. Workplace change in the acute hospital sector is examined in the context of the historical evolution of the NHS and recent national policy developments that underpin workplace reform. It is based mainly on analysis of developments since 1991, allowing comparisons to be drawn between Conservative and Labour government periods in office. The focus on the acute sector reflects the continuing dominance of acute hospitals within the NHS in terms of staff employed, health service expenditure and policy priorities (e.g. staff shortages and waiting times). The approach of this study can be outlined in relation to three more specific objectives of the book. First, it provides a detailed up-to-date analysis of developments in employment relations practice, pay bargaining reform and work reorganization within the acute hospital sector. The focus is on understanding why initiatives have been adopted within individual NHS trusts, and how managers have introduced politically sensitive reforms to employment practices, and on assessing the views of the main participants to these attempts to reconstitute NHS employment practices.

Linked to this objective, a central component of the book is detailed case study research, in three NHS trusts, which examines employment relations policy, pay bargaining reform and work reorganization. An important consideration in pursuing this research agenda has been the limited amount of detailed empirical work focused on alterations in NHS employment practices and the practical outcomes of these policies. Most published research has concentrated on traditional institutional mechanisms of collective bargaining reform and trade union organization, to the exclusion of broader issues of human resource management policy (Lloyd 1997; Thornley 1998). These issues include work organization and labour utilization policies, systems of performance management and policies on employee involvement and communications. In addition, although the type of HR policies adopted and the role of personnel specialists in implementing this agenda has been explored (Procter and Currie 1999; Truss *et al.* 2002), these studies concentrate on formal management policies and provide little insight into worker responses and the process that is adopted to bring about workplace change. The concern of this research has been to understand how government policies are mediated at the workplace by the responses of managers, workers and trade unions. This is crucial for understanding workplace change.

The second objective of the book is to advance policy analysis on employment relations in the NHS, especially in terms of pay determination and work organization. Employment relations as a field has a long tradition of policy orientated research, and many research questions are framed within wider policy debates. This is especially relevant for a public service like the health service because the government as employer has a direct impact on the employment policies implemented within the workplace. The most pressing research questions are therefore shaped by government policy; for example, the impact of the internal market or the consequences of the performance targets established for NHS trusts on management and worker behaviour. Kelly (1998: 17–18) has expressed concern that policy orientated research in industrial relations tends to neglect theoretical concerns and is tailored to managerial concerns about whether a policy is effective. The implication that such research is invariably managerialist is dismissed by Edwards (2001: 4). He suggests that examining the contradictions of management policy, such as the handling of absenteeism, can generate important insights into workplace behaviour.

The third objective of the book is to develop an integrated understanding of employment practice change in the NHS and thus straddle the boundaries of institutional employment relations, human resource management and public administration. These areas of study share many characteristics; they are rooted in multi-disciplinary analysis and often focus on policy orientated research. The field of employment relations (or industrial relations as it has traditionally been termed), has drawn attention to the influences beyond the workplace that shape the employment relationship. The existence of conflict and co-operation, and an asymmetry of power between workers and managers, has ensured a continuing concern with the manner in which workers have defined their interests collectively within trade unions (Kelly 1998). These considerations remain pertinent to an understanding of health service employment relations. The workforce remains highly unionized, and it will be argued that influences beyond the workplace have a strong influence on health service employment relations.

Human resource management (HRM) is less amenable to definition, and the term HRM is often used interchangeably with employment relations (see Bach and Sisson 2000; Edwards 2001). For the purpose of this book HRM is defined in a generic sense as an approach to employment management that uses a variety of policies and practices related to the management of people, rather than in a narrow sense as a particular high commitment style of managing people. It differs from employment relations, however, in its dominant interest in management practice. In particular it is associated with a tight coupling between human resources and business policy with an integrated set of personnel policies that support the business strategy of the organization (see Bach and Sisson 2000; Storey 2001). HRM is also usually focused on the workplace and the responses of individual employees to management policies. For the purposes of this study HRM draws attention to the extent that health service employees are being managed on a more individual basis; the degree to which employment management is being led by HR specialists; the influence that they command within NHS trusts; and in what ways employment management policies and practices support trust managers' 'business' strategy.

Public administration has roots in political science, constitutional law and administrative science (Ranson and Stewart 1994: 32). This reflects long-standing concerns with the efficient administration of public services as prescribed by legislation and an emphasis on the distinctive character of public administration arising from the implementation of political choices in an equitable and accountable manner. Public administration has therefore been suspicious of drawing a firm line between management and politics. Traditional public administration, however, has been challenged by an emphasis on public management, located within business schools (Gray and Jenkins 1995: 82). The introduction of general management, the internal market reforms and public–private partnerships forms part of a broader attempt to replicate private sector 'best practice' and indicate the influence of the so-called *new public management.* This study draws on insights from public administration and public management to examine the ways that the NHS 'management revolution' has enabled managers to break free from central political control and to assess the implications for professional staff.

Research focus

Many of the characteristics of state employment that have traditionally differentiated it from the private sector derived from the unique role of the state as employer. These relate to the diverse functions of the state, distinctive forms of accountability that are embedded within bureaucratic forms of organization and the occupationally diverse character of the workforce (Edwards 1986: 146–54; Fredman and Morris 1989). It also includes the 'political contingency' (Ferner 1988) – the need for governments to be sensitive to their electoral constituency – and these concerns are to the fore in the government's role as an employer.

Fredman and Morris (1989) suggest that these unique features of state employment resulted in the state being a distinctive employer that tried to set an example to the private sector. Elsewhere Morris (2000: 169) argues:

> Until 1979 the implementation of the 'good employer' philosophy in Britain meant job security; the encouragement of trade unionism and collective bargaining; pay determined by reference to appropriate private sector comparators; and, latterly, the promotion of equal opportunities.

Fredman and Morris (1989) argue that the election of the Conservative government in 1979 led to a decline in the model employer tradition because its commitment to market-based principles undermined collective organization and overturned the basis of the model employer tradition. Consequently the dominant strand of debate has focused on the extent to which public sector employment relations have been transformed since 1979. Corby (2000) suggests that the most radical employment relations changes have occurred in the civil service, for instance on pay determination, while Morgan and Allington (2002) highlight an increase in job restructuring (i.e. a two-tier workforce), an assault on collectivism and poor pay outcomes.

Fredman and Morris's arguments need to be extended in two ways. First, a recognition that state employment relations are distinctive needs to be decoupled from the assumption that the state has been a 'model employer'. In the UK, examination of the historical legacy has indicated that the model employer tradition developed in a partial and uneven manner (Bach 1999a; Carter and Fairbrother 1999). In particular, the state was a model employer if judged in procedural terms such as support for trade union recognition and collective bargaining, an emphasis on fair procedures and greater concern for issues of equal employment policies, but much less so in terms of substantive outcomes (Thornley 1995). This historical legacy continues to exercise an important influence over state policy, with both Conservative and Labour governments seeking to portray themselves as model employers. The Labour government has reiterated that the first pillar of effective human resource management is to make the NHS a model employer:

> The model employer or '3 star' employer embraces a composite of best policies, practices and facilities. The *HR in the NHS Plan* paints a picture of the model employer and through a series of accredited phases, assists each NHS organisation to progress towards the ideal. (Department of Health 2002a: 4)

It is therefore important to investigate how far the state continues to emphasize an appeal to the procedural aspects of the model employer tradition in the management of health service staff and how these policies are interpreted by managers and workers at workplace level.

Second, the policies associated with the state as model employer idea were grounded in an analysis of civil service employment, but major differences in employment relations exist between central government, local government and the health service (Bach and Winchester 2003). These variations arise from differences in financing arrangements; forms of political accountability and political sensitivity; and the character of the workforce and their representative organizations. Consequently the distinctive features of public sector employment provide a necessary starting point for analysis of employment relations, but require further development. The central argument of this study is that the most effective understanding of health service employment relations is derived from an analysis of the distinctive characteristics of the NHS that arise from its financing, centralized control and the professional character of the workforce. This analytical framework is developed in Chapter 2 and will inform a series of research questions that are set out below.

Management strategy and structure

Successive Conservative and Labour governments have tried to reform management practice in the health service to enhance efficiency and improve labour utilization. This process was reinforced by the Griffiths reforms, the internal market and the performance framework adopted by the Labour government, focusing attention on the strategies and organizational structures adopted by senior managers. Frequently, analytical frameworks developed in the private sector have been applied to the public sector. The role of increased competitive pressures, especially globalization, has been viewed as a catalyst for change in employment practices in the private sector, and the extent to which managers can exercise a degree of strategic choice in shaping their employment policies has been a dominant issue (Kochan *et al.* 1994; Katz and Darbishire 2000).

Kessler and Purcell (1996) have extended this analysis to the public sector. They argue that it is necessary to assess whether the research on the link between organizational structure, management strategy and employment practices which developed in the private sector is relevant to the experience of the public sector. The starting point for this approach has been the establishment of the multi-divisional organizational structure within the public sector, including the NHS (Bach 1995). The experience of the private sector indicates that the development of multi-divisional organizational structures influences a range of employment decisions, particularly the role of the personnel function, the degree of decentralized collective bargaining and the stance towards trade unions (Purcell and Ahlstrand 1994; Marginson *et al.* 1995).

Their analytical framework for the public sector retains the key elements of the strategic choice model. It focuses on the relationship between upstream and downstream decisions within employer units (i.e. NHS trusts). It suggests that first order decisions on the mission and scope of activities undertaken by the organization influence second order decisions on organizational structure and control. In turn these decisions define the parameters for the discretion exercised by managers on third order decisions which comprise employment choices over whether to focus on individualism or collectivism, cost minimization or employee development, upskilling or deskilling, etc. The application of this framework, however, revealed that a range of socio-economic, legal and political factors constrained these choices in the public sector (Kessler *et al.* 2000).

The strategic choice framework has been very influential in the consideration of the employers' role in shaping industrial relations practice. Three issues need to be considered in assessing its value for public sector analysis. First, the strategic choice approach emphasizes agency over structure. It suggests that managers have the power and political influence to develop organizational structures and employment practices in line with their own preferences (Child 1997). The emphasis on the choices available to managers may exaggerate the discretion available to them and underplay the structural constraints they confront.

The emphasis on structural constraints is particularly relevant to the health sector when the range of political, economic and workforce characteristics identified in Chapter 2 are considered. This is not to argue that managers have no discretion, but to suggest that strategic choice frameworks may exaggerate the scope for autonomous management action. A second, related point is that it is not self-evident that managers will use their discretion to act in a strategic manner and adopt HR practices that are viewed as beneficial to both the organization and the individual (Guest 2001: 106). As Sisson (1995) has argued in his interpretation of UK employment relations developments, the system of corporate governance encourages short-termism, and managers muddle through rather than exercise strategic choice. NHS managers have had to grapple with achieving financial targets in conjunction with unpredictable political interventions and a process of almost continuous reorganization. It is possible therefore that short-termism has imbued management practice, militating against strategic management.

A third, equally fundamental issue concerns the nature of strategy itself. Strategic choice approaches reflect, in Whittington's (1993) terms, the classical view of strategy focused on rational top-down planning. Within the strategy literature, however, there has been a shift in emphasis towards the importance of strategy implementation (Purcell 2001). As Pfeffer (1998: 14) argues, 'firms often pursue a strategic fix to what are fundamentally operational problems'. Nonetheless for politicians, strategies provide political kudos by sustaining an appearance of decisive remedial action to address public criticism of public services. The classical view of strategy fits the highly centralized form of the NHS. Government ministers therefore remain wedded to the classical view, with a series of strategies for nursing, human resources, and information management, incorporated within the overall NHS plan. It cannot be assumed, however, that these strategies are integrated at national level or effectively put into practice at the workplace.

A related issue concerns the role undertaken by the personnel function in strategy formulation and implementation. The question of whether the personnel function has shifted from an operational to a strategic function has been a dominant theme of employment relations analysis (Sisson 2001). In general, there is a perception that public personnel specialists are less effective than their private sector counterparts, and a series of myths and misconceptions may prevent able personnel specialists entering the public sector (Lupton and Shaw 2001).

Within the NHS there has been a long-standing debate about the role of the personnel function (now invariably referred to as the HR function) and the impact of health service reform on its role and influence. Uneven investment in the HR function, and an administrative legacy reflecting highly centralized and standardized personnel practice, alongside political constraints, has ensured that personnel in the NHS has often been confined to a narrow operational role with limited influence (Bach 1995; 1999b). The Department of Health (2002a: 32) has emphasized that building HR skills among all managers and ensuring the credibility of the HR function are important elements of their HR strategy. It acknowledges, however, that there is a long way to go, because:

> human resource management in the NHS is still too often tarnished by its former role as the pejorative 'personnel' function. (2002a: 3)

This interpretation that the NHS personnel function has been unable to develop a strategic role that would foster changes in employment practices has been contested (Currie and Procter 2001; Truss *et al.* 2002). A key issue remains, however, in clarifying what the role of a strategic HR function comprises within an organizational context that places constraints on the policies adopted by trust managers. What is clear is that in a labour intensive organization confronted with a large restructuring agenda, the role and influence of the HR function will have an important effect on employment relations.

The management of employment relations

The establishment of trust hospitals in the 1990s was presented by the Conservative government as an opportunity for trust managers to reshape employment relations. A thinly disguised objective was to diminish trade union influence in the NHS (Seifert 1992: 400). Across the economy, human resource management techniques involving forms of direct communication and staff involvement have increased substantially (Millward *et al.* 2000: 118). Cully *et al.* (1999: 88) reported that in 72 per cent of workplaces managers expressed a preference for consulting directly with employees, rather than with unions. These management practices often coexist alongside trade unions, although whether they are intended to substitute for collective voice remains unresolved (Bacon and Storey 2000; Guest 2001). Bacon and Storey, in their multi-sector study that included three NHS trusts, noted that trust managers held back from wholesale derecognition of trade unions. Managers suggested that such a move would have engendered distrust, creating apprehension among employees, and that such a step was not necessary because they had imposed workplace changes without using the sanction of derecognition (2000: 414). It was evident therefore that trade union influence had diminished significantly.

Carr (1999) in his 1997 survey of 46 trusts found that managers had withdrawn recognition from a number of small unions (with few members) in 34 per cent of cases. In most cases derecognition involved a downgrading from negotiation to consultation rights. The striking finding of Carr's survey was that 65 per cent of trusts had increased communications, with the main growth being in individual communication. He maintained that these measures were not intended to diminish the role of trade unions, but it is difficult to gauge management motives using a survey based methodology. The evidence on managerial attitudes towards trade unions in the NHS during the 1990s was relatively sparse, reflecting a generalized assumption that joint regulation remained firmly entrenched within the health service (e.g. Thornley 1998: 428).

More recently, reflecting Labour government policy, these issues have been reformulated into a concern with the emergence of workplace social partnerships, although the origins, aims and outcomes of these arrangements has varied significantly between trusts (Heaton *et al.* 2001; Industrial Relations Services 2001a). In some cases it has been argued that this is merely a new label for employee involvement to gain worker and union consent for change (Lugsden 2001); in other trusts outcomes were partly related to inter- and intra-union relations (Heaton *et al.* 2001). Reduced adversarial relations with management were noted in some cases and potential opportunities to enhance union influence highlighted (Munro 2002). Overall, however, these studies remain cautious about the overall effect on union influence. A concern of this research is therefore to examine management–union relations. To what extent are managers altering their approach towards the involvement of trade unions in consultation and negotiation forums? Has there been an increase in direct involvement and communication and what does this signify for trade union influence at the workplace?

Trade union influence at the workplace depends not only on managerial behaviour but also on the actions of trade unions. Fairbrother (2000), focusing on developments in the civil service and local government, has argued that public sector restructuring has been a catalyst for union renewal arising from organizational decentralization and the concomitant growth of local bargaining activity. This process is associated with the development of local representative structures that are more independent from centralized union structures, fostering increased membership participation.

Surprisingly, however, the renewal thesis does not identify the distinctive characteristics of public sector trade-unionism. In particular the continuing importance of central government decision-making within a political process ensures that public service trade unions will endeavour to influence the policies of the government in relation to the public sector. This impacts on union purpose, tactics and the type of pressure that they can bring to bear that may be orientated as much to the political domain as to the labour market in terms of bargaining power (Johnston 1994). Articulation and co-ordination of union action between different levels within public service unions is important and extends beyond the focus on the workplace. As a result the devolution of management practice does not detract from the influence of central government in shaping public sector employment relations, and this leads McIlroy (1995: 138) to term public sector union decentralization as 'coercive fragmentation' because:

> Apart from the evidence of erosion of organisation, decentralisation diminishes the real utility of national coordination and the deployment of external power unavailable in the enterprise. It is a sign of weakness not strength.

There are strong echoes here of the debate that has focused predominantly on the private sector about whether unions are becoming 'hollow shells' in which union structures and collective bargaining processes remain in place, but trade unions are so weakened that they have only a limited capacity to represent their members effectively. One key indicator of union membership strength relates to levels of union density. Within the public sector the most rapid decline has been within the health sector with an annual rate of membership decline of 4.5 per cent per annum between 1990 and 1998, a similar rate of decline as in the private service sector (Millward *et al.* 2000: 143).

This type of evidence suggests that union renewal may not be the dominant trend in the public sector, especially in the health service. Waddington and Kerr (1999: 187) indicate that Unison structure and organization is weaker in health than elsewhere, and they report high levels of dissatisfaction with local union organization among union members. These difficulties may be exacerbated by partnership arrangements that distance union members from shop stewards, creating distrust of union representatives (Heaton *et al.* 2001: 118). Similar weaknesses in union organization, and a dearth of union activists, have also been noted in studies of acute hospitals (Carter and Poynter 1999: 508), highlighting the fragility of union organization. Less is known about other health service trade unions, although a survey of RCN stewards suggested that management support for their role remained strong (Kessler and Heron 2001).

Carter and Poynter (1999: 507) point out that weak workplace union organization has been masked, and at the same time reinforced, by a concentration of bargaining at national level. A similar process may be occurring at present, with government expenditure increasing NHS staff numbers and boosting trade union membership levels, while disguising underlying patterns of union organizational weakness. Moreover, staff shortages and a process of work intensification that was noted in the 1990s (Green 2001: 73) could be expected to have an adverse effect on the capacity of trade unions to develop and sustain workplace organization. Professional staff in particular may be unwilling to participate in trade union activities, if they perceive their involvement as increasing the workload for their colleagues and jeopardizing service standards. Questions remain about whether managers continue to view trade unions as integral to the process of employment reform and the capacity of trade unions to shape this process.

Pay determination and work reorganization

In recent years there have been major changes in the way that pay is determined and labour utilized. There has been a decline in the coverage of collective bargaining and an increase in pay determination systems that depend more on managerial discretion. An additional component of workplace reform has been changes in employer labour use strategies that have taken a variety of forms (Cully *et al.* 1998; Gallie *et al.* 1998).

There has also been a significant shift from industry-wide to organization based systems of pay determination (see Arrowsmith and Sisson 1999; White 2000). Within the health service during the 1990s the dominant concern was the level at which collective bargaining was conducted and the balance that was to be struck between centralization and decentralization.

In the private sector there has been a highly decentralized system of collective bargaining since the 1970s, so it was not surprising that Conservative government ministers in the period 1979–97 advocated a more decentralized system of collective bargaining, arguing that it would be more sensitive to local labour market conditions and managerial needs (Winchester and Bach 1999: 45). The Labour government since 1997 has also been concerned to reform the system of pay determination, confronting similar dilemmas about the appropriate balance between centralized and decentralized pay determination (Department of Health 1999a).

The Conservative government encouraged trust managers to develop local pay and conditions. The term local pay has been widely used but has an ambiguous meaning. It can variously refer to the settlement at trust level of a component of the annual wage round; the development of trust-specific terms and conditions of employment for particular occupational groups; or, most radically, the establishment of a revamped pay and grading system for some or all of the occupational groups within a trust. More than one component of local pay may coexist within an individual trust.

It is necessary to disentangle these separate components of local pay, to be precise about trust based developments and to evaluate current debates about the future of pay determination in the health service. The Conservative government forced trusts to negotiate a component of the annual pay increase at local level during the mid-1990s. Although the outcomes in terms of pay settlements have been documented (Nurses' Pay Review Body 1996; 1997), our knowledge about the process of pay determination at trust level is much more limited, relying primarily on survey based data (e.g. Thornley 1998). In particular, the type of information used within the local negotiation process, the extent to which final settlements were agreed with the staff side or imposed by management, and the impact of local negotiations on the climate of employment relations are pertinent issues as the NHS enters a further period of pay determination reform.

In terms of the development of local pay structures few trusts moved wholesale away from the existing Whitley terms and conditions of employment. The few exceptions were trusts that introduced a single pay spine, or established an appraisal based payment system, or piloted a competency based pay and grading system (Buchan *et al.* 1998: 68). The durability of these pay systems, the numbers of staff covered by them, and the cost of their introduction remains unclear. There are also variations between trusts in the occupational groups that were incorporated into local pay arrangements (e.g. Corby *et al.* 2001: 38; Grimshaw 2000). It is not clear why trust terms and conditions applied to some groups rather than others and to what extent the introduction of local pay for certain occupational groups has been viewed by trust managers as a short-term opportunistic response, or a precursor to wholesale reforms of trust terms and conditions of employment (Grimshaw 2000: 960).

The development of local pay and subsequent trust based initiatives on pay determination can be used to examine the degree to which trust managers were able to develop their own approach to local pay, and explore the main influences on their approach to pay determination, illuminating the question of 'strategic choice' and sub-sectoral characteristics raised earlier. In contrast to the high profile issue of local pay the degree to which trust managers reorganized working practices received less attention in the mid-1990s.

Analysis of employer practice has frequently differentiated between two labour utilization strategies: numerical flexibility, concerned with adjusting the number of workers to meet fluctuations in demand, and functional flexibility that signifies the range of tasks undertaken by employees. In the health service the suggestion that different forms of flexibility can be adopted among particular portions of the workforce to maximize labour utilization became an influential idea, popularized through Atkinson's (1984) model of the flexible firm (for a critical review see Kalleberg 2001).

Within the health service both numerical and functional forms of flexibility have received some attention, not least in concerns about the emergence of a 'two tier workforce' whether arising from competitive tendering, or more recently the consequences of the private finance initiative (Bach 2002: 329). Part-time employment has often been associated with forms of numerical flexibility. The managerial aims and implications for nurses have been investigated and the under-utilization and under-development of their skills noted (Edwards and Robinson 2001; Lane 1999). These findings sit uneasily alongside recent Labour government emphasis on flexible working patterns that promote the NHS as a model employer and which are viewed as integral to recruitment and retention initiatives (Department of Health 2002a).

A separate long-standing concern of policy-makers has been to alter work organization to encourage 'new ways of working' and break down demarcations between occupational groups. For some commentators the commercialization of the public sector has led to Taylorite work processes being applied to the state sector including the NHS (Cousins 1987; Webb 1999). These writers contend that the increasing pressures on employers to minimize costs has ensured increased managerial control and the removal of worker discretion within the labour process. The type of initiatives associated with these developments is linked to job design and the examination of tasks undertaken by workers, to assess whether tasks can be redistributed among existing or newly established occupational groups.

A distinction can be drawn between changes in grade mix that may represent a substitution of qualified for less qualified staff and is primarily budget driven, as opposed to skill-mix changes that attempt to match and align the skills and competencies of professional staff to improve the service provided to the patient (MSF 1992). In the last decade there has been a slight change in grade mix within nursing, with the proportion of nursing staff reducing slightly (Buchan and Seccombe 2002). These aggregate changes, however, may disguise more radical changes at individual workplace level (e.g. Poynter 2000). Support for the proposition that work is being transferred from more qualified to less qualified staff is often linked to the delegation of work from doctors to nurses, the growth of health care and other assistant roles and the development of generic working which combines portering, cleaning and catering tasks (Grimshaw 1999; Leys 2001: 193–4; Munro 1999: 199). The Labour government has enthusiastically embraced such an approach and has committed itself to increasing the number of health care assistants by 27,000 by 2005 (from a 2002 baseline), and a key objective for the workforce is to

> Increase workforce capacity and productivity through skill mix and continuing professional development; moving work from doctors to other healthcare professionals and from healthcare professionals to the support workforce, supported by pay modernisation, and service redesign. (Department of Health 2002b: 23)

These changes have been facilitated by the *NHS Plan* (Department of Health 2000a: 59) that encouraged the development of a standard guideline or protocol for each condition that medical and other staff are expected to follow. The emergence of clinical governance has also encouraged more transparency and uniformity in the organization of medical work (Harrison 2002).

Other commentators contest this interpretation, arguing that increased managerial control has been exercised indirectly primarily by increasing the intensity of work. This has been achieved by altering the context in which nursing work occurs by increasing activity levels forcing nurses to work harder (Ackroyd and Bolton 1999). Similar arguments have been advanced by Allan (1998) in his study of the Queensland hospital system. He argues that intensifying work has been a distinct form of labour adjustment used in the health sector and that hospital staff are particularly vulnerable to work intensification pressures because of their professional ethos and their reluctance to take industrial action.

An almost diametrically opposed account of developments in work organization is related to moves towards a 'knowledge' society in which task complexity is increasing and the general trend is towards a more educated workforce undertaking more complex tasks (see Storey and Quintas 2001). In contrast to the emphasis within Taylorism on deskilling, increased managerial control and fragmentation of work, emphasis is placed on trying to reduce the number of discrete tasks involved in patient care by combining tasks and focusing more on redesigning work around patient needs. As the *NHS Plan* argues, 'successful services thrive on their ability to respond to the individual needs of their customers ... services have to be tailor-made not mass produced' (Department of Health 2000a: 26). This line of argument has been termed patient focused care (PFC) and is reflected in the Labour government's emphasis on focusing on the whole patient journey.

Patient focused care has its origins in the restructuring of health care in a small number of hospitals in the USA during the 1980s (Buchan 1995). Its overall approach is to simplify patient care by reducing the number of process steps and limit the staff that come into contact with patients by a process of multi-skilling and cross-training. The hospital environment is restructured, with services and staff clustered into decentralized units, and the amount of patient and staff movement is reduced. The aspect of PFC which has received the most attention is the emphasis on multi-skilled and cross-trained staff. It is claimed that in traditional hospitals staff, particularly nurses, spend as little as a third of their time in direct patient care, and less as staff become more senior. The advantage of PFC is that it reduces the number of staff involved with patients, which improves patient care and efficiency as well as creating more satisfying jobs (Hurst 1995). There is limited evidence on the adoption of patient focused care in the UK, but some of the same emphasis on improvements in work organization that address nurses' concerns about recent patterns of restructuring is evident in the interest in Magnet hospitals (Department of Health 2002a: 37).

This study examines forms of work reorganization, focusing on the development of generic working and its implications for ancillary and nursing roles. Changes in work organization are examined to establish whether they have fulfilled managerial expectations of greater 'flexibility', and explore the impact for the staff concerned of reforms to working practices.

Research methods

An understanding of the impact of government reforms, on local employer practice and management–worker behaviour, requires a detailed examination of workplace developments. A central component of this book is based on three case studies of acute NHS trust hospitals. There has been extensive analysis of national policy developments within the NHS which examines the origins and implementation of the NHS reforms at national level (Klein 2001; Webster 2002), but less research on the detailed impact of these reforms at trust level.

To make sense of the relationship between workplace practice and national developments it was necessary to complement workplace studies with national-level data. Interviews at national level were conducted with civil servants, senior managers and trade unionists to gain a better understanding of the national health policy and employment relations agenda, as a basis for interpreting workplace developments. National data sources enabled the case study trusts to be contextualized and placed within a wider sampling frame – the NHS in England – to indicate the extent to which they are representative of developments elsewhere. Case studies are not designed to be statistically representative, but the analytical insights generated are intended to be generalizable to other organizational settings (see Scott 1994: 30; Yin 1994). National data was drawn from government, employer and trade union sources. The pay review bodies and management consultants also undertake surveys and provide guidance on employment issues for their constituents. The plethora of audit mechanisms established by successive governments, including the Audit Commission, National Audit Office, Commission for Health Improvement and Select Committee inquiries, also provided valuable comparative data on specific issues.

The case studies selected were designed to be broadly representative of developments across England. The process of political devolution instigated by the Labour government has led to significant differences emerging in health policy and HR strategy between England, Scotland, Wales and Northern Ireland that are beyond the scope of this book, which focuses on England. The analytical framework proposes that the characteristics of the sub-sector will be the dominant influence on management practice and workplace reform. The purpose of the case studies was to test out this proposition and to examine the scope that remains for the exercise of a degree of strategic choice that may account for local variation. Differences between individual trusts could be expected to be linked to their position within the local health economy (i.e. financial position, size and range of services); variations in the organization and structure of management, including the influence of the HR function, and finally differences in the approach towards employment relations, including the stance towards trade unions. The selection of organizations used a number of criteria to aid this process. The trusts selected varied in size and the mix of service provision, and they were drawn from more than one region of the country. The London region was excluded because its distinctive labour market and other pressures are not indicative of developments across the NHS in England. To the extent that Conservative and Labour government reforms across the sector have transformed employment practices, this should have been apparent in the majority of trusts by 2002. More insights into workplace behaviour can often be generated from failed or only partially successful innovations than from self-proclaimed 'leading edge' organizations.

Ancillary and nursing staff were the primary focus of the fieldwork because they have been subject to more extensive reforms of pay determination and work organization than other health service occupational groups (Buchan *et al.* 1998; Munro 1999). The contested boundaries between ancillary and nursing work have provided the focus for managerial attempts to 're-profile' the workforce, and to develop local terms and conditions of employment. Together these occupational groups comprise approximately half the health service workforce, and their employment conditions remain a prominent policy issue. Nonetheless, given the wide diversity of occupational groups in the health service, some reference is made to other occupational groups, such as medical staff, throughout the book.

Data collection

The main fieldwork for this study was conducted between 1995 and 2001, with five additional interviews conducted in 2002. The advantage of longitudinal research undertaken over a 7–8-year period was the ability to return at regular interviews to the case study trusts and to re-interview key stakeholders. A period of study leave enabled the first intensive period of fieldwork to be conducted between January and September 1996 with follow-up interviews in the summer of 1997. The second main phase of fieldwork was conducted between April and September 2001. Up to a month was spent at each trust, and over the period of the fieldwork the proportion of time spent in each was approximately the same.

The main data sources within each trust included public and semi-public documents, such as the trust's and individual directorates' business plans, minutes of joint staff consultative committees, trust newsletters, workforce information and cuttings from local and specialist health press. In addition, private documentation was examined, including confidential 'warts and all' business strategy documents, management consultancy reports, papers to the trust and management boards and notes of the various management working parties on employment relations issues. In the second phase of fieldwork other documentation became available, such as staff opinion surveys.

In each case trust board members, senior personnel managers, managers responsible for nursing staff and ancillary staff, staff representatives from the main trade unions and their full-time officers, and a sample of employees were interviewed. On average these interviews lasted between one and two hours, and were almost always taped. The case study interviews were supplemented by national-level interviews with trust chief executives, directors of human resources, civil servants and national and regional trade union officials. In total 103 semi-structured interviews were conducted, approximately 80 per cent of interviewees being from within the case study trusts.

Structure of the book

The central premise of this study is that workplace behaviour is shaped by the distinctive characteristics of the health service. For analytical and organizational purposes these arguments are developed by a division between the nationally orientated analysis that encompasses Chapters 2–4, and the workplace based material that is concentrated in Chapters 5–8. Chapter 9 provides the conclusions and revisits the questions raised in Chapter 1. In keeping with the twin aims of addressing both policy and conceptual issues, each chapter reflects a differing balance of policy and conceptually orientated material.

Chapter 2 develops the analytical framework by exploring the distinctive characteristics of the NHS in terms of finance, the role of the state and the professions. Irrespective of variations between individual workplaces that are explored in later chapters it is argued that these characteristics of the NHS provide the bedrock for understanding NHS employment relations. Chapter 3 concentrates on the most important development in the NHS over the last twenty years in terms of workplace behaviour: an unfolding management revolution that has mutated several times under succeeding Conservative and Labour governments. The chapter considers the managerial reforms of the Conservative government period and the internal market of the mid-1990s, alongside developments under Labour governments since 1997. It places these developments in the context of debates about the new public management and management strategy. Chapter 4 traces the development and reform of pay determination and working practices in the NHS.

The following four chapters examine these themes in relation to the reform process at workplace level. The focus is on presenting and analysing the findings from the case studies, linked to a common set of themes that were addressed at each case study site. The case studies are not however presented on a case by case basis. This is because the analytical framework developed in Chapter 2 emphasizes the similarity of challenges facing NHS trusts and the manner in which national policies constrain local practice. The primary purpose of the cases is to elicit themes that are common to the NHS and to examine the interplay between national and local developments. The book does provide some comparison between each trust, but the focus is on the managerial response to similar pressures.

The material is presented in a thematic way. Chapter 5 provides an introduction to each workplace and examines how government reforms based on prescriptions associated with the new public management have shaped management organization and practice. Chapter 6 considers how the evolving national employment relations agenda has been implemented at workplace level particularly in relation to the approach towards performance management and management–trade union relations. Chapter 7 addresses issues of pay determination, including the Conservative government sponsored pursuit of local pay and subsequent developments in pay determination under Labour governments. Chapter 8 considers managerial attempts to improve labour utilization by examining issues of work reorganization and attempts to develop forms of generic working. The final chapter draws out the main findings, assesses the analytical frameworks used in the first half of the study, and elaborates the overall policy implications of the research.

2 THE GOVERNANCE OF HEALTH SERVICE EMPLOYMENT RELATIONS

There can be few organizations whose restructuring has been as controversial and as subject to so much media scrutiny as the reforms of the NHS over the last twenty years. Health service reform is not confined to the UK; across all continents governments are struggling to reconcile increased patient expectations with the reluctance of employees and employers to contribute more resources to maintain the growth of health services. The distinctiveness of the UK experience, however, is the degree to which health sector reform has formed a central component of the domestic political agenda for more than two decades.

For the Conservative governments of the 1980s radical restructuring of the public services symbolized an ideological hostility towards the public sector and signalled the end of the post-war consensus over the welfare state. Far-reaching market-style reforms of the NHS in the 1990s consolidated the management reforms of the previous decade. The Labour government elected in 1997, after eighteen years out of office, also placed NHS reform high on their political agenda. The Labour government enthusiastically embraced the managerial reforms of the Conservative period, bolstering centralized systems of performance management while modifying the more ideological components of their predecessors' market-style reforms (Bach 2002). After their re-election in 2001, and with continuing public disquiet about the state of the NHS, a more chastened Prime Minister staked his government's credibility on its capacity to improve public services. The Labour government committed itself to substantially increased investment in the NHS to deflect calls for alternative methods to finance health care.

As a labour intensive service industry, it is the NHS workforce that is in the frontline in translating government aspirations into improved patient services, but both Conservative and Labour governments have been critical of the producer domination of public services (Office of Public Services Reform

2002). Employment relations reform has been a central component of the attempts to break down demarcations between occupational groups, alter professional roles and ensure that public services become more performance- and user-orientated. For Conservative governments, these outcomes were to be brought about by policies of compulsory competitive tendering and the subsequent discretion granted to trusts to set their own terms and conditions of employment. Local pay was envisaged as the catalyst for wide-ranging employment relations reform.

The Labour government broadened the employment relations agenda beyond the discredited policy of local pay and launched a series of high-profile human resource management initiatives in the NHS, indicating that HRM was central to its modernization agenda (Department of Health 1998; 2000a). In a tighter labour market context, government documents emphasized the importance of recruitment, retention and improving the working lives of NHS employees to ensure that sufficient, motivated staff were in place to achieve government targets (Department of Health 2000a). This approach was coupled with very substantial increases in NHS expenditure in its second term of office, which enabled the government to argue that increases in NHS expenditure had removed finance as an impediment to reform.

This chapter outlines the analytical framework for understanding NHS employment relations. It draws out the distinctive features of health service employment relations and the manner in which these characteristics are embedded in, and influenced by, state policy and patterns of regulation. These characteristics include the fiscal and political context and the distinctive features of the workforce in terms of the long-standing influence of professional staff and trade unions. A central argument of this study is that the focus on the employer unit, the NHS trust, has to be complemented by an analysis of the wider political and economic context in which NHS trusts are located, to gain a fuller understanding of the process of employment relations reform. This context has tended to be under-played because Conservative government rhetoric emphasized the autonomous nature of trusts, sentiments echoed more recently by Labour governments' emphasis on 'earned autonomy' and 'Foundation Hospitals'. Consequently the unit of analysis has tended to be the individual trust rather than the characteristics of the health service.

The characteristics of the National Health Service

The dominant theme in recent analysis of public services reform has been an emphasis on the ascendancy of the new public management (Bach and Della Rocca 2000; Hood 2000; Pollitt and Bouckaert 2000). Although the term has been associated with a variety of organizational practices, it signifies an ideological belief that management practices originating in the private sector can be applied across the public services to improve their efficiency and effectiveness. The key message indicated by the shift within the policy and academic community from public *administration* to public *management* is that instead of a focus on the specific characteristics of the public sector – its funding, forms of accountability, and political and economic environment – and how this shapes management practice, attention shifts to the manage-ment techniques which are being applied to public sector organizations. Issues of *agency* (management behaviour in particular) and managers' 'stra-tegic choices' become the primary focus of analysis while it downplays the wider institutional structures within which managerial decisions are located.

Within the new public management (NPM) literature, historical patterns of state intervention are ignored because the state is viewed as essentially exogenous to the process of workplace reform. According to the influential study by Osborne and Gaebler (1992) the state produces a blueprint for reform but, having set the reform process in motion, it allows 'the entre-preneurial spirit' to flourish. By implication the *internal* characteristics of the state, its historical forms of development and the economic and political environment in which state intervention occurs, are not important influences on the reform process. New public management *techniques* and the *values* that they reflect are viewed as applicable to all countries and types of organiza-tion: 'we believe that our ten principles underlie success for *any* institution in today's world – public, private or non-profit' (Osborne and Gaebler 1992: 21, emphasis in original).

A defining feature of employment relations as a field of study, however, has been its recognition that relations between employers, employees and trade unions are part of a system of employment regulation in which internal and external influences interact to shape the employment relationship. This shifts attention away from a sole preoccupation with the human resource management techniques used within individual workplaces, to a considera-tion of how management practices and HR techniques are set within a wider historical, economic and political context. These arguments have been developed more fully for the private sector. There is a widely held view, not-withstanding organizational diversity, that employment relations in the UK has been strongly influenced by a system of corporate governance orientated to short-term results which has meant that it has been an inhospitable context for investing in human resource management (see Bach and Sisson 2000: 8–9).

As the public sector has been exhorted to follow the example of the private sector, some aspects of UK private sector corporate governance have been grafted onto existing public sector practice. Examples affecting NHS trusts include the threat of takeovers and mergers, the adoption of multi-divisionalization forms of organization, trust boards with executive and non-executive directors and the requirement to achieve short-term financial and waiting time targets. These developments have influenced managerial behaviour, but not necessarily in the ways envisaged by policy-makers because they are 'hybrids' which are superimposed on existing patterns of public sector management. Long-standing patterns of state intervention and organisational practice have left an indelible mark on the management process and, even as new reforms are brought forth, the residue of previous initiatives continues to influence management practice in a cumulative manner. As Cooper *et al.* (1996) argue, reform processes build up layers of sediment, and this geological metaphor implies that underlying values and behaviours remain embedded in the organisation, even as restructuring continues apace.

This is evident in the case of the NHS, in which three integral features of its organizational structure and management have a crucial bearing on workplace reform. The first relates to the UK welfare state, the fiscal environment in which governments operate and the impact on NHS expenditure. The second is linked to the centralized control of the NHS and the manner in which state control has facilitated an audit explosion (Power 1997) in the NHS. The third relates to the state ceding control of the NHS to professional staff at the inception of the NHS and how this has altered over time. It is the interaction between these three sets of processes that gives NHS employment relations its specific characteristics and has a crucial bearing on workplace reform.

The political economy of health care expenditure

The UK health care and welfare systems are deeply rooted in the political and economic institutions of the nation state. Esping-Andersen (1990) distinguishes between three types of welfare state. He argues that the expansion of the service sector with less scope for productivity improvements than in manufacturing industry affects all welfare states. Post-industrial employment and welfare trajectories differ, however, giving rise to three different worlds of welfare capitalism. Germany is the ideal typical representation of the corporatist welfare state, Sweden exemplifies the social democratic tradition and the United States characterizes the liberal tradition with Britain placed in this category. This signifies minimalist public provision with benefit levels kept low to reinforce the work ethic; employment is viewed as the overriding legitimate form of citizenship and means of survival in the market economy. Although the NHS has a universal character which sits uneasily alongside the minimalism of the liberal categorization for the UK, waiting lists and other forms of rationing indicate that the NHS has never provided universal citizenship rights in practice. Elements of self-help, such as exit to the private sector or individuals living with unmet needs, remain a necessary part of the 'economy' model of the NHS.

Moreover, in contrast to social insurance health systems that create entitlement to an identifiable range of *services* that are subsequently reimbursed, the NHS provides a non-specific entitlement to *access*. The NHS attempts to meet citizen needs to the best of its ability within the resources available (Moran 1999: 61).

These differences are reflected in different levels of public expenditure in terms of the proportion of government expenditure as a percentage of gross domestic product (GDP). OECD data indicates that in 2000, for Germany, the proportion was 43 per cent, for Sweden 54 per cent, for the USA 29 per cent and for the UK 38 per cent (Atkinson and van den Noord 2001, Table 1). The significance of Esping-Andersen's typology therefore is that it indicates the reluctance of states defined as liberal to commit themselves to high levels of public expenditure. In the UK, although important variations exist between Conservative and Labour governments' expenditure patterns, all governments have remained within a policy framework which has supported a low tax culture. One of the defining features of New Labour has been an emphasis on maintaining low levels of direct taxation, to dispel its image as a party of high taxation (Gamble and Kelly 2001: 182). This implies, in a publicly funded, tax based health system, pressure to keep a tight rein on health care expenditure, especially the pay bill, which constitutes its largest component. Furthermore, in contrast to the archetype liberal welfare state, the United States of America, the health service funding gap has not been bridged by private expenditure, which at 17 per cent remains very low in comparison to other OECD countries (Wanless 2001: 46).

Despite modest expenditure, uncertainty about the financial viability of the NHS has been long-standing. Less than ten years after its inception, the

Guillebaud Inquiry (1956) examined the rising costs of the health service. Throughout its existence cost containment has been to the fore, exercised by covert rationing and other measures. During the 1950s an arbitrary ceiling of about £400 million was imposed on the direct taxation contribution available to the NHS. Expenditure above this level was expected to derive from efficiency savings and other sources such as charges (Webster 2002: 32). Until the mid-1970s this fragile equilibrium remained intact, but it was challenged more radically during the 1980s with the election of a Conservative government explicitly committed to reducing public expenditure. The election of the Labour government in 1997 reflected a shift in the political climate from a primary concern with containing health care expenditure to a growing public concern that insufficient public expenditure was being directed into the NHS.

The proportion of expenditure on health care has been increasing, but this disguises important annual fluctuations indicating a strong 'stop–go' pattern, reflecting the post-war trajectory of the UK economy. As Table 2.1 indicates, in the early 1990s there was a surge of NHS expenditure accompanying the introduction of the internal market, but after 1995, expenditure growth slowed markedly. In its 1997 election manifesto, the Labour Party argued that it would retain the spending plans of the previous government for its first two years in office. This was justified partly by the need to reduce the substantial budget deficit it inherited, and partly to sustain its 'business friendly' credentials by reducing expectations of an immediate hike in public sector pay. This strategy was effective if judged in these terms, but led to a squeeze on expenditure that was described by the former Chancellor Kenneth Clarke as 'eye-wateringly tight' (cited in Stephens 2001: 194). Between 1997 and 2001, public expenditure as a proportion of GDP averaged under 40 per cent compared to 44 per cent of GDP for the whole 1979–97 period (Mullard 2001: 310).

By late 1999 the government was besieged by tales of the financial crisis in the NHS. This led to Tony Blair's statement in early 2000 that the UK should increase its share of gross domestic product that it spends on health care to the average of the European Union (EU) by 2006. This pledge reflected concern that the UK devotes a lower proportion of its GDP to health care than other industrialized countries as is apparent from Table 2.1. This legacy of under-funding was confirmed in the Report by Derek Wanless, former chief executive of NatWest Bank, who was commissioned by the Chancellor of the Exchequer to quantify the resources required for a publicly funded, comprehensive, high quality health service (Wanless 2002).

The NHS employs more than 1.2 million people in the UK, and staff expenditure comprises around two-thirds of current expenditure. Expenditure

Table 2.1 *Total expenditure on health, percentage of GDP in selected OECD countries 1960–2000*

	1960	1970	1980	1990	1995	1997	1998	1999	2000
Australia	4.3	4.9	7.0	7.8	8.2	8.4	8.5	8.4	8.3
Canada	5.4	7.0	7.1	9.0	9.1	8.9	9.1	9.2	9.1
France				8.6	9.6	9.4	9.3	9.4	9.5
Germany	4.8	6.3	8.8	8.7	10.6	10.7	10.6	10.7	10.6
Ireland	3.6	5.1	8.4	6.6	7.2	6.9	6.8	6.8	6.7
Italy				8.0	7.4	7.7	7.7	7.8	8.1
Japan	3.0	4.5	6.4	5.9	7.0	7.2	7.1	7.4	7.8
New Zealand		5.1	5.9	6.9	7.2	7.5	7.9	7.9	8.0
Spain	1.5	3.6	5.4	6.6	7.7	7.6	7.6	7.7	7.7
Sweden	4.5	6.9	9.1	8.5	8.1	8.1	7.9		
UK	3.9	4.5	5.6	6.0	7.0	6.8	6.8	7.1	7.3
USA	5.1	6.9	8.7	11.9	13.3	13.0	12.9	13.0	13.0

Source: OECD Health Data, 2002.

constraints have therefore had an important influence on staffing levels and the mix of staff utilized within the health service. The interim Wanless Report (2001: 183) reported that the UK relied heavily on international migration, but still employed fewer doctors and nurses per head of population than other European countries. Of the 27 OECD countries for which data is available, the UK had the lowest density of physicians per 1,000 population in 2000 with the exception of Korea and Turkey (OECD 2002). As Table 2.2 indicates, of the major OECD countries, only Japan approaches the UK's low physician density. In terms of certified nurses in the late 1990s, the UK had 4.5 per thousand population, compared to 6.0 in France, 9.6 in Germany and 10.2 in Sweden.

A related dimension of state expenditure concerns the requirements placed on trusts in their stewardship of public expenditure. As part of the internal market reforms introduced from 1990, hospitals were reconstituted as public corporations. This involved very significant changes in the accounting regime, which has been viewed as unduly harsh in comparison to the privatized utilities and the scope for manoeuvre granted to private companies (Shaoul 1996; 1999). Shaoul suggests that the financial obligations placed on trusts, have exacerbated their financial difficulties and forced them to squeeze their labour force (Shaoul 1999: 46). At the core of this analysis is the capital accounting regime within the NHS. The Conservative government argued in the early 1990s that the NHS estate was poorly

Table 2.2 *Practising physicians, density per 1000 population in selected OECD countries 1960–2000*

Country	1960	1970	1980	1990	2000
Australia	1.1	1.2	1.8	2.3	2.5 (1998)
Canada		1.5	1.8	2.1	2.1
France	1.0	1.3	2.0	2.6	3.0 (1998)
Germany	1.4	1.6	2.3	3.1	3.6
Ireland				1.6	2.3 (1999)
Italy	0.7	1.1	2.6	4.7	6.0
Japan	1.0	1.1	1.3	1.7	1.9
New Zealand	1.1		1.6	1.9	2.2
Spain				2.3	3.3
Sweden	1.0	1.3	2.2	2.9	3.1
UK	0.8	0.9	1.3	1.4	1.8
USA	1.4	1.6	2.0	2.4	2.8 (1999)

Source: OECD Health Data, 2002.

managed because capital in the NHS was effectively a 'free' good. The solution, as outlined in *Working for Patients* (Department of Health 1989), was that trust managers would be required to service their debt through capital charges. Crucially, trust assets were valued at current values rather than historic values, raising the interest and dividend payment levels. This can be compared to the treatment of the privatized water companies in which the assets were valued at £9 billion but given to them for £4 billion. Hutton comments:

> NHS trusts have been saddled with £10.3 billion of assets without any concession over the valuation, no debts have been written off, and the growth of income is only marginally above inflation. Only the treatment of the universities rivals it for rank inequity and meanness. (Hutton 1996: 17)

An additional feature of the accounting regime concerns the statutory financial duties placed on NHS trusts. They have to break even after paying interest taking one year with another; they must make a 6 per cent return on the value of their assets; and they must operate within their external financing limit (EFL), which is set annually by the NHS Executive. Since the early 1980s all governments have required the NHS to deliver annual efficiency savings of around 3 per cent, with budgets reduced accordingly. This regime has continued with the Labour government confirming that 'we expect to see improvements in NHS productivity of 2% per annum' (Department of Health 2002c: 37). Research within NHS trusts has suggested that managers are preoccupied with achieving efficiency savings and that the financial regime was 'over-determined' with no need for two profit targets (Lapsley *et al.* 1998).

The legacy of parsimonious funding from the mid-1990s meant that trusts had an accumulated deficit of £77 million in March 2000. By the following March, of the 356 trusts in England, 47 had cumulative deficits of more than 0.5 per cent of income, and of these, 33 were judged to have significant financial difficulties that required preparation of a recovery plan to be monitored by the Regional Office (National Audit Office 2002). A significant proportion of increased health expenditure will therefore continue to be used to clear past deficits.

During 2001–02 almost 40 per cent of the increase in resources was channelled into additional wage increases for hard-to-recruit groups, such as particular nursing grades (Department of Health 2002e; Incomes Data Services 2001: 14–15). These pay bill increases have been augmented by the cost of implementing the working time directive, the agreement to cap average working hours for junior doctors at 56 hours per week and increased pension costs for NHS trusts. In addition, much of the increase in resources has been allocated to particular initiatives, such as the establishment of NHS Direct, rather than linked to increases in baseline funding for trusts. Managers have been concerned about the laborious process involved in bidding for relatively small amounts of money that are often provided on a non-recurring basis.

These continuing financial pressures need to be considered alongside well documented pressures on the NHS in terms of increased activity levels (Table 2.3), demography, the availability of new medical technologies and drug regimes, and the increased expectations of the public (Harrison and Dixon 2000). Capital spending on public services (even including PFI investment) as a proportion of GDP has fallen continuously since 1975; a trend that continued during the first two years of Labour government (Clark *et al.* 2001: 2). Although the NHS has moved into a much more favourable expenditure context Wildavsky's (1979) phrase about 'doing better, feeling worse' captures the paradox whereby more resources put into health ratchets up public expectations, placing more pressure on staff. Consequently, the combination of long-term under-investment in the NHS, low staffing levels in comparison to other OECD countries and the altered accounting regime ensured that during the fieldwork period budgetary pressures remained prominent.

Table 2.3 *NHS hospital in-patient admissions in England 1990/91–2000/01*

Year	Admissions	Year-on-year change
1990–91	8,188,087	
1991–92	8,724,328	+6.5%
1992–93	9,078,863	+4.1%
1993–94	9,492,652	+4.6%
1994–95	9,857,320	+3.8%
1995–96	10,247,000	+4.0%
1996–97	10,190,689	−0.5%
1997–98	10,537,535	+3.4%
1998–99	10,708,972	+1.6%
1999–00	11,025,944	+3.0%
2000–01	11,001,095	−0.2%

Source: Parliamentry Debate, 13/12/01 Column 982W.

Centralization

The second distinctive feature of the NHS concerns its highly integrated character. This mirrors the centralized form of the UK state which has enabled governments to instigate more far-reaching reforms of the public services than in any other European country (see Bach *et al.* 1999). Freeman (2000: 41) distinguishes between three forms of integration: executive, central and public. *Executive* integration refers to the power of national governments and the degree to which they are constrained by administrative and judicial regulations. Within the British unitary system of governance few constraints are placed on the executive because there is no specific public sector employment statute that regulates employment matters. Conservative and Labour governments with large parliamentary majorities have been relatively free to pursue a radical agenda safe in the knowledge that the opposition was weak and that they were largely unhindered by administrative or judicial constraints. For the NHS this has meant that even though NHS trusts act as separate employers, even at the height of the rhetoric about decentralization under the internal market arrangements in the mid-1990s, the Secretary of State for Health remained responsible for the policies and administration of the NHS overall (Morris 1999). This proved to be a considerable political constraint on management policy.

Central integration refers to the extent to which policy-making authority is concentrated at national level rather than regional or local levels. In contrast to federal states the British unitary system cedes great power to the executive because of the central control of public policy from Whitehall and the absence of complex coalition politics that arise within systems of proportional representation. This degree of centralization is reflected in the control of public expenditure. Leaving aside the more dispersed financing and control of public services within federal states, even in comparison to other unitary states (Denmark, France, Netherlands and Norway) the British state is unusually centralized in its functional control of expenditure. In the case of health services, the British state's central funding, distribution and control of expenditure remains exceptional (see Atkinson and van den Noord 2001).

Moran (1999: 32) highlights the political bargaining that surrounded the creation of the NHS, and what he terms 'a command and control planning system'. This arose from the state's willingness to nationalize the hospital system to ameliorate the financial difficulties of the voluntary hospitals, which, coupled with the medical profession's hostility to municipal control of the health system, enabled the merger of a disparate range of hospital provision into a single integrated health service. Aneurin Bevan's famous quote that 'when a bedpan is dropped on a hospital floor its noise should resound in the Palace of Westminister' is a more accurate portrayal of the NHS of today than fifty years ago. In the 1950s the NHS was 'national' in name only because it comprised a loose coalition of hospitals with wide geographical variations in the facilities available. Service planning arrangements and financial redistribution from South to North gradually established a more even provision of health services from the early 1970s (Webster 2002: 84–7). It was not, however, until the 1980s and 1990s, in a more politically charged environment for the NHS, that Conservative and Labour governments reinforced the centralized structures in the NHS via corporate style management arrangements and used them to force through a radical agenda of reform.

Finally, *public* integration refers to the extent of government authority over private interests, such as health service professions and hospitals, and the degree to which these interests are integrated into a public service. Plainly, the NHS is highly integrated on the public dimension as it is financed through general taxation, hospital facilities are publicly owned and staff are employed by the state. The partial exception is GPs who have formal independent practitioner status, but they depend for their livelihood on the NHS and, in recent years, the Labour government has encouraged the establishment of salaried GPs.

Combining Freeman's three dimensions highlights the highly centralized and integrated nature of the health system in the UK. Three implications flow from these institutional arrangements. First, the inherent political sensitivity associated with health care reform in all countries has been heightened in the case of the NHS. The unity of funding and control has prevented the diffusion of responsibility for health care reform that exists in more pluralist health systems. In social insurance systems, such as France and Germany, there are a number of separate institutions linked to financing and reimbursement decisions. In terms of provision, many European and other countries have a more pluralist mixture of public and private hospital provision. It is much harder in these countries to pinpoint the centre of the health system and responsibility for health care in a way that is apparent in Britain (Bach 2001).

Second, a distinctive characteristic of the UK experience has been that attempts to restructure public services have formed a central part of the political agenda of all governments since 1979. Intense public scrutiny of public services, especially the NHS, has ensured that its performance has remained pivotal to the electoral fortunes of all governments. Reducing the size and scope of the public sector was central to Mrs Thatcher's appeal to the electorate in 1979 in the aftermath of the infamous 'Winter of Discontent', and the internal market reforms of the early 1990s ensured that the NHS remained centre stage. The Labour Party warned in 1997 that, if elected, 'it had 24 hours to save the NHS'. In 2001, the Labour Party's (2001) election manifesto stated that 'Renewal of our public services is at the centre of New Labour's manifesto' (p. 6). According to MORI data the proportion of voters regarding the NHS as the most, or second most important issue facing Britain rose from 27 per cent in 1990 to 37 per cent in 1996 to 48 per cent in 2001 to 72 per cent in February 2002 (cited in Cooper 2002: 24). As a consequence, detailed daily monitoring and guidance from the Department of Health remains a defining feature of the health service management environment.

Third, this degree of integration and political centralization has facilitated the growth of what has been termed the Audit Society (Power 1997). This signifies the increased number of individuals and institutions which find themselves exposed to more intensive audit requirements: 'In short, a growing population of "auditees" began to experience a wave of formalized and detailed checking up on what they do' (Power 1997: 3). These mechanisms formed an integral part of the reforms of the health service. As the NHS became more fragmented under the internal market reforms of the 1990s with the establishment of separate NHS trusts, more auditing of outcomes was instigated. This ensured that formal devolution of managerial authority to trusts did not weaken political control and accountability. Consequently the establishment of performance indicators, broadening the remit of the Audit Commission to include the NHS and other audit processes, such as medical audit, proliferated under successive Conservative governments.

The advent of a Labour government in 1997 did not overturn these trends, quite the reverse, they intensified and embedded audit mechanisms further within the NHS. The reintegration of the NHS has allowed these audit mechanisms to work more effectively and there has been more intensive scrutiny of trust performance. This reflects the centrality of performance management to the Labour government's reforms of the NHS. Whereas Conservative governments believed that competitive pressures would improve NHS performance, for Labour, auditing trust performance against set targets with severe penalties for individuals and organizations that fail to meet them has been the preferred approach. Additional audit mechanisms and regulatory institutions have been created by the Labour government. These include: the Commission for Health Improvement, which carries out inspections of trusts and has taken over the responsibility for the star rating system; the National Institute for Clinical Excellence, which establishes treatment guidelines for medical staff; the Modernization Agency, which benchmarks and implements 'best practice'; and finally a plethora of initiatives which trust managers have to implement with targets set for their achievement (e.g. Improving Working Lives).

The top-down character of these performance targets which line managers and the workforce have little scope to influence may have led to a sense of disempowerment among staff, especially frontline professional staff. They are sandwiched between increased patient expectations and the pressure to fulfil government targets, and face continuing shortages of staff. Moreover, the monitoring of trust and individual performance, and the often prescriptive manner in which guidance has been issued, conveys to the 'auditees' that they are not trusted by government or by the managers charged with ensuring that performance outcomes are achieved (Hunter 2002). This is a particularly sensitive and threatening issue for the NHS, as professional staff are imbued with a professional ethic of self-regulation and an ethos that suggests their actions are designed to serve patient needs. This has important implications for an organization that is dominated by professional staff.

Professionalism in the workforce

The third distinctive feature of the NHS has been the centrality of professional staff to the organization and delivery of health care, and this has given NHS employment relations a particular form. This is reflected in the high

Table 2.4 *NHS hospital and community health services staff in England 1991–2001*

Whole time equivalent	1991(i)	1995	1997	1999	2001	Estimated change 1991–2001
Total employed staff	800,812	755,570	758,060	782,110	837,200	+4.5%
Medical and dental (excluding locums)	44,612	52,580	57,100	60,340	64,060	+43.6%
Nursing, midwifery & health visitors (ii)	385,520	348,110	350,810	361,870	388,290	+0.7%
Qualified	255,440	246,820	246,010	250,650	266,170	+4.2%
Unqualified (iii)	96,130	96,000	101,960	108,850	120,020	+24.8%
Nursing, midwifery & health visiting learners	32,120	4,580	2,250	1,880	2,100	−93.4%
Scientific, therapeutic & technical staff (ii)	87,540	93,950	100,440	107,090	115,770	+32.2%
Qualified allied health professionals	31,320	33,860	36,920	39,340	42,080	+34.3%
Other qualified scientific, therapeutic & technical staff	39,960	42,530	44,680	47,500	51,010	+27.6%
Unqualifed scientific, therapeutic & technical staff	16,260	17,320	18,450	20,050	22,680	+39.5%
Management and support staff	274,690	260,930	249,710	252,800	269,080	−2.0%
Ambulance	14,580	14,480	15,180	15,250	16,320	+11.9%
Admin & estates	156,470	168,730	166,960	172,770	188,530	+20.4%
Support	97,990	74,540	66,800	64,200	63,650	−35.0%
Others	5,650	3,180	770	580	590	−89.5%

(i) In 1995 the classification of staff changed from staff groups based on pay-scale classification to occupation codes. The figures for 1991 are adjusted to enable direct comparisons to be made.

(ii) Totals may not equal the sum of component parts due to rounding and the inclusion of unclassifiable staff.

(iii) The health care assistant staff group did not exist prior to 1995, so have been included with unqualified nurses for comparability purposes.

Source: Department of Health 2002d.

levels of education among NHS workers; 20 per cent are graduates compared to 12 per cent of the UK workforce overall (Wanless 2001: 184). It is also evident from the composition of the workforce detailed in Table 2.4. Medical and dental staff constitute almost 8 per cent of the workforce, with nurses, midwives and health visitors the numerically dominant group comprising about 44 per cent of the workforce. The only staff category in which professional staff do not constitute a majority of the workforce is within the 'Management and support staff' category that constitutes approximately one-third of the workforce.

Although the data needs careful interpretation due to alterations in categories used and the emergence of new occupational groups, some clear trends emerge. First, the workforce has been fairly stable over the last decade with reductions in workforce numbers in the 1990–95 period being reversed at the end of the decade. In comparison to the large increases in patient activity (Table 2.3), this admittedly crude comparison is suggestive of substantially increased workloads for health service staff over the last decade. Second, there have been very significant changes in the composition of the workforce, with ancillary staff particularly hard hit by the impact of compulsory competitive tendering, reflected in the large decreases in the 'support' staff category. There has also been much more rapid growth among professional support staff and non-registered nursing staff than among registered nursing staff. This is particularly evident in terms of professional and non-registered nursing staff, the latter category includes health care assistants (HCAs). Disaggregated data indicates more than doubled numbers from 13,000 to 27,000 between 1995 and 2001 in England, although some of this increase may arise from reclassification of nursing auxiliaries (Buchan and Seccombe 2002: 29).

It has long been acknowledged that professions such as medicine have a pivotal role in shaping patterns of service delivery and work organization. Their high status has been based on the ability of specific occupational groups to lay claim to areas of specialist expertise and to monopolize the use of that knowledge. Professions protect their monopoly powers by the erection of educational and legal barriers and justify their position via an ideology of service and altruism (Abbott and Meerabeau 1998).

Mintzberg (1979) coined the phrase *professional bureaucracy* to indicate that professional organizations combine professional dominance with elements of bureaucratic structures. Although inter- and intra-occupational competition for resources and status has been a pervasive feature of hospitals, these differences were resolved by complex political negotiations alongside administrators that largely supported professional service providers.

Professionals and administrators worked in tandem: the professions shaped the evolution of the NHS and provided the specialists that delivered the service while the NHS bureaucracy provided careers and job security for professionals (Laffin 1998: 4).

These conditions have altered markedly in the last two decades, and there has been a preoccupation with the many challenges to professional status. Some of these relate to broader societal changes with increased education levels and less deferential societal attitudes contributing to a loss of prestige and trust (Giddens 1990). The growth of consumerism is another component of these changes, reflected in postmodern arguments that identity is increasingly derived from consumption rather than employment (Lyon 1999). This type of consumerism results in health being viewed as another consumer product, and governments require professional staff to be sensitive to the requirements of 'customers' rather than to define patient needs exclusively in terms of professional knowledge (Harrison 2002: 477–8).

The Conservative government elected in 1979 reflected this emerging hostility towards producer interests and advanced this agenda in a number of ways. The health service professions were viewed as hostile to reforms of the health service, and their control over the policy agenda was systematically weakened. Conservative and Labour governments increasingly relied on the proliferating number of organizations concerned with policy analysis ('think tanks'), industrialists, management consultants and special advisers for policy advice, sidelining the professions. For example, between 1997 and 1999 the Department of Health and its agencies spent more than £22 million on management consultants (Dillon 2000: 4).

In the 1990s the loss of authority of professions was reinforced by high-profile public scandals. The status and influence of the medical profession in the UK was damaged by a series of malpractice cases, most importantly the paediatric cardio-vascular surgery scandal at the Bristol Royal Infirmary that revealed long-standing professional incompetence and a secretive individualistic culture (Kennedy 2001). These revelations encouraged the Labour government to increase the audit and state regulation of the medical and other professions, eroding the tradition of self-regulation (Harrison 2002).

What are the implications of the changing professional character of the workforce for NHS employment relations? First, an important dimension relates to the changing occupational boundaries within and between professional groups. Nurses are pivotal to many of these occupational boundaries and have often been characterized as semi-professionals (Etzioni 1969) because their training is shorter, their status and expert knowledge is less legitimized and they have less autonomy from supervision of their work than the medical profession. A countervailing influence was the control of the statutory body, the United Kingdom Central Council for Nursing, Midwifery and Health Visiting (UKCC) that ensured nurses' largely self-regulated entry standards, controlled the entry gate for registered nurses and performed a disciplinary function for its membership. Its replacement in 2002 by the Nursing and Midwifery Council with increased lay membership represents a dilution of professional self-regulation.

The reforms of nurse education at the end of the 1980s, termed Project 2000, was a further central component of a professionalizing strategy because it resulted in a change from an apprenticeship model of training towards a university based model in which student nurses would be supernumerary. Project 2000 raised the qualification levels for nurses and, by placing nurse training within universities, distanced nurse training from the immediate service priorities of hospital managers. This was at a time when the power base of nursing was under threat from the new public management reforms of the Conservative government, introduced under the guise of general management (Traynor 1999).

The outcomes for nursing have been contested. Long-standing concerns about the manner in which the gendered nature of nursing undermines its influence have been coupled with issues about nurses remaining in a hierarchically subordinate position to medical staff (Perry 1993; Salvage 1985). In addition, the division within nursing between registered and unregistered nurses has enabled a managerially sponsored growth of health care assistants which may encroach on some areas of nursing practice. At the same time, however, the reduction of working hours for junior doctors and government initiatives to boost the status of nurses by the creation of nurse consultants has led to many tasks being taken on by nurses that were previously undertaken by junior doctors. The changing boundaries within nursing and between nursing and other occupational groups therefore have an important bearing on NHS employment relations.

A second issue relates to concerns about flexibility. From within the more managerially orientated health policy literature, occupational roles defined by professions and reinforced by separate recruitment, training and pay structures have been interpreted as creating managerial difficulties in terms of rigidly demarcated roles, ensuing poor staff deployment and tensions between different occupational groups. The problem is viewed as especially acute because of the proliferation of specialist occupational groups within hospitals which is exacerbated by the expansion of sub-specialisms. For example the Royal College of Nursing has identified more than seventy different nursing specialisms *with their own knowledge base and skills* (e.g.

paediatric oncology nursing). The development of specialist knowledge and the associated differentiation and fragmentation it has created has been beyond the capacity of health systems to reintegrate, creating duplication and professional rivalry (Glouberman 1996: 18). As Hunter (2002: 61) has noted:

> The NHS is not, and never has been, a unitary organization. Rather it is a coalition of multiple groups, each jostling for supremacy ... The NHS may be likened to a huge arena in which the various groups play out their power struggles, although these are not always overt.

It has frequently been argued by employers that these separate occupational 'silos' militate against forms of team-working and hamper flexible working practices while reinforcing professional tribalism. The Conservative government's championing of local pay and the Labour government's proposed reforms of the NHS pay system share the aspiration to break down demarcations between occupational groups. As the Labour government has stated:

> Changes in working practices will be fundamental to delivering these improvements. In the way staff are employed and paid the NHS retains too many of its 1940s employment practices – overly demarcated and inflexible – and has learned too little from other model employers about the benefits of employment flexibility, linked to appropriate rewards and incentives.
> (Department of Health 2002c: 34)

A third theme that emerges is focused more directly on the labour process and suggests that nurses and doctors are being subjected to the same type of control over work practices that has long been applied to other types of occupational group. In historical terms the Labour government had to persuade the medical profession to accept the effective nationalization of health care. In return for accepting salaried status and state employment, within an overall funding envelope, hospital doctors were largely free from state and managerial intervention in terms of operational performance and regulation of their work, jealously guarding their clinical autonomy (Klein 1990 cited in Moran 1999: 32). The rise of the new public management and the establishment of a cadre of professional managers has challenged the autonomy of medical staff (Exworthy and Halford 1999: Harrison 2002). Most attention has been paid to the way in which the managerial values and techniques have challenged professional values by reorientating service delivery away from professionally defined norms (e.g. individual service need) towards managerially defined norms, particularly cost effectiveness and achieving government defined targets. The conflict of values that such a shift in organizational values can bring in its wake is clearly visible from Traynor's (1999) interviews with nurses and nurse managers. HR communication strategies were being used to engender feelings among staff that they belonged to a corporate identity (the trust) with a reduced emphasis on the importance of professional roles and identities (Traynor 1999: 118).

It is too stark to portray the issue of professional values and the management policies that have been enacted to reshape professionalism as a simple conflict between managerialism and professionalism. The values of public sector managers are distinct from those of private sector managers and their emphasis on service is closer to the values of professionals than to those of managers in the private sector (Steele 2000). Professional staff are not uniformly hostile to management and recognize the importance of the effective use of resources, while medical staff retain a capacity to resist managerial incursion into spheres of professional influence (Kitchener 1999). It remains the case, however, that attempts to reshape professional roles have been an integral feature of the reforms of employment practices over the last two decades.

Health service trade unions

Finally, the myriad of distinct occupational groups with separate training, pay and career structures is reflected in tensions over professional status, job boundaries and pay and their organization into separate, rival trade unions. To a limited extent a complex multi-union environment has been simplified by a series of trade union mergers over the last decade. Nonetheless, an important feature of trade union structure in the NHS is that several of the most influential trade unions are not affiliated to the TUC and combine the functions of trade unions and professional associations, recruiting only within the health sector. The British Medical Association (BMA) and the Royal College of Nursing (RCN) are the most influential, with memberships of 111,000 and 334,000 respectively (Certification Officer 2002: 64). These organizations have been termed 'professional unions' to signify that they do not rely exclusively on collective bargaining but instead attempt to control labour supply by limiting membership to registered professionals with an orientation towards the defence of job demarcations and long-standing pay differentials (Burchill 1995). Using Kelly's (1996: 80) distinction between

Table 2.5 *Components of union militancy and moderation*

Component	Militancy	Moderation
Goals	Ambitious demand (scale and scope) with few concessions	Moderate demands with some or many concessions
Membership resources	Strong reliance on mobilization of union membership	Strong reliance on employers, third parties or the law
Institutional resources	Exclusive reliance on collective bargaining	Willingness to experiment with/support non-bargaining institutions
Methods	Frequent threat or use of industrial action	Infrequent threat or use of industrial action
Ideology	Ideology of conflicting interests	Ideology of partnership

Source: Kelly, 1996.

moderate and militant trade unions, these professional trade unions would be clustered towards the moderate end of the continuum (Table 2.5).

By contrast Unison, with 1.3 million members spread across the public services, has the largest trade union membership in the health service and would be more closely identified (albeit with some caveats) at the militant pole of Kelly's typology. It was formed in 1993 from the merger of three public service unions; the Confederation of Health Service Employees (COHSE), the National Union of Public Employees (NUPE), and the National and Local Government Officers' Association (NALGO). It organizes most of the union members among clerical and administrative staff (former NALGO members), the majority of ancillary staff members (mainly NUPE), and has a substantial membership among non-registered nursing staff (auxiliaries and health care assistants) in acute and non-acute settings. Unison is vigorously seeking to increase its membership among registered nursing staff where it faces intense competition from the RCN. In addition, the two general unions, the Transport and General Workers' Union (TGWU) and the General and Municipal Boilermakers' Union (GMB), recruit among ancillary staff but had few members in the case study trusts. Manufacturing, Science, Finance (MSF) (now part of Amicus) recruits technical workers and included the Health Visitors' Association.

As Table 2.4 indicates the differences in trade union orientation could be expected to impact on their approach towards a range of employment issues, as can be seen in the different stance between Unison and the RCN, the two trade unions most central to this study. As Burchill (1995) points out, professional unions are distinctive not least because they experienced rapid growth in membership during the 1980s when other unions faced membership decline. They have also faced a tension between pursuing a traditional trade union agenda of maximizing pay and conditions for the membership based on labour market power, as opposed to pursuing broader policy and professional issues which require wider forms of political mobilization and lobbying. These tensions are reflected in the structure and operation of the RCN, exemplified by separate Employment Relations, Nursing Policy and Education departments (Kessler and Heron 2001: 373). The RCN has been active in policy issues that affect their members' capacity to deliver high standards of professional care, and this professional orientation accounts for a long-standing reluctance to take industrial action and an unwillingness to open up their membership beyond the core registered nursing workforce.

This elitist orientation has been reflected in their approach to issues such as skill-mix, where there has been a concern about professional 'dilution', international recruitment that has been orientated to the implications for patient care more than the wages of those being recruited, and *Agenda for Change* that has focused on the professional development of nurses as much as the outcomes in pay terms. The RCN has been less willing to confront Conservative and Labour government policy as illustrated by the less forthright opposition to local pay than Unison and its initially muted response to PFI (Bach 2002: 330). Nonetheless there are signs that the demarcation between professional and trade union activities is being diluted. For example, in 1995 during the dispute over local pay (Chapter 4) the RCN membership voted for a new Rule 12 which allowed for 'action by members of the College in furtherance of an industrial dispute'.

Unison represents a less homogenous membership than the RCN, many of whom are low paid. Its structure reflects the attempt, when it was established, to develop a new approach to union government based on the principle of proportionality that aimed to ensure that the union's governance structures were representative of its membership (Terry 1996). Tensions remain within Unison in reconciling the different traditions of local organization and lay control that informed NALGO in comparison to the more centralized full-time officer tradition that characterized NUPE. These differences reflect differences in approach about the most effective way of responding to the restructuring of public services (Fairbrother 2000: 61). The differences with the RCN ensure that lay activist pressure is exerted more directly, not least in the election of the general secretary. These differences are reflected in a more ideologically opposed stance towards issues of local pay and the private finance initiative, and a capacity to mobilize workplace members, especially in its strongholds among ancillary workers.

It is not surprising that despite the distinctive origins and character of the RCN and Unison the approach of each union influences the other. For example, the capacity of Unison to take national industrial action in the NHS is constrained by the orientation of the RCN. Unison, however, has been developing its professional services, trying to give a high profile to the concerns of particular NHS occupational groups such as nurses, although this task remains hampered by the lack of organization by profession within Unison. Similarly the RCN has focused more attention on developing its steward network, albeit with mixed results (Kessler and Heron 2001). The RCN and Unison confront many of the same challenges: both unions appear to be able to articulate membership concerns at national level but confront weaknesses in organization at the workplace, limiting their ability to influence employers at trust level. Whether this intensifies competition for members or provides scope for more co-operative inter-union relations remains to be seen.

Consequently, the distinctive professional character of the NHS workforce, and an ideology of professionalism, has influenced the behaviour of the NHS workforce and their ambivalent response to government health service reforms. These concerns have been articulated by NHS unions. They have mobilized nationally against government policies and in some cases galvanized workplace union organization to reinforce national campaigns

This chapter has examined the specific characteristics of the health sector. The pattern of workplace reform can only be understood in relation to these distinctive features of the health service context. First, budgetary constraints have been a perennial feature of the economy model of the NHS that has been translated into low staffing levels in the NHS in comparison to other OECD countries. Successive governments, underpinned by Treasury concerns about the cost of the NHS, have forced managers to implement cost efficiency programmes, but the effectiveness of such reforms has been influenced by wider management and organizational reforms considered in Chapter 3. Second, the centralized form of the British state and the integrated nature of the health service created scope for governments to shape directly the direction of health policy and management to a degree that has few parallels in other European countries. Fiscal pressures and centralizing tendencies have to be placed alongside the third distinctive characteristic of the health sector, the influence of professional staff in the workforce, especially the medical profession, that has played a key role in shaping the evolution of the health service. The professional character of the workforce has also influenced strongly the form of trade unionism within the NHS.

This chapter has started to identify the reforms that successive Conservative and Labour governments have implemented in the health service and some of the consequences for the workforce. As Table 2.4 indicated there have been some increases in professional and medical staff employed to cope with a rising and more complex workload. Nonetheless, considering the large increases in aggregate activity levels (Table 2.3), employment levels among key occupational groups have increased less rapidly than workload over the last decade. This is suggestive of a process of work intensification, an interpretation borne out by other data (Green 2001). In Chapter 3 the management and organizational reforms that may account for these developments are examined, and the degree that they corroborate or undermine the key characteristics of the health service identified in this chapter is considered.

3 REFORMING NHS MANAGEMENT PRACTICE

It has become commonplace to argue that the public sector has undergone a transformation in management practice and values over the past twenty years. This chapter examines the management revolution within the NHS under successive Conservative and Labour governments. It explores the development of general management, the establishment of the NHS internal market and the policies instigated since 1997 under Labour. It locates these developments within the debates about the emergence and impact of the new public management (NPM).

The consideration of the role played by management in the restructuring of the public services has become a dominant preoccupation of policy, but the form and significance of these reforms has been contested (Clarke *et al.* 2000; Cutler and Waine 1997; Ferlie *et al.* 1996). In essence the new public management rests on the twin doctrines of using private sector management techniques to enhance organizational performance, and shifting away from a bureaucratic procedural orientation towards a focus on measurable results (Hood 2000). Dunleavy and Hood (1994) summarize these developments as moving 'down group' (de-emphasizing differences between the private and public sectors) and shifting 'down grid' (from a focus on administrative process to outcome requirements). For Cutler and Waine (1997) this overall approach was given concrete expression in the NHS through the introduction of corporate management arrangements following the Griffiths Report (Griffiths 1983); the establishment of performance indicators and competitive tendering initiatives; the development of the NHS internal market and reforms to public sector pay determination.

Management in the public domain

The new public management agenda has highlighted the degree to which public services management practice is distinct from that in the private sector. It has become fashionable to suggest that this distinction has become less evident and that some convergence between the two sectors has occurred (for an overview see Boyne 2002). Ackroyd *et al.* (1989) disagree, arguing that public service management is distinctive because of the relationship between public service workers and their clients in which they exercise a high degree of autonomy and professional judgement. Management style is shaped by this labour process and is described as *custodial management* because it preserves the customary standards of service provision, as defined by professionals, within a wider framework of political choices. Advocates of a new public management claim that these values have been eroded, and rightly so, by the recent restructuring of the public services.

The importance of recent reforms does not diminish the distinctive characteristics of public service management which need to be forcibly restated to counter the orthodoxy of those who wish to 'reinvent government'. A number of commentators suggest that public service management differs fundamentally from that in the private sector, in terms of objectives, the context in which it operates and the constraints upon performance (Ranson and Stewart 1994; Mintzberg 1996).

The implications are that a number of enduring features of the public sector continue to shape management practice. First, in terms of the organizational context public sector organizations are distinctive because they are more transparent and open in the manner that they operate. Managers are an integral part of the political process, translating collective values expressed through the ballot box into policy initiatives. Politics cannot therefore be removed from management, and the public service management process is more open to external influences, remaining sensitive to the vagaries of the electoral cycle and the shifting policy priorities of government (Farnham and Horton 1996: 8–10). As noted in the last chapter this is especially so in a highly centralized and politically sensitive service such as the NHS. The management process is not simply a technical activity, but a political one in which managers interpret political signals, deriving from a variety of stakeholders, and shape policies to suit their local needs, while delivering for government the targets required of them. As one trust chief executive commented:

Politics is often seen as a dirty word in NHS management, but it is a key part of our job; people who say they are divorced [from it] don't really understand their job. (Interview notes, August 2001)

It could be anticipated, however, that this would make the pursuit of coherent management strategies difficult because of the permeability of management practice, the influence of multiple stakeholders, and the short-time horizons that confront managers.

Second, public sector organizations have distinct goals that place constraints on how managers operate and necessitate distinctive managerial processes (Ranson and Stewart 1994). Their primary purpose is set by government and includes goals that are absent from the private sector in terms of equity, access and accountability (Ferlie *et al.* 1996: 226). The relationship with the customer also differs substantially from customer interactions in the private sector because there may be no direct monetary exchange, much of the value received is collective, public value, and the organization may be trying to ration the service rather than maximise its sales (Mintzberg 1996). In terms of achieving these goals, despite attempts to link resource use more closely to performance, public services remain cash limited and face a range of budgetary pressures. It is not simply that public service managers are likely to face greater resource constraints than private sector managers, but rather that their scope to respond to these difficulties is severely constrained. Many of the options available to private sector managers, for example, to increase prices, to divest themselves of particular services, to enter new markets or raise additional income, are severely circumscribed by political choices and regulatory rules.

Third, public sector organizations have a distinctive workforce with particular values, characterized as a public service ethos (Pratchett and Wingfield 1996). This refers to a blend of values which shape behaviour that includes being service rather than profit motivated, a loyalty to collective values of community that extends beyond the boundaries of their employing organization and an acceptance of the legitimacy of other features of the public domain such as political accountability (Pratchett and Wingfield 1996: 108–9). The result is that those who provide public services are trusted by the communities they serve. These values are fostered by the distinct occupational identities and labour market characteristics of many public service professions. Because the health service workforce is dominated by professional staff, these values permeate the organization. Frequently, long periods of training are required in which workers are socialized into a particular set of values that are sustained by common policy networks and, in the case of professions, systems of self-regulation. As the Audit Commission (2002: 16) has highlighted, individuals seek jobs in the public sector because it provides roles in which they 'can make a difference'. These values may be most closely associated with traditional public service professions, but managers as well are viewed as less materialistic than their private sector counterparts (Steele 2000). Consequently, the shift towards externally imposed contractualism, policies of performance-related pay and other financial incentives are unlikely to enhance staff commitment or organizational performance (Boyne 2002: 102; Le Grand 1997). It is the combination of these factors that makes the public sector management process distinctive.

Enter new public management

The 'new public management' movement has its ideological roots in public choice theory with its emphasis on 'producer capture'. It is suggested that public bureaucrats engage in bureau-maximizing behaviour to increase their status and remuneration (Niskanen 1971; for a critique see Self 2000). Conservative and Labour governments have been critical of the producer domination of public services. In a phrase that echoes earlier Conservative sentiments, the Prime Minister's Office of Public Services Reform suggested:

> They [public services] have to be refocused round the needs of the patients, the pupils, the passengers and the general public rather than the problems of those who provide the service. (Office of Public Services Reform 2002: 8)

New public management policies are therefore framed to curb the entrenched power of the professions. The underlying ideological orientation is towards legitimating the role of managers as the custodians of public service organizations by emphasizing their unique competencies and stressing their managerial accountability for individual and organizational performance.

A first element concerns the establishment of a cadre of managers to enforce a more 'business-like' approach with stronger managerial and financial controls. These managers are ceded greater operational control but are also more subject to centralized forms of audit. New public management is therefore simultaneously more centralized and decentralized. It separates 'steering from rowing' (Osborne and Gaebler 1992: 34–7) with policy goals set and monitored by the centre with service delivery devolved to separate agencies. To achieve their performance goals, required changes in employment practices include tighter control of staff through clearer performance targets, linked to individual performance related pay, and more forceful management of issues such as absenteeism. In addition, pay determination should be devolved to enhance management authority and rewards more closely to local labour market conditions and organizational requirements.

A second element focuses on the devolution of managerial responsibilities from central government to local level within reformed organizational structures. The establishment of NHS trusts was accompanied by the formal devolution of employment practices to trust managers. The devolution of responsibility for personnel practice was accompanied by concerted efforts to develop personnel expertise, not only among personnel specialists but also by developing the human resource capabilities of line managers. Devolution of managerial responsibilities therefore opened up the possibility of the development of a more strategic personnel function at trust level (Bach 1995).

A third element stresses that public sector managers have to shift from management by hierarchy to management by contract with competitive mechanisms used to put pressure on managers and employees to enhance performance and alter employment practices. Under Conservative governments market-type mechanisms such as competitive tendering and the internal market were developed that forced managers to compete to provide services. The Labour government has been more sceptical of market forms of competition, preferring to encourage managers to compete for earmarked resources linked to the attainment of performance targets (Newman 2001: ch. 5).

Interpreting NPM: strategic choice or regulation inside government?

The significance of the new public management for employment relations is that the emphasis on new organizational forms coupled with operational devolution opens up the spectre that managers may be able to act more strategically in the policies they adopt for their workforce. Strategic choice frameworks, however, that focus on the employer unit neglect the distinctive characteristics of the NHS outlined in Chapter 2. This is a more secure starting point for consideration of management practice that is shaped by the public service regulatory regime applied to the NHS and the requirements of the audit explosion (Cope and Goodship 1999; Hood *et al.* 2000; Power 1997). This refers to the manner in which NHS trusts are being guided, controlled and monitored to ensure that they subscribe to a central government policy framework that is overseen by arms-length public service agencies with authority to enforce their mandate. The prominence of central regulation, noted in Chapter 2, has three implications for the consideration of employment practices. First, NHS trusts are the employing unit and therefore remain the focus of attention, but in contrast to the strategic choice framework that concentrates on local management policies, the importance of government regulation places greater weight on the interplay between workplace developments and the influence of the regulatory framework in shaping trust practice.

Second, the focus on the NHS regulatory regime reinforces the importance of the sector – health – for understanding workplace employment relations. Although variations in employment practices are to be expected between trusts for historical reasons and arising from different management capacities, it is the *similarities* between trust policies that are likely to be at least as significant as the differences. This argument bears similarities to DiMaggio and Powell's (1983) analysis which considered why there is homogeneity of organizational practices within a field (akin to a sector) rather than variation, a process termed isomorphism. They examine the pressures that lead organizations to seek common solutions, which provide legitimacy for management actions, ensuring continued influence and access to resources. Many of their predictors of isomorphic change are pertinent to the NHS.

Coercive isomorphism stems from political influence exerted by organizations on which they are dependent; the government is able to impose requirements on trust managers, for example targets for absence levels or waiting times. *Mimetic* isomorphism refers to the modelling of one organization's policies on another. Labour government policy has emphasized the importance of benchmarking good practice and reducing variations in performance. The Modernization Agency and the Audit Commission are two agencies that seek to spread best NHS practice across the NHS. The SHRINE network and the national HR conference perform a similar function for human resource management interventions. *Normative* isomorphism signals the existence of standards that pervade a particular field, and DiMaggio and Powell viewed the professionalization process as the primary mechanism. The existence of professional groups that operate across the NHS, sharing a specific body of knowledge and a common training, located within professional networks that can diffuse knowledge rapidly, is a powerful source of normative isomorphism. Consequently one could anticipate many similarities in terms of the employment practices adopted rather than the variations implied by the strategic choice framework.

Third, the emphasis on the public service regulatory framework draws attention to issues of trust. Tonkiss and Passey (1999: 258) have argued in relation to voluntary organizations that relations of trust that 'pertain to ethical relations that are not conditioned by an external framework of controls' are being replaced by relations of confidence, 'which are secured by contract or other regulatory forms'. Similar implications flow from Le Grand's (1997: 149) analysis that policy-makers no longer view public service workers as altruistic knights, but rather as self-interested knaves that bring forth low-trust policies based on contractual relations. The implication is that as the state no longer places trust in individual health professionals more bureaucratic and systematized forms of control are developed to demonstrate to a sceptical public that they can be *confident* about systems of regulation that safeguard service standards. The implications for staff ethos and morale are only now being recognized. As the Public Administration Select Committee (2002: 16) noted:

> There is also the question of the effect of an externally-imposed measurement culture on the ethos of public service. There is a danger that such a culture can erode trust and damage the values of professionalism.

These analyses resonate with Fox's classic analysis of employment contracts (Fox 1974). Fox contrasted high-trust relationships based on status with low-trust relationships based on contract. In high-trust relationships the parties trust each other to fulfil a set of obligations which are not precisely defined. The continuous honouring of these obligations reinforces and strengthens the high-trust relationship. In low-trust relationships, an opposite dynamic operates with the presumption among managers that employees will act opportunistically and 'cheat'. This leads to a battery of control structures – tight supervision, formal rules and clearly defined obligations. These measures are perceived by the workforce to indicate that managers do not trust them and are resented. Low trust begets low trust in a downward spiral which reinforces the low-trust dynamic, by encouraging self-interested behaviour which unleashes further control mechanisms. It is relatively easy to shift an organization from a high-trust to a low-trust dynamic, but much harder to reverse this pattern.

To summarize, the implementation of the new public management has profound implications for NHS management practice. The strategic choice and public service regulatory perspectives draw different conclusions about the consequences of the NPM. It is only by examining the development of management practice in the NHS that the value of these competing perspectives can be assessed.

Towards new public management in the NHS

During the 1950s and 1960s the NHS grew rapidly, influenced by technological innovations in medicine, social changes and sustained economic growth. These trends were reflected in concerns to develop the organization and management of the NHS to ensure effective control of resources. Barnard and Harrison (1986) highlight two key trends. First, there was the development of more formalized management hierarchies with defined management roles. One of the earliest and best known attempts resulted from the recommendations of the Salmon Report that nursing management should become a function in its own right with the development of an extended nursing hierarchy (Salmon 1966). Second, from the mid-1960s new management specialisms emerged which clamoured for influence with other existing groups. In the support services functional managers of domestic, laundry and catering services were introduced, linked to the increased specialization of nursing and the shedding of 'non-nursing' tasks. This trend was reinforced by the interest in scientific management, with work study techniques and bonus schemes established for ancillary staff, to boost their pay and productivity (National Board for Prices and Incomes 1971).

The 1974 reorganization attempted to develop a more integrated health service by creating area health authorities which were coterminous with local authorities. The principle of consensus management was adopted in which all members of a multi-disciplinary management team enjoyed nominally equal status. Its evolution aimed to reconcile the views of diverse professional groups and to accommodate the emergent functional specialisms. This system proved ill-adapted to the difficulties of achieving consensus in a harsher economic climate and the more conflictual industrial relations climate of the late 1970s. The concept of a chief executive, however, had been explicitly rejected because of the complexity of the health care environment and because it was viewed as incompatible with professional independence. The injection of a chief executive role into the NHS was likely to prove controversial.

In 1979, the Conservative government entered office determined to curb public expenditure and improve efficiency in the public sector. Better management was assigned a high priority with efficiency improvements expected to flow from tighter control of performance and the generation of more information to aid decision-making. During this period NHS performance indicators were developed which enabled, for the first time, comparisons to be made between health authorities, providing the antecedents for financial and other targets that trust managers are required to fulfil. The most important initiative was triggered by the recommendations of the Griffiths Report (Griffiths 1983). Roy Griffiths, Managing Director of Sainsbury's, led the inquiry, which was envisaged by Mrs Thatcher as an investigation of manpower problems. These had been highlighted by the 1982 strikes and exacerbated by the rudimentary state of workforce planning in which there was no overall system of control and planning of staff numbers (Halpern 1983; Webster 2002: 168). Griffiths, however, broadened its remit because he suggested that manpower problems were integral to the management process. The inquiry was completed in approximately six months and its recommendations took the form of a 24-page letter to the Secretary of State orientated towards recommendations rather than analysis.

The central proposition of the Griffiths Report was that a distinct general management role modelled on private sector practice should be established in the NHS at each organizational tier to provide leadership and motivate the workforce. These ideas were rooted in criticisms of consensus management. In a particularly acerbic paragraph Griffiths asserted:

> if Florence Nightingale were carrying her lamp through the corridors of the NHS today she would almost certainly be searching for the people in charge.
> (Griffiths 1983: para. 5)

Griffiths aimed to strengthen the unit level by establishing unit general managers with greater discretion to develop organizational structures linked to local requirements.

At the apex of the NHS, Griffiths criticized the blurred responsibilities between the Department of Health and the NHS and proposed the establishment of an NHS Management Board reporting to an NHS Supervisory Board. The Supervisory Board was to be the equivalent of the board of directors, chaired by the Secretary of State, with overall responsibility for NHS policy. The Management Board was responsible for implementing policy and was particularly concerned with finance and performance review. It was expected that the chairman would be drawn from outside the NHS, an implicit rejection of the assumption that NHS management was distinctive.

Finally, the Griffiths recommendations incorporated a more developed role for the personnel function, including a separate personnel director for the Management Board. Despite the labour intensive character of the NHS, the centralized and inflexible national pay bargaining machinery left limited scope for the development of local personnel initiatives, confining personnel to a fire-fighting role. This situation had been compounded by the shortage of suitable personnel officers and health authorities' reluctance to fund adequately the personnel function (McCarthy 1983a). Griffiths argued that:

> Devolution in personnel matters will imply a strengthening of the personnel function at each level and its close support of line management. (Griffiths 1983: para. 24)

Consequently the Griffiths reforms provided an important stimulus for the development of the NHS personnel function that started to shift from an advisory role towards becoming part of the corporate management team (Buchan 2000: 320).

The impact of general management

The government and senior managers reacted warmly to the proposals, but a frosty response was forthcoming from professional staff. The RCN waged, and lost, a high profile campaign whose central message was that 'nursing should be run by nurses'. The medical profession, while wary about the threat to clinical freedom posed by general management, anticipated that many of these posts would be filled by clinicians on a part-time basis, a view encouraged by Griffiths' emphasis on clinicians entering management. Public service trade unions viewed the introduction of a more commercial management approach as inappropriate and likely to result in worse pay and conditions, more centralized control and the weakening of democratic accountability (NALGO 1984). The government ignored these objections and instructed health authorities to establish the general management function by the end of 1985.

The first assumption of the Griffiths Report that a strengthened management role would improve decision-making and allow a more decisive style of management was partially borne out at unit level (Pollitt *et al.* 1991). There was little evidence of a more strategic approach to decision-making, however, because general managers were overwhelmingly concerned with a narrow, finance-driven agenda and reacting to short-term political imperatives. This situation was exacerbated by the number of national priorities (47), which was widely agreed to be unmanageable. Nurses' concerns were largely realized; few nurses were appointed to general management positions, and they were frequently excluded from the district management boards. A lead for these changes had been provided by Griffiths, who recommended that the chief nursing officer be excluded from the Supervisory Board.

The management changes at the centre of the NHS revealed some of the limitations of Griffiths' reluctance to acknowledge the distinctiveness of public service management practice. General management was conceived as a way of separating the politics of policy-making at 'head-office' level (via the Supervisory Board) from the management of the NHS led by the Management Board. The artificial nature of this division led to the abolition of the Supervisory Board, but this left an ambiguous relationship between the Management Board and the Department of Health (Webster 2002: 172). The abrupt resignation of Victor Paige, brought in from the private sector as the first chairman of the Management Board, highlighted the difficulties when he argued that the Griffiths Report was 'flawed', complaining that:

> Ministers take all the important decisions, political, strategic and managerial. Because of that, the intention to devolve executive accountability and authority from the Secretary of State did not happen. Indeed within existing policies and practices it never could. (Paige 1987: 7)

The NHS Management Board was remodelled to become the NHS Management Executive (Management was subsequently dropped from its title) and the tension between management and policy resolved by giving the NHS Executive responsibility for both functions in 1995. This, however, created an uneasy relationship between the Department of Health and the NHS Executive (Day and Klein 2001).

The implementation of the Griffiths recommendations represented a relatively early example of the adoption of the precepts of the new public management in the NHS. Three issues can be highlighted which are relevant in evaluating the scope for strategic management practice within trusts. First, the experience of general management suggests that many of the prescriptions associated with new public management may be difficult to apply. Griffiths assumed that clear objectives could be set, allowing management devolution and performance monitoring. This failed to recognize sufficiently the complexity and political nature of the NHS environment in which professional standards shape the establishment of objectives which are frequently contested. General managers were reluctant to challenge doctors because they were acutely aware that if they lost the confidence of medical staff their own tenure would end abruptly. The continuing autonomy of medical staff blunted Griffiths' vision of a single chain of command with all decisions vested in general managers. This interpretation challenges the 'transformational' role assigned to managers in the NPM literature. It also highlights wider questions about the capacity of governments to set targets for the NHS that are acceptable to all stakeholders and transparent, thereby reducing the scope for opportunistic behaviour.

Second, the scope for strategic management practice by senior NHS managers was curtailed because the separation of policy decisions from operational management decisions was less clear-cut than Griffiths assumed. The experience of the NHS Supervisory and Management Boards illustrated the difficulties of this approach. Political intervention in management decisions was also evident in the prescriptive nature of the implementation circular, government pressure to appoint outsiders to general management posts and the central vetting of district health authority structures (Edwards 1993: 87). The distinction between policy and operational decisions was therefore hard to sustain in a publicly funded organization with a high political profile in which the government approves senior management appointments.

Third, the imposition of general management illustrates the ideological assumptions surrounding the new public management. Griffiths was irritated by the suggestion that selling groceries was not comparable to treating patients, and he argued that similar management principles could be applied to all organizations because private sector profit targets 'do not immediately impinge on large numbers of managers below board level' (Griffiths 1983: 10). The Social Services Select Committee was more sceptical because of the dominance of professional staff within the NHS which they anticipated would prove resistant to 'mechanistic management hierarchies' (Social Services Committee 1984: ix). This implied that other management initiatives based on private sector 'best practice', such as devolved pay bargaining, could be expected to meet with similar difficulties.

Contracts, markets and reform

As the 1980s proceeded the Conservative government became convinced that managerial changes were a necessary but not a sufficient condition to achieve fundamental reforms of the NHS. The solution proposed in the 1989 White Paper *Working for Patients* (Department of Health 1989) was for the stimulus of competition to improve efficiency. The Conservative government therefore aimed to shift public debate from a concern about the level of resources to a focus on the effective utilization of the NHS budget. It was asserted that the invisible hand of the market would achieve the following: pressurize clinicians and other staff to take more notice of their use of resources; instil market principles and business planning into the fabric of the NHS;

undermine restrictive practices and erode national pay bargaining; increase user influence over health care services; and deflect criticisms of the NHS from politicians towards the performance of local managers. The advocates of market principles were influenced by public choice theory, which suggested that in the absence of market information and competitive pressures administrators would yield to the demands of organized interest groups (Mather 1991).

At the core of the internal market was the separation of the purchasing of health care from its provision by a range of competing providers. District health authorities (DHAs) were recast into the role of purchasers, assessing the needs of their resident populations and buying a range of services for them, using contracts with providers to establish activity levels, prices and quality standards. Health authority budgets remained cash limited and were reduced in proportion to the transfer of funds to the other type of purchaser, GP fundholders. They were provided with a budget to purchase a defined range of primary and hospital based services on behalf of their patients.

On the provider side, *Working for Patients* envisaged that all health providers would eventually become self-governing trusts (subsequently termed NHS trusts) and compete for contract income. Trusts were to be managed by boards of executive and non-executive directors. The government's intention was that the management of trusts would mirror private sector practice with greater autonomy over financial and personnel matters than had traditionally existed. Trusts would be able to employ their own staff on trust terms and conditions of employment, devise their own consultation and bargaining arrangements, dispose of surplus property and borrow subject to an external financing limit set annually by the NHS Executive. These 'freedoms' were linked to a new accounting regime which required them to break even and make a 6 per cent return on the value of their assets.

The power of the Secretary of State to intervene directly in operational management issues was strengthened (Hughes 1991) and the mandate of the Audit Commission was extended to the NHS, reflecting the increase in public sector regulation noted earlier. For medical staff, performance evaluation was increased by the introduction of medical audit and by the role given to managers in assessing merit awards and agreeing job plans with consultants. The centralization of the NHS was actually increased with local authority representatives removed from health authorities and the role of community health councils reduced.

Reaction to *Working for Patients* centred initially on the issue of trusts. Government ministers argued that the increased autonomy associated with trust status would create more flexible management and faster decision-taking geared towards local needs, resulting in better patient care. Opposition to the establishment of trusts reflected concerns about the further advancement of managerial priorities to the detriment of professional values (British Medical Association 1989). For trade unions generally, trusts were 'opting-out' of the NHS, and because they would be autonomous and managed along commercial criteria, trust status was the Trojan horse that would lead inexorably to the privatization and fragmentation of the health service. As this process unfolded they predicted that their members would be subject to poorer terms and conditions of employment as trade union influence and national pay bargaining were eroded.

The internal market: a regulated market?

The internal market was intended to stimulate competition and enable resources to be allocated to more efficient providers. As labour costs are the largest component of trust expenditure, the degree of competitive and financial pressure arising from the internal market was expected to impact on the restructuring of employment practices. The form of the internal market and the impact of the market-style reforms were shaped by the features of the health service identified in Chapter 2, and this produced a series of unintended consequences.

In a similar fashion to the Griffiths reforms, the internal market was imposed on the NHS over a short period of time. This demonstrates the capacity of governments in a highly centralized state with an integrated health service to implement a system of 'dictated competition' (Light 2001). This term signifies that the terminology of markets was used as a form of central regulation to alter incentive structures and challenge professional norms of behaviour. Cost efficiency criteria incorporated into contractual relations between purchasers and providers were intended to take precedence over clinically defined service requirements. The traditional role of professional staff was eroded. Medical and para-medical staff were particularly concerned about the way in which a service ethos was being replaced by a competitive ethos. This ethos discouraged co-operation and prevented the exchange of information and advice that characterized the health service prior to the internal market (Lee-Potter 1997: 247–8; Potter 2000).

In key respects the internal market was fostered and steered by central government regulations. Direct political control was exercised by appointing the chairs of all trust boards and health authorities that were accountable to the Secretary of State for Health. Regional health authorities were consolidated and then absorbed into central government. Information about the impact of the NHS reforms was scarce because there was no central government evaluation of the internal market. The dismantling of the regional health authorities, senior trust managers' emphasis on 'commercial confidentiality', and the erosion of data quality and availability within a more fragmented NHS, exacerbated these informational shortcomings (Buchan 2000: 321). This enabled the government to pursue a policy of 'success by declaration' (Light 2001) (see, for example, NHS Management Executive 1992). Consequently the internal market functioned with limited information, of poor quality, and great uncertainty about the costs of NHS services (Paton *et al.* 1998: 101).

Heightened political sensitivity about the reforms, and a poorly structured market, resulted in increased central control and political directives. For trust managers this led to a disjuncture between the rhetoric of 'trust freedoms' and the reality that managers perceived about their limited room for manoeuvre. The government sought the gains from competition but feared the political consequences of trusts becoming financially insolvent or making service reductions. When the internal market was introduced in April 1991 the political sensitivity of the changes, close to a general election, led the government to slow down implementation, with the first year intended to be a period of 'steady-state', implying a gradual transition from the previous system. As one trust manager commented bitterly:

> However no-one had told the first wave Trusts that the brave new world was not upon them. The decision that the spirit of the reforms would be jettisoned occurred after our Trust managers had made their plans. The rug was pulled from under the feet of those first wave trusts which had sought to take a lead. (Small and Baker 1994: 175–6)

This caution continued, with the Conservative government vacillating in terms of whether it wished to see something akin to a real market developing in the NHS or whether it intended to stifle competition and regulate the market.

These difficulties were compounded by the existence of weak purchasers and strong providers. Trust managers manipulated contract prices to cross-subsidize between services and purchasers, scarcely conducive to a competitive market environment (Ellwood 1996). NHS trusts had the advantage of being larger organizations than purchasing authorities, with more resources available to assess their costs, and they were aware that it was almost impossible for purchasers to adequately monitor contract performance. As one seasoned commentator noted:

> I have observed one management group in a hospital take a deliberate decision to reclassify endoscopic procedures carried out in a minor treatment suite as day surgery cases. This would increase the nominal contract income they attracted compared to being recorded as outpatient attendances. While this was the most naked example of fixing the figures, no doubt others have gone on, not least because of the wide range of activities carried out in hospitals and the lack of detailed data quantifying them. (West 1997: 142)

Nonetheless the impact of fiscal constraints remained apparent. Health authorities faced with limited budgets had an incentive to pass the problem of what has been termed 'overproviding' (i.e. trusts undertaking unfunded activity) to trust managers. This appeared to be borne out by health authorities' preference for block contracts that only loosely coupled activity levels to resources provided (Paton *et al.* 1998: 78).

It was very difficult for purchasers to shift work away from their main provider trusts, not only because of the informational vacuum which would make it difficult to justify publicly such decisions, but also because the historical development of the NHS has been towards integrated district general hospitals providing a comprehensive range of services, effectively acting as local monopoly providers of services. This trend was reinforced by the accelerating process of trust mergers, and a long-term decline in bed numbers, that ensured there was very little spare capacity in the NHS.

Purchasers wished to support their local trust while maintaining the pressure on them 'to do more for less'. Low-trust behaviour was a feature of the conflictual relationships that developed between purchasers and providers, reflecting the relative underdevelopment of the purchaser role and its lower status compared to trust management (Hargadon 1993; Wall 1993). Trust managers unreasonably refused information to purchasers, while purchasers intervened in the operational concerns of trusts. This situation was reinforced by the financial constraints faced by both parties.

The case study evidence explored in later chapters examines the ways in which a more regulated and centralized approach to the internal market emerged, blunting the radical intent of *Working for Patients* and potentially diminishing the discretion available to trust managers, especially in reforming employment practices.

New Labour: from marketization to modernization

The election of a Labour government in 1997 after eighteen years of continuous Conservative government marked an important juncture for the NHS. The Labour government aimed to balance its instinctive hostility to the internal market reforms, alongside its enthusiastic endorsement for other components of the Conservatives' management revolution. The government maintained that 'over the past 20 years, various management changes within the public service have improved value for money and quality in the way services are delivered' (Cabinet Office 1999: 11). They were also confronted with the difficulty of reconciling their pledge to abolish the internal market while at the same time reassuring managers and staff, wearied by the continuous process of reform, that further structural changes would not arise from Labour's health agenda (Paton 1999).

In its White Paper, *The New NHS: Modern, Dependable* the government criticized the internal market, which it argued had incurred high administrative costs and encouraged a secretive and competitive ethos arising from the annual system of contract negotiations (Department of Health 1997). Primary Care Groups (PCGs) replaced GP fundholding and were made mandatory for all GPs to prevent the 'two-tierism' associated with fundholding. PCGs have evolved to become autonomous Primary Care Trusts (PCTs), merging purchasing and providing roles. They also hold the primary and hospital care budgets, commissioning services from other providers, but provide primary and community services directly. This process started in April 2000 and is expected to be completed by April 2004. As part of its attempt to devolve resources to the 'frontline', PCTs will control 75 per cent of the NHS budget by 2004 (Department of Health 2002c: 29). The next stage in this policy evolution is the integration of health and social care by establishing Care Trusts.

The abolition of the internal market was accompanied by an intensification of the management revolution. Whereas the previous Conservative government had relied primarily on market mechanisms to improve performance, the Labour government was more sceptical, preferring to intensify the audit culture. The government emphasized the need for improvements in service quality, reinforced by new regulatory institutions and a stronger focus on performance management.

The New NHS outlined measures to ensure high standards of care at trust level and to promote improvements in clinical practice, a process termed clinical governance. Within trusts, chief executives' statutory responsibility for financial performance was extended to incorporate quality of care. The implication was that whereas during the 1980s and 1990s managers had tried to draw clinical staff into management by encouraging clinicians to become budget holders, the duty of quality would, for the first time, require chief executives to take a direct responsibility for the quality of clinical services. This potentially signalled a large shift in the frontier of control from medical staff to trust chief executives.

This measure was complemented by the establishment of the National Institute for Clinical Excellence (NICE) in 1999 that undertakes evidence-based appraisals of new clinical interventions and produces guidelines on the clinical and cost effectiveness of treatments that should be employed in the NHS (Rawlings 1999). In addition to central guidelines on clinical treatments the Labour government has established central service guidelines. National Service Frameworks (NSFs) specify how particular conditions (e.g. heart disease, cancer) should be organized and treated locally. The increased standardization of clinical practice is justified by reference to the goal of reinforcing the national character of the NHS and reducing inequalities of outcome. A symbolic illustration of this emphasis on uniformity has been the requirement for hospitals to scrap their distinctive logos to ensure 'consistent branding' across the NHS (Waugh 2001: 5). To enforce national standards the government established the Commission for Health Improvement (CHI) with a remit to examine clinical governance in practice, including system failures, reviewing the work of every trust, health authority and PCT every four years. As a type of Ofsted for the NHS, the government emphasized that it would be less confrontational and more developmental than its counterpart for schools (Klaushofer 2000), but some of its early investigations precipitated the departure of trust chief executives (see Thompson 2001). CHI and other forms of accountability could be expected to increase the pressure on staff as they attempt to achieve government defined performance targets. Taken together the trilogy of NICE, CHI and NSFs constitute the building blocks of corporate governance and have been interpreted as probably 'the most systematic strategy for controlling doctors ever attempted in the NHS' (Harrison 2002: 474).

Human resource management: working together

The Labour government viewed human resource management as integral to their management reforms in a manner that contrasted with the Conservative government's narrower preoccupation with local pay. *The New NHS* acknowledged the importance of staff development and involvement which in the past had 'not been a high priority' but pledged a new approach 'to better valuing staff' (Department of Health 1997: 50). With a legacy of poor human resource planning, low unemployment and widespread negative perceptions of working for the NHS (see Arnold *et al.* 2001), the government confronted endemic problems of recruitment and retention among many health care professions. As the NHS Executive bluntly acknowledged:

> Not all local employers have placed HR on their strategic agenda in a way which encourages a well thought out approach. As a result, development of human resource management capacity and best practice in human resources has been patchy . . . The lack of a clear strategic framework which locks human resource management effectively into the government's health care policies and service development objectives has been a major impediment to progress. (NHS Executive 1997: paras 3 and 7)

The government's HR priorities were set out in *Working Together* (Department of Health 1998), the first time that the NHS had set out a comprehensive approach to employment relations. The document contained three strategic aims. The NHS had to 'ensure . . . a quality workforce, in the right numbers with the right skills', 'demonstrate we are improving the quality of working life for staff' and 'address the management capacity and capability required to deliver this agenda'. These aims were to be achieved by placing requirements on trust managers to develop policies, for example to tackle harassment, violence and racial discrimination, with target dates set for their achievement. The aims within *Working Together* continued to develop over the course of Labour's first term in government. A subsequent equalities framework required employers to offer flexible working patterns to ensure a proper work–life balance (Department of Health 2000b). A number of initiatives relating to recruitment and retention were launched, including an emphasis on increasing training places and more controversially increasing international recruitment (see Industrial Relations Services 2001a). Central to these efforts has been the *Improving Working Lives* (IWL) initiative that requires NHS employers to achieve the IWL standard by April 2003 and forms part of the HR performance framework. One component of creating a healthy workplace concerned the management of absence, with trust managers required to achieve a reduction of 20 per cent by 2001 and 30 per cent by 2003.

Many of the policies were targeted at individuals, although an emphasis on partnership working and staff involvement aimed to alter the culture of employment relations in the health service. The government has viewed partnership as a means to restore the idea of the 'good employer' to make the NHS 'the employer of first choice', although the main emphasis within government policy has been on direct rather than indirect (representative) forms of staff involvement. The requirements in *Working Together* were modest, focusing on developing an involvement policy, including relevant questions in each trust's annual staff survey and reviewing induction arrangements. These requirements did not suggest that involvement would become integral to the core concerns of senior management, and 'reviewing staff involvement' and 'establishing a partnership agreement' were the lowest priorities in terms of progress on thirteen HR goals in a survey of 75 trusts (Industrial Relations Services 1999: 5–6).

Nevertheless these initiatives were a tangible sign that the government viewed HR issues as integral to its reform agenda. *Working Together* was explicitly aimed at chief executives and chairs to raise the profile of HR issues and was an implicit recognition that the HR profession in the NHS lacked the authority to make human resource management issues a priority for trusts. Although the strategy emphasized the local delivery of targets, the balance between central guidance and local discretion was tilted strongly in favour of central direction. This took the form of numerous guidance documents that detailed the initiatives to be taken, how they were to be achieved and who had to be involved in their implementation. Whether hard-pressed human resource managers had the time to address the HR agenda and the extent to which the government would insist that all the targets were achieved in the prescribed timescales remained an open question.

The *NHS Plan*

By early 2000 the Labour government was on the defensive about the state of the NHS, with few tangible signs that health care had improved. The government responded with the *NHS Plan* (Department of Health 2000a), which was launched in July 2000 as a blueprint for improving the NHS. Like Mrs Thatcher a decade before, Tony Blair and the Downing Street Policy Unit were heavily involved in drawing up the *NHS Plan*, linking his personal credibility to the success of the reforms. The *NHS Plan* emerged fully formed with 144 pages of detailed aims, targets and inspection mechanisms and with the signatures of 25 key NHS stakeholders who looked forward to 'working with the Government in modernizing the NHS and ensuring change is delivered across health and social care' (Department of Health 2000a: 6).

It had an ostensibly modest vision, focused on delivering tangible improvements for patients, but it candidly outlined the shortcomings of the NHS. It was peppered with statements about a lack of national standards, demarcations between staff, the absence of clear incentives and the dearth of support and intervention to improve performance. This admission of partial failure not only legitimated the detailed reform agenda, it also signalled that the government would not tolerate any attempts by professional interests to modify the reform agenda. The *NHS Plan* was therefore Tony Blair's version of Mrs Thatcher's famous dictum, 'There is No Alternative'.

The Plan was the most comprehensive guide to New Labour's approach to the NHS. Existing systems of performance management were reinforced with NHS trusts issued annually with performance ratings (stars) linked to clinical effectiveness, patient experience, efficiency and capacity and capability. The ratings are graded from 3 stars, the highest level of performance, to zero stars, the poorest level of performance. Depending on the level of performance, trusts receive different levels of autonomy. The concept of earned autonomy and the option for the top performing trusts to apply for 'foundation' status stemmed from the *NHS Plan*, although it did not specifically mention foundation hospitals. Nevertheless repeated criticism that the government's centralized approach, focused on short-term political imperatives, was undermining managerial and public support for the *NHS Plan* (Calman *et al.* 2001) led the government to change tack.

This was signalled by the publication of *Shifting the Balance of Power* (Department of Health 2001a) that committed the government to decentralization and devolving power to the frontline. Foundation status was integral to this shift of emphasis, and the proposed 'freedoms' in terms of pay flexibility, accessing capital finance and retention of land sale monies (Department of Health 2002c: 30) echoed the early days of the trust movement. The willingness of the Treasury to loosen central control and allow greater financial independence remained uncertain, and these proposals also generated strong resistance from trade unions and professional associations.

Discussion

The analysis in this chapter suggests that management practice in the public services remains distinctive. This arises from the embeddedness of the NHS within a particular regulatory environment that is shaped by the characteristics of the NHS outlined in the previous chapter. It cannot be disputed that the techniques and values associated with the new public management have swept through the public services, but the outcomes appear less certain. General management had a fundamental impact on the management process within the NHS. It contributed to more effective implementation of central policy directives and allowed greater scrutiny of a range of activities, reinforcing the quest for increased efficiency. A stronger management ethos developed which was at the expense of professional staff, particularly nurses, who saw their influence at local level diminish. Managerial actions, however, remained constrained by unpredictable political interventions from above and clinical discretion and influence from below. The management revolution remained incomplete.

The establishment of the internal market tried to overcome these limitations by the addition of competition and market based restructuring. The ambiguities and short-termism inherent in an annual contracting process and budgetary constraints created incentives for trust managers to act opportunistically. This behaviour was reinforced by an inflexible financial framework with strict performance targets and uncertainty about the degree of regulation of the internal market. Trust managers were encouraged to use the greater flexibility in managing human resources to respond to these financial uncertainties with a potentially significant impact on the patterns of employment relations.

In contrast to the predictions of the new public management and strategic choice analysis, the internal market was associated with more centralized control over managers and more intrusive political intervention arising from the plethora of central directives that defined and regulated the market. This analysis is borne out by a survey of over 1,000 public service managers (20 per cent were from the NHS), undertaken during the internal market period (Talbot 1994). It revealed that there was considerable scepticism about the rhetoric surrounding new public management. For example, one of the findings was that public service managers' ability to resist political interference had declined sharply, the direct opposite of the result that would have been predicted by advocates of NPM. This outcome was attributed to the decentralization and fragmentation of the public services which seemed to weaken the bonds between managers. Because they worked in smaller units in which crucial decisions on performance pay or contract renewal involved political appointees, managers became more susceptible to political interventions.

The shift to explicit contracts between purchasers and providers may have become a transmission belt for enhancing managerial control over the workforce, providing a legitimation of management practice which can be blamed on an external party (e.g. the purchaser). These features of the internal market indicated a radically altered context for staff management. Uncertainties about contract income could have reinforced pressure on trust managers to economize on the wage bill and, second, trust managers may have developed forms of flexible employment practices which maximized their ability to respond to fluctuations in income. It is less clear whether the uncertainty associated with the internal market facilitated or inhibited managers in devising innovative employment practices.

The election of New Labour reinforced the management revolution. Its emphasis on strengthening the role of local managers and increasing their control over the workforce sits uneasily with the increased central government regulation of the NHS. The increases in the number and influence of regulatory organizations and the proliferation of potentially contradictory targets has left many health service workers feeling that they have limited discretion in shaping service delivery. This is especially incongruous as the *NHS Plan* states (para. 6.1) that the NHS is a 'high trust' organization and suggests that 'The NHS is an organization glued together by a bond of trust between staff and patient or, what some have called, "principled motivation".' The Labour government's anxiety about its capacity to improve the NHS sufficiently rapidly reinforced the emphasis on top-down change which many health service workers may have interpreted as a lack of trust in them.

The last two decades have witnessed a continuous process of management reorganization that has radically altered the context in which the workforce is managed. Trust managers have been subject to a range of performance targets and market-based incentives that have been overlain on existing features of the health service, especially centralized political control, financial constraints and the influence of professional staff. As the following chapters document, these contradictory pressures had a major impact on the reform of employment practices.

4 Pay Bargaining Reform

Since its establishment in 1948 the NHS has been subject to a series of reforms to its structure and management. In tandem with these changes industrial relations have evolved, with the growth of trade unions and more conflictual relations between the government and health service workers. By the 1970s these developments had stimulated increased managerial consideration of employment relations matters. In turn, there were numerous proposals, but limited action, to reform the institutional structures of pay determination. A national system of pay determination has remained intact, trade unions and professional associations have exerted an important influence over employment and policy matters, and the workforce has regarded with suspicion alterations to existing occupational hierarchies.

During eighteen years of Conservative government from 1979 to 1997, far-reaching changes to employment relations institutions and practices were an integral feature of their NHS reforms. The establishment of the internal market accelerated these developments, with NHS trusts granted discretion to employ staff on locally determined terms and conditions of employment. Since 1997, the Labour government has also embarked on pay bargaining reforms that are just as radical as those contemplated by their predecessors. This chapter examines the development of pay determination in the NHS and employer and government approaches to the management of pay. The historical evolution of national pay determination is outlined as a basis for evaluating more recent reforms of bargaining practice in the NHS, notably the partial shift to local pay bargaining and *Agenda for Change* (Department of Health 1999a).

Health service pay determination: the shortcomings of Whitleyism

The health service has been characterized by formal negotiation arrangements that were established across the public sector and referred to as 'Whitleyism'. This term derived from the Whitley subcommittees that examined the deterioration in public sector employment relations during the First World War and proposed a system of employment relations based on a number of principles. National pay and terms and conditions of employment were advocated, determined at national level by employers negotiating with trade unions in joint industrial councils. These arrangements incorporated explicit support for trade union membership and a belief in national collective bargaining (Carter and Fairbrother 1999: 122–5; Burchill and Casey 1996: 43–5).

In the late 1940s the Whitley model of national negotiations for pay and conditions of service was extended to the NHS. Originally nine functional councils were set up to determine the pay and conditions of particular occupational groups, with a general Whitley council establishing conditions of service common to all NHS staff (subject to ministerial approval). The problems associated with the Whitley arrangements quickly became visible, and during the 1950s there was frequent recourse to arbitration, which was not confined to pay issues (Loveridge 1971). These problems illustrated the limits of free collective bargaining and reflected the intimate involvement of the Treasury and the Ministry of Health in NHS wage fixing (Clegg and Chester 1957).

Many of these problems were masked by sustained economic growth which enabled increased resources to be devoted to the NHS and a rapid expansion in the numbers employed, ensuring high levels of job security. Nonetheless, imperceptibly at first, and then with a speed and magnitude that took both trade unions and NHS administrators by surprise, pay disputes and industrial action became a familiar feature of the NHS landscape from the late 1960s, culminating in the protracted industrial action of the Winter of 1978–79 and again in 1982 (Seifert 1992: 269–71). It appeared that dramatic changes in health service industrial relations had occurred in tandem with broader developments across the public sector (Winchester 1983: 176).

The origin of these changes was rooted in the severe political and economic problems of the British economy in the 1970s. Incomes policies and reductions in public expenditure followed, alongside measures to improve the efficiency of the health service. National and local disputes increased markedly, with a substantial increase in union membership and activity at local level. The number of days of strike action in the NHS rose from 500 in 1966 to 9,000 in 1969, and to 98,000 in 1972 (Merrison 1979: 460). Government incomes policies provoked the 1972–73 ancillary workers' strike, because government claims that low-paid workers would be protected from their consequences proved to be a hollow promise (Carpenter 1988: 349). The 1974 NHS reorganization, with its extended hierarchy and more specialist managerial roles, contributed to this altered industrial relations climate, and during the mid-1970s hospital consultants and junior doctors were also involved in industrial disputes (Merrison 1979: 460). These disputes left in tatters the assumption that health workers' commitment to the NHS would prevent them taking industrial action and indicated that a qualitatively different type of employment relationship was emerging in the NHS. It was rooted less in consensus, based on professionally defined standards of service, and more on managerially established norms of efficiency and effectiveness.

These developments were reflected in the changing character of health service trade-unionism. Centralized, bureaucratic patterns of organization were being supplemented by more radical workplace representatives, whose role was formalized by the decision to develop shop steward systems in the 1970s (Hancock 1979). The fierce competition for members between trade unions reflected their complex structure and the absence of clear membership demarcation. This rivalry reflected in part the tension between TUC-affiliated unions, such as the National Union of Public Employees (NUPE), and non-TUC organizations (especially the RCN), which combined the functions of trade unions and professional associations (Bosanquet 1979). There was also strong competition between the TUC affiliates, the intensity of which varied between geographical locations and types of service (ACAS 1978).

Increased industrial relations activity at the workplace did not detract from the continuing dominance of national-level institutions. It was at national level that industrial relations grievances, even if expressed primarily at the workplace, could be resolved. As a result, throughout the 1970s and 1980s policy discussion centred on the shortcomings of the national system of pay determination and proposals to reform it. However, foreshadowing more recent problems with local pay determination and the lengthy gestation of the *Agenda for Change* initiative, reform proposals failed to generate fundamental alterations to the Whitley system. The principle of national agreements was not disputed, although some local flexibility was viewed as desirable. As the 1979 Royal Commission on the NHS concluded:

> Standardised, centrally negotiated terms and conditions promote the unity of a national service and relieve staff and management of the complexities of local bargaining on basic matters such as pay and hours of work. However, some questions need to be settled locally, and it may not be easy to decide where the line between national and local negotiations should be drawn. (Merrison 1979: 165)

The legitimacy attached to collective bargaining institutions is intimately connected not only to outcomes, but also to the degree to which the parties are seen as representative of their respective constituencies. The legitimacy of both the staff and management sides within the Whitley councils has been frequently questioned since 1948, leading to intensive intra-organizational bargaining and attempts to alter the composition of each side (McCarthy 1976). The management side has been dominated by Department of Health officials and health authority appointees of the Secretary of State, with an under-representation of health service managers. McCarthy (1976) argued that it was vital that a sense of corporate identity was developed among the management side, who lacked commitment to the task they performed. This reflected, in his well known phrase, 'employers who do not pay and paymasters who do not employ' (McCarthy 1976: 11). As a result the legitimacy of the pay determination machinery among managers was undermined. They complained that their role was merely to implement poorly structured national agreements.

These representational difficulties reflect fundamental dilemmas about who should represent employers and the scope for autonomous management practice. Bosanquet (1979) argued that this predicament reflected the inevitable dominance of central government, especially the Treasury, in maintaining control over the NHS pay bill, and the direct control exercised by the Secretary of State, who was answerable to Parliament for pay matters. A different conclusion drawn was that trying to reform the Whitley system was self-defeating and that a more radical devolution of pay determination was required (Dyson 1979).

The rivalry and competition for membership between unions reflects distinct occupational identities and interests of particular professions, and the division between TUC affiliated and non-affiliated organizations (TUC 1981). Union representation on the staff side also posed problems because the distribution of seats largely reflected 1950s membership levels. McCarthy (1976) proposed a reduction in the number of recognized organizations and greater use of proportional representation in determining Whitley council membership. This was rejected by the TUC-affiliates which feared losing seats to the single-profession non-affiliated trade unions. These differences continued to fester until the heat was partially taken out of the issue with the establishment of the Nurses' Pay Review Body in 1983.

Alongside representational difficulties, both sides agreed that the Whitley system had produced complex, prescriptive agreements that allowed insufficient flexibility at local level. It was not only that the Whitley system contained a myriad of specific allowances, but also that the existence of separate functional councils reinforced these differences between occupational groups. Once Whitley agreements (or pay review body awards) were accepted by the Secretary of State, they were then authorized by detailed statutory regulations. Managers could offer only what was laid down in these regulations. A mechanism existed to vary terms and conditions by making a special application to the Secretary of State, but this proved to be a lengthy process (Trinder 1990: 11). Managers complained that they were unable to respond to local labour market conditions in order to resolve shortages except by resorting to grade drift; that is the shift of employees to higher paid grades. Recruitment and retention problems were also exacerbated by the narrow differentials between supervisory and other staff who took on additional responsibilities (Foster *et al.* 1985: 23). A related concern was the absence of any scope to link pay to individual performance.

Two policy developments were significant in the mid-1980s. First, the advent of general management, discussed in Chapter 3, encouraged management to seek more control over the pay bill. This process was reinforced by the introduction of competitive tendering for support services (cleaning, catering and laundry services). Regardless of whether a service was retained in-house or outsourced, this policy led to substantial reductions in the workforce and accompanying pay-roll savings (Colling 1999). These cost reductions arose from job losses, worse pay and conditions and work intensification. The imposition of mandatory tendering provided managers with an incentive to alter working practices, erode national terms and conditions and, in their judgement, establish more clearly defined and monitored performance standards. Service managers, anxious to retain services in-house, wanted more local flexibility to compete effectively against the private sector, forcing concessions from trade unions. Even when basic rates were protected, hours of work, bonuses, holiday and sick pay entitlements were often reduced (Bach 1989). The deterioration in pay and conditions was invariably greater for women workers; private contractors rarely pursued the equal opportunity policies typically associated with the model employer tradition (Escott and Whitfield 1995).

Second, following industrial action in 1982, the government established an independent pay review body for nursing and other professional staff in the expectation that they would never again join other health service workers in sector-wide pay campaigns. Its establishment contributed to the resilience of national systems of pay determination. Although it provides government with a platform for expounding its policy priorities and the opportunity to reject or modify their recommendations, it also reports and often legitimizes the contrasting views of trade unions and professional interest groups (Winchester and Bach 1995: 322–4).

Among the proposals for reforming NHS pay determination there was a remarkable degree of consensus that collective bargaining, as opposed to pay review or indexation, was the most appropriate form and that comparability should continue to play an important role (King's Fund/NAHA 1985; McCarthy 1983b; TUC 1981). These positions reflected a pragmatic appraisal of what was possible, a distrust of the unilateral control that review bodies ceded to central government, and a commitment to the principles of collective bargaining despite concerns that cash limits were eroding the ability of the Whitley system to operate effectively.

A long-standing issue has been the appropriate balance between national and local pay determination. A totally localized system was rejected, maintaining the consensus on the advantages of national pay determination. The King's Fund/NAHA (1985) report recognized that the definition of the bargaining unit was problematic. Equating 'local' with a district health authority made little sense in pay terms, as a variety of labour markets existed for each occupational group. These difficulties were compounded by the existence of the review bodies, coupled with the belief that NHS management lacked the competences to handle such a radically devolved system. The government's position was viewed as contradictory. Not only was there anticipated Treasury resistance to devolved pay, but health authorities in the south of England required additional monies to recruit and retain scarce staff. Finally, there was a consensus that the NHS required a system in which there would be a framework of national agreements, with scope for local bargaining to permit workplace flexibility, the policy position endorsed nearly two decades later in Labour's *Agenda for Change* proposals.

Conservative government policy and the shift to local pay

The heightened debate about the reform of NHS pay determination in the 1980s was encouraged by government ministers who frequently criticized the existing national systems of pay determination. They maintained that national arrangements were insensitive to variations in local labour-market conditions, they did not offer management sufficient flexibility in meeting different organizational requirements, and they discouraged an explicit link between pay and individual performance. It was the organizational fragmentation and market-based restructuring associated with the internal market in the 1990s, however, which challenged directly the traditional patterns of centralized pay determination (Bach and Winchester 1994).

From the middle to the end of the 1980s, the government sought to encourage a more decentralized and flexible system of pay determination within the existing framework of national agreements. This was mainly in response to labour market shortages of qualified staff, but also reflected an emphasis on rewarding individual performance. The main group affected by performance related pay were general managers who were also placed on short-term contracts and had their negotiating rights removed. These changes strengthened the control that the government could exert over this key group of staff as their job tenure depended on their ability to fulfil the government's performance targets.

As skill shortages increased during the late 1980s the Department of Health advocated the use of pay supplements for hard-to-fill posts, especially for particular nurse specialities. The policy of flexibility within nationally agreed pay deals, however, had its limitations. There were concerns that pay supplements led to rapid growth in additional payments over which the Treasury had little control, but which did not appear to tackle the supply side shortages among certain occupational groups. The Nurses' Pay Review Body expressed reservations about the scheme and were sympathetic to staff side arguments that labour market supplements would simply shift shortages around the country (Thornley and Winchester 1994: 260).

The most significant change for nursing staff arose, however, from the revised pay and grading system implemented from 1988 that replaced the structure that had remained largely unaltered since 1948. A new clinical grading structure was implemented that was designed to grade nurses according to skills and responsibility, rather than as previously by the post the individual occupied. The objective was to increase flexibility by ensuring that nurses could progress beyond ward manager level without being forced into managerial or teaching roles. The new grading structure was developed and agreed by the Nurses' and Midwives' Nursing Council based on research within the NHS, and the Nurses' Review Body attached a financial value to the new grades.

The implementation process, which involved the assimilation of a large and diverse workforce onto a new grading structure, was inevitably complex, but no-one had anticipated the scale of the difficulties or the bitterness that it would provoke. These problems stemmed from the initial difficulties of determining the cost of the new pay system and the high expectations that had been created among nursing staff in the lead-up to implementation. Differences in the interpretation of the criteria created varying patterns of grading at local level, and dissatisfaction was fuelled by the suspicion that many grading decisions were influenced by financial constraints. As a result over 135,000 nursing staff, one quarter of the nursing workforce, lodged grading appeals and the procedure could not deal with the volume of applicants, leading to lengthy delays in resolving appeals that undermined support for the pay scales themselves (Buchan *et al.* 1998: 65; Thornley and Winchester 1994: 253; Nurses' Pay Review Body 1992: para. 12).

The establishment of NHS trusts foreshadowed more radical changes to employment practices because of their discretion to determine their own terms and conditions of employment and to establish organization-specific systems of industrial relations. Especially significant was the creation of a new staff group of health care assistant (HCA) outside the national Whitley framework. NHS trusts faced the constraint imposed by the NHS and Community Care Act 1990, which provided for existing staff to transfer to trust employment with their contractual rights intact. Consequently, while trust managers had discretion to devise trust terms and conditions packages for new employees, existing staff could opt to remain under the terms of the relevant pay review body or Whitley council.

An additional complication was a lack of clarity about what the term 'local pay' signified. Successive Conservative governments appeared to endorse different conceptions of local pay as policy priorities and circumstances altered. In the late 1980s the government equated local pay with regionally based variations in pay rates and less restrictive national agreements. In the early 1990s the emphasis shifted to individual performance related pay and, in the face of unrelenting medical and nursing opposition, a further shift in emphasis occurred towards the element of the annual pay increase decided at local level. This issue dominated government policy during the mid-1990s alongside the development of trust-specific pay and grading systems for some occupational groups.

The uneven development of local pay between 1991 and 1997 can be divided into three phases. Between 1991 and early 1994, there was much speculation and rhetorical support for local pay, but few significant developments. From early 1994 to the end of 1995 there was a more intensive period of development, with strong encouragement from the NHS Executive that trust managers should establish local pay. This led to a lengthy dispute in

1995 and to a compromise reached in September 1995 that signalled the third phase of more uneven development until the general election in May 1997.

Phase 1—1991–94: The phoney war

After the internal market came into existence in April 1991, it was anticipated that there would be a significant move away from national terms and conditions of employment led by NHS trusts with personnel specialists playing a key role. Managers adopted a more cautious and pragmatic stance. Almost all trusts continued to pay their staff national rates, even if some staff were placed on trust contracts. Conditions of service remained essentially unaltered, although some trusts tinkered with annual leave and many revamped their disciplinary and grievance procedures. Speculation that trusts might withdraw recognition from some trade unions did not materialize, and bargaining structures were devised in expectation of a move towards local pay bargaining (Corby 1992; Industrial Relations Services 1993). The Select Committee on Health (Health Committee 1992: xv) found individual cases in which managers were moving away from Whitley negotiated agreements, but they concluded that:

> Trusts' caution in introducing radical changes to staff pay, terms and conditions owes much to the considerable attention necessarily given to introducing the many other new administrative and management arrangements ... many Trusts lack the management negotiating skills and support systems to administer local pay systems.

Writing towards the end of this phase Bach and Winchester (1994) developed an analytical framework to explain why local pay bargaining had been slow to develop and anticipated that health service managers would continue to 'opt-out' of local pay. Three factors were highlighted, which mirror the characterization of the NHS outlined in Chapter 2. The first arose from the budgetary context in which the reforms were implemented. The second stemmed from the political sensitivity of health service reforms and the role of local pay, and the third related to the occupational identities of key professions and the strategies of their respective trade unions.

The first issue concerns the economic environment in which local pay was promoted. Economic recession and record levels of government borrowing led to a squeeze on public expenditure which slowed the pace of change. For trusts there was no pressing need to move away from national rates of pay to recruit and retain staff. The grave economic situation, compounded by Britain's forced exit from the exchange rate mechanism, led to the imposition of a 1.5 per cent limit for all public sector pay rises in 1993. This undermined the ability of trusts to develop innovative pay structures, as invariably, pay innovations require increased funding to facilitate change.

Second, the highly centralized and integrated character of the NHS made reforms of the health service pay system politically sensitive. In the lead-up to the 1992 election there was concern to minimize the electoral consequences of the internal market. Many trust managers wanted to see the outcome of the election before nailing their colours to the mast of radical changes in employment practices. This political uncertainty for managers was heightened by the absence of a clear lead from the NHS Executive which NAHAT (1994: 11) argued amounted to a 'policy vacuum on the future shape of NHS pay'. There was little central guidance on personnel issues, and the low priority assigned to employment matters contrasted with the rhetorical support for local pay. For example, a celebratory account of the first six months of the internal market reforms failed to mention employment matters (NHS Management Executive 1992).

Political vacillation was evident in the resilience of national pay determination arrangements which sent mixed signals to managers about local pay. The government did not attempt to abolish the Whitley system but preferred to let it 'wither on the vine', and the review bodies continued to operate. The former NHS director of personnel was highly critical of this approach, suggesting that if trust managers would not develop local pay voluntarily then it should have been forced on them by the abolition of the Whitley system and the review bodies (Caines 1993).

Moreover, there were also considerable uncertainties within trusts about whether the organizational capacity existed to develop effective local pay determination. The legacy of national bargaining meant that reward management expertise was absent at local level; it was the least effective aspect of the NHS personnel function according to Guest and Peccei (1993). Personnel departments were hindered by their lack of resources, inadequate management information and the absence of a satisfactory system of job evaluation (Buchan and Seccombe 1994).

Third, the diversity of the workforce and its professional character accentuated these difficulties. NHS trusts employ a wide range of occupational groups, often located in different workplaces with distinct industrial relations traditions, and these professional status divisions have made it difficult to reform the staff side at national level. Similar difficulties could have been anticipated at trust level, complicating local consultation and bargaining arrangements. More importantly, professional associations and trade unions have given the highest priority to the retention of national salary and grading structures. In their view they not only define terms and conditions of employment, but also shape career expectations, influence mobility patterns and safeguard professional standards of service. Brown and Rowthorne suggested that 'fragmented bargaining within individual public services could be expected to give rise to an increasingly uneven quality of service nationwide' (1990: 13). For these reasons local managers anticipated opposition from trade unions if they sought to establish local pay and conditions of service.

Phase 2—Spring 1994 to autumn 1995: full speed ahead?

By early 1994 the re-elected Conservative administration had foiled attempts to prevent hospitals becoming self-governing trusts and sought more actively to push the issue of local pay. A letter from the NHS Chief Executive, Alan Langlands (1994), to trust chief executives in June 1994, instructed them to have local pay machinery in place by February 1995. The letter was widely interpreted as implying that the NHS Executive blamed trusts for the slow pace of change. The Langlands letter anticipated the pivotal role of the Nurses' Pay Review Body recommendations in the struggle to launch local pay. It was a signal to the review bodies that more rapid progress was expected shortly and that they should encourage local pay developments in their 1995 recommendations.

If the political signals about local pay were becoming more explicit, the economic context also appeared more propitious. In autumn 1993 the government announced a three-year pay bill freeze for the public sector in which pay increases would have to be self-funded by productivity increases. It was more flexible than the earlier 1.5 per cent limit, however, because it encouraged managers to trade pay increases for efficiency gains through job losses, or changes in work organization, and these discussions could be carried out in a meaningful way only at trust level.

Nonetheless, the degree to which trusts were able to manage local pay had not altered substantially. A survey of 180 trusts during 1995 examined the progress that trusts had made towards local pay and conditions. Two-thirds of trusts met the NHS Executive's October 1994 deadline for local action plans, but the proportion of staff affected by local pay remained low. Although 75 per cent of the trusts which responded had introduced local terms and conditions for some staff, only a small proportion were on trust contracts, and most of the changes were minor adjustments to national terms and conditions (Industrial Relations Services 1995).

The Nurses' Pay Review Body confirmed that progress had been limited and argued that a longer transitional period would be required than they envisaged in their previous report. It was explicit, however, about the prospects for local pay in 1995–96:

> These are transitional recommendations for a transitional year. We would prefer not to make a recommendation in this form next year. By that time we expect to see a framework established for effective local pay determination, with clear prospects for achieving pay increases based on local achievements and needs. (Nurses' Pay Review Body 1994:16)

The strong endorsement of local pay arose in part from the changing composition of the Nurses' Pay Review Body in which members with private sector experience of decentralized bargaining were more influential than hitherto. It also reflected the Review Body members' wider frustrations that the Department of Health had failed to address nurses' pay.

These sentiments were substantiated in February 1995 when the Nurses' Pay Review Body recommended a two-tier approach to pay determination: a national pay award of 1 per cent and a local element to be negotiated at trust level, which it was anticipated would increase the overall pay rise to between 1.5 and 3 per cent. The irony was that the review body – an institution of national pay determination – became the catalyst in the government's strategy to implement a system of local pay. The RCN felt betrayed by *their* review body, which they believed had abandoned its impartiality and become a stooge for the government and its drive towards local pay. This anger was fuelled by the contrasting fortunes of the medical profession, which received a national 2.5 per cent award and were largely exempt from local pay.

The trade unions threatened industrial action, with the RCN balloting its members to achieve a rule change permitting limited industrial action. The RCN and Unison made a similar demand: an unconditional local pay offer of 2 per cent. The dispute continued throughout the summer despite more trusts, under pressure from the NHS Executive, making an offer of 3 per cent in total (combining the national and local element) without attaching conditions. But with ballots for industrial action looming the NHS Executive reached agreement with the main trade unions, but not the RCN, in which the trade unions accepted the principle of local pay determination within a national framework which up-rated national salary scales annually, based on the outcome of local negotiations in the previous year.

The dispute highlighted three issues. First, the influence of the professions and their trade unions in shaping developments in the NHS was evident, and the tensions between the trade unions, particularly the RCN and Unison, were rekindled with particular force. On the surface this was puzzling. Both unions were opposed to local pay, at least in public, and they appeared to have the same objective: an unconditional local pay increase of 2 per cent. However, the longer-term aims of the organizations diverged sharply. RCN's primary objective was to safeguard the future of the Nurses' Pay Review Body. To maintain its dominant position, it was unwilling to enter into talks with other trade unions. The RCN believed that if enough trusts offered 3 per cent it would have effectively negated the local element and sent a signal to the review body to return to its 'proper' role in 1996 (Hancock 1995). Unison had long-standing criticisms of the review body that were reinforced by the 1995 dispute. Its officials believed that the review body lacked independence, did not help to eradicate the problems of low pay and was 'elitist' in providing a focus in pay and policy debate on the position of qualified nurses to the exclusion of other groups in the NHS (Unison 1996). Unison wanted an end to the division between review body and non-review body staff and sought ways in the dispute to pursue this objective.

Second, the centralization of policy in the NHS, despite the emphasis on trust freedoms, was reflected in the dominance and interventionist stance of the Department of Health during the dispute. This was reflected in the inability of NHS trusts to develop a representative voice, with NHS management representation divided between two rival organizations that adopted different positions on local pay (Butler 1995). This resulted in the voice of NHS management remaining weak. The NHS Executive was dominant and provided increasingly prescriptive advice to trust chief executives about how they should manage the dispute. In April trusts were warned by the NHS personnel director:

> Ministers have expressed concern that there have not been more pay offers. If you have not yet made an offer, it is important that you do so as soon as possible. (Jarrold 1995)

This was followed up by guidance to trusts: to make offers of 3 per cent without conditions; to pay staff on account, prior to a settlement to demonstrate the commitment of managers to local pay and to undermine employee resistance; and advice to purchasers highlighting that increases in NHS funding would allow reasonable pay rises in line with review body recommendations (NHS Executive 1995ab). This strong central direction was particularly ironic as the dispute was nominally about establishing local pay arrangements.

Third, the dispute highlighted more fundamental problems of pay determination under the internal market that had their roots in the fiscal constraints confronting trusts. The government placed the highest priority on affordability criteria, undermining the principle of comparability, but the relationship between pay, contract prices and trust income was unclear. During the dispute there was considerable uncertainty as to whether trusts could afford the 'going rate' of 3 per cent; there were considerable variations between trusts depending on factors such as contract pricing decisions, the scope for further 'efficiencies' and existing cash reserves. The focus on affordability also impacted on employees' conceptions of fairness as individual review bodies adopted different stances on comparability and affordability criteria leading to different pay outcomes. The anger of nursing staff was undoubtedly fuelled by unfavourable comparisons with the decisions of the Doctors' and Dentists' Review Body.

Phase 3—Autumn 1995 to spring 1997: the demise of local pay

The agreement of September 1995 allowed both parties to claim that they had achieved their aims. The NHS Executive argued that the principle of local pay had been accepted with the threat of industrial action lifted. The up-rating agreement reinforced central control by the NHS Executive as it effectively undermined the value of any trust deviating substantially from the NHS 'going rate'. By September Unison was anxious to settle because it was unlikely that their members would have endorsed a strike ballot over local pay. Nonetheless the national framework meant that the long-standing differences in pay settlements between review body and non-review body staff were effectively removed, with important implications for the future shape of pay determination arrangements. The RCN, which had refused to participate in the talks, voiced its opposition to the deal, ostensibly because they remained opposed to the principle of local pay.

The national framework agreement dominated developments in NHS pay determination until just before the 1997 general election (when it was abandoned as too complex) and dissipated much of the drive towards local pay. The Conservative administration was divided and limping towards its electoral demise, and with the Labour party committed to the restoration of a national pay framework, the political momentum for local pay subsided. In 1997 the Nurses' Pay Review Body report was peppered with references to its disappointment at the slow pace at which local pay determination had developed. Nonetheless it appeared to abandon its pursuit of local pay, recommending a national award that effectively precluded further locally negotiated increases (Nurses' Pay Review Body 1997).

The Review Body's own survey evidence found increased activity in terms of local pay *settlements*, but there were no significant differences in the pay offers made to nursing staff on trust contracts, compared to those on Whitley contracts, or much variation between trusts in their pay offers. In terms of the development of local pay *structures* a survey of 137 trusts in 1997 found that 35 had made some significant departures from national terms and conditions in relation to annual leave, premium payments and sick pay (Industrial Relations Services 1997). Thornley's study, based on responses from Unison lead stewards, found that approximately 80–85 per cent of registered and unregistered nurses remained on Whitley terms and conditions, and of those that were on local contracts they largely mirrored Whitley grades and settlements (Thornley 1998: 420).

Labour government policy and *Agenda for Change*

The Labour government on entering office confronted a discredited policy of local pay alongside some increase in local agreements. At the same time the national system of pay review bodies remained intact, leaving a confusing mixture of national and local activity (Corby *et al.* 2001). The Labour government viewed the existing pay system as a significant impediment to the modernization of the NHS, and its criticisms echoed its broader concerns about public sector pay determination arrangements (Cabinet Office 1999). *Modernising Government* suggested that radical changes in pay determination were needed to ensure that public servants were 'rewarded fairly for the contribution they make' and to encourage 'more of the best people to join and stay' (Cabinet Office 1999: 58). Recurring themes to achieve this objective included an emphasis on tackling discriminatory pay systems, addressing recruitment and retention problems, altering pay systems to move away from automatic annual increments to competency based progression and a stronger focus on systems of performance management.

Agenda for Change

The Labour government's proposals for a comprehensive modernization of NHS pay systems, set out in *Agenda for Change* (Department of Health 1999a) identified a number of existing problems relating to flexibility, fairness and performance. The government argued that the existing pay system hindered flexibility because it 'does not recognize that modern forms of health care rely on flexible teams of staff working across traditional skill boundaries' (p. 3), and that it reinforced professional demarcations by a 'focus on status not skills' (p. 6). These problems, it was suggested, arise from rigid grading definitions reflecting outmoded clinical practice which makes it hard to establish and reward new flexible roles appropriately. Similar criticisms, relating to the clinical grading structure for nurses, were highlighted in *Making a Difference* (Department of Health 1999b: 14–15).

Agenda for Change highlighted the inequity of staff undertaking similar roles receiving differential rewards. Compliance with equal value law has been an important stimulus for the reform of the pay system. The NHS has faced hundreds of equal value claims because of the existence of separate pay structures for different occupational groups which have been judged to be indirectly discriminatory to women (Incomes Data Services 2000a). The vigour with which NHS trade unions pursued equal value claims also reflected trade union frustration at the systematic undervaluing of work undertaken predominantly by women. The best known test case concerned the speech therapist Pam Enderby, who claimed parity with male clinical psychologists and pharmacists. After 14 years of legal judgements and concerted Conservative government opposition the Labour government negotiated a settlement with MSF (now part of Amicus), the union representing the speech and language therapists affected, which amounted to £12 million (MSF 2000a). The Labour government has been sensitive to these problems because of the budgetary implications of equal value cases and their commitment to diversity.

There was also a government concern that existing pay arrangements did not provide an appropriate link between rewards and progression. The government highlighted the £200 million spent on automatic increments annually but noted that the NHS 'lacks incentives to encourage staff who gain new skills and make productivity gains' (p. 6). Moreover, many staff remained stuck at the top of their grade; another form of unacceptable pay inequity. The government therefore sought to link progression to new responsibilities and competencies, thus improving the link between education and development and pay progression.

The main proposals outlined in *Agenda for Change* were the replacement of separate pay structures for different occupational groups, with the establishment of three new pay spines with local grading to cover all staff; one for doctors, one for NHS professionals, primarily nurses and professions allied to medicine, and one for other staff, mainly ancillary and administrative staff. This is intended to ensure equal pay for work of equal value and allow more flexible job roles, but this depends on ensuring that the pay awards for each of the three pay groups are linked. Recommendations on pay awards will continue to be made by the doctors' review body, the nurses' review body with an extended remit to encompass some other professional groups, and a third negotiating body to cover all other staff. This implied a significantly altered role for the existing review bodies. For the first time, a single national job evaluation system has been proposed and trusts will be required to assess jobs locally according to agreed national criteria. Pay progression will no longer be based on automatic service-based increments; instead progression will be based on 'contribution' linked to a system of competencies. Conditions of service are also to be amended with 'core' conditions laid down nationally, and other terms to be negotiated locally. The government also signalled that it wanted to remove a range of allowances which staff receive for working particular shifts or undertaking specific tasks and incorporate these allowances into basic pay.

Converting *Agenda for Change* from a generalized set of propositions into a workable blueprint that satisfied the aspirations of the government, not least the Treasury, employers and diverse trade union interests, proved to be a complex and time-consuming task. Following joint agreement with the trade unions on the principles in October 1999, it was originally envisaged that implementation would commence by spring 2001, but the target date has slipped several times and implementation in a number of pilot sites will not commence before spring 2003. All parties, however, are keen to avoid the problems associated with previous attempts at pay reform, especially the poorly structured nurses' clinical regrading exercise.

The Department of Health has been committed to involving trade unions in the development of the proposals, and the centrality of their involvement reflects the limited pay expertise within the health service HR community. Two of the key working groups established early in the negotiations (on competency pay progression and conditions of service) were led by senior national trade union officers. As other groups have been established, for example the development of a Knowledge and Skills Framework (KSF), trade union involvement has expanded. This is in marked contrast to the Conservative period when the trade unions were totally excluded from policy-making and were scarcely consulted on major reform proposals. A further departure from the Conservative government approach is the intention to test the new system in a number of trusts, termed 'early implementers'. Staff side support within each trust is a prerequisite for selection as an early implementer (Foster 2002). Nonetheless the confidential nature of the negotiations and the principle that 'nothing is agreed until everything is agreed' has made it difficult for both sides to brief fully their constituencies, although union activists have been kept abreast of developments.

The Department of Health has argued that pay reform will improve recruitment and retention by enabling more rapid career progression and higher advertised rates by consolidating a range of allowances into basic pay; raise productivity by eroding barriers to staff working in multi-skilled teams; and achieve high standards by ensuring rewards are allocated to those who achieve high performance. It is the 'skills escalator' that is central to developing new ways of working with pay incentives to help staff extend their skills and move up the escalator, while roles and workload are delegated down the escalator to generate efficiency and skill-mix benefits (Department of Health 2002a: 4).

The degree to which the Treasury is convinced that these outcomes are attainable has influenced the level of resources that it is prepared to commit to pay modernization at a time when demands on public expenditure have continued to increase. It is anticipated that *Agenda for Change* will add 3–5 per cent to the current NHS pay bill. The NHS pay bill is a large component of public expenditure; the combined medical, dental, nursing and para-medical pay bill in 2001 was estimated by the government as £17.5 billion (Department of Health 2001b; 2001c). At the same time the lengthy negotiation process has raised expectations among the NHS workforce. Trade union agreement, and membership endorsement by ballot or other forms of consultation, will require evidence of tangible benefits.

During 2001 and 2002 trade unions became increasingly frustrated that their ability to evaluate the impact of *Agenda for Change* for their members was being hindered by the uncertainties about the funding of pay modernization. In June 2002, the RCN threatened to suspend their involvement from the process if delays continued and funding assumptions were not clarified. It was not until the publication of the third Comprehensive Spending Review in July 2002, however, that these issues could be resolved. These frustrations were exacerbated by concerns that more immediate problems, such as unfair grading decisions, are being left unresolved because the government argues that all reforms should arise as part of the *Agenda for Change* discussions. This led the Nurses' Pay Review Body (2002: 4) to warn the government of serious consequences for morale, recruitment and retention if implementation was delayed significantly.

Pay modernization: key issues

The lengthy gestation period reflected the complex issues to be resolved, and the commitment to partnership working inevitably increased the timescales involved. There has been the requirement to establish a 'felt-fair' national job evaluation system that can cope with the range and complexity of the NHS workforce. A review of six existing job evaluation schemes within the NHS reported that different schemes generated very different rank outcomes (Jones 1999). Although the study had some methodological problems the results remain striking. For example, in a comparison of 37 jobs in the NHS, that of personnel officer was ranked as high as 9th and as low as 26th in different schemes. This indicated the requirement to develop an NHS-specific scheme. It was extensively benchmarked against more than 400 different jobs to ensure that consistent evaluation across the NHS could be established.

Implementation issues at trust level remain paramount to ensure that it does not generate either an uncontrolled increase in the NHS pay bill, or large numbers of grading appeals, as occurred under the clinical regrading exercise for nurses in the late 1980s. A repetition of the difficulties surrounding clinical grading remains a dominant concern of trade unions and managers, but lessons have been drawn from the implementation of clinical regrading. The use of early implementers, technical support from the Modernization Agency, an appeals mechanism based on computer software rather than managerial interpretation, greater union involvement and crucially broader rather than narrower grades should militate against a repeat of the mass appeals of the nurse regrading exercise.

By summer 2002 the main elements of the final system were becoming clearer. Many of the original principles remained in place, but a crucial difference was that the initial expectation that the pay system would cover all staff had been diluted. Consultant medical staff were offered a new contract and a 10 per cent pay increase over three years, increasing the pressure on other unions to achieve similar outcomes. The three-year deal also highlighted the Treasury's commitment to moving towards longer-term pay deals in the public sector to underpin modernization, by enabling a focus on pay reform rather than the annual bargaining round (Treasury 2001: 29). The confirmation that medical staff were not formally part of *Agenda for Change* left a seven- or eight-grade structure for other staff (excluding top managers) expressed as two separate pay spines. The Department of Health was also seeking to find new ways of rewarding staff for working unsocial hours, and continuing recruitment and retention difficulties ensured that premiums for hard-to-fill posts had become a more central issue. In addition, plans to establish Foundation Hospitals with greater freedom to set pay complicated pay negotiations (Buchan 2002).

The approach to pay progression remains a pivotal issue. The government's instinctive preference for some form of performance-related pay clashed with the trade unions' emphasis on maintaining incremental progression. A resolution of this issue has been proposed in terms of pay progression linked to competencies supported by the NHS-wide Knowledge and Skills Framework. These types of pay systems focus on the underlying behavioural requirements expected of the employee to fulfil their role. Competency based systems are associated with fewer, broader pay bands which replace a multitude of narrow grades and allow greater managerial discretion in the design of jobs and their position within the overall salary structure (see Kessler 2000). This type of pay system requires a number of underpinning support mechanisms, including a systematic approach to training and development to enable competency acquisition and a performance appraisal system to measure how competencies are being used, because ultimately competence is about performance (Institute of Personnel and Development 1997: 26). Employers and trade unions have been supportive of the KSF because it is designed to improve staff development and encourage the development of new roles linked to other initiatives, such as the lifelong learning strategy. Nonetheless trade unions are wary that the link between pay progression and competencies must not be used as a form of backdoor performance related pay. The number of thresholds or 'gateways' within each pay band that staff have to pass through to progress to a higher salary is integral to the balance that is ultimately struck between 'automatic' and competency based progression.

The *Agenda for Change* proposals highlight the influence of the features of the NHS identified in Chapter 2. The affordability of pay modernization has been a dominant concern of civil servants and local managers anxious that recent agreements (e.g. on junior doctors' working hours) and planned changes to medical staff contracts bequeath huge costs on local trusts. Conversely trade unions have been frustrated about the lack of clarity about the resourcing of the new system. The political sensitivity of the NHS has impacted on pay modernization, with the government anxious to ensure that the timetable for pay modernization, and the benefits that accrue to employees, are synchronized with the comprehensive spending review and the electoral cycle. Finally, the professional rivalries within the workforce and the attempt to break down professional boundaries between occupational groups is central to the government's perspective on pay modernization as the Secretary of State for Health stated:

> Pay reform will help us deliver faster and better services for patients by breaking down the barriers to flexible working in the NHS, facilitating the creation of new patient centred roles and new ways of working. (Milburn 2001)

For the main trade unions involved, long-standing differences in emphasis, clearly expressed in the 1995 dispute, have been evident. Unison has been concerned to improve and harmonize upwards the pay and conditions (e.g. annual leave, hours of work) of its low-paid members, and to erode the dominant political position of the RCN within the Nurses' Pay Review Body by opening it up to a wider range of semi-professions. Many low-paid Unison members may gain from reductions in working hours, and non-registered nursing staff could also be beneficiaries because the skills escalator may raise their wages to reflect the work they undertake rather than their traditional lowly occupational status.

A central preoccupation of the RCN has been on how pay modernization will replace the discredited clinical grading structure and facilitate professional career development. There has been some concern about the dilution of *their* Review Body as its coverage is extended to other para-medical and assistant roles. For this reason the RCN has placed a strong emphasis on the incorporation of medical staff within the job evaluation system to enable nurses to benchmark and link their roles to those of doctors. As registered nurses increasingly take on roles previously performed by junior doctors the expectation is that if nurses can demonstrate that some of the job evaluation scores are similar to junior medical staff this will bolster arguments about comparability. For the RCN and many of the professions there are complex and divisive issues to be resolved relating to allowances and unsocial hours payments to ensure that increased 'flexibility' does not disadvantage particular membership constituencies.

Pay modernization has also highlighted many of the long-standing issues associated with NHS pay reform. First, the balance between national pay determination and local flexibility has been a perennial issue, but the policy of the mid-1990s discredited local pay bargaining, as well as other locally negotiated flexibility elements. *Agenda for Change* aims to rehabilitate local flexibility within a national context as a catalyst for developing new ways of working. The Labour government wants to go further, with an emphasis being placed on local variations, for example, arising from differences in local labour market conditions. This is intended to boost pay in hard-to-recruit areas, but trade unions will need to be reassured that it will not undermine the integrity of the national framework.

The government's plans for three-star rated hospitals to have the option of becoming Foundation Hospitals presents one of the most significant threats to *Agenda for Change* because it raises the spectre of a return to trust hospital 'freedoms' and local pay. This could ultimately undermine a *national* pay framework, especially if the government's emphasis on a more diverse system of health provision emerges. As Unison has stated:

> The suggestion that *Foundation Hospitals* should be given the freedom to introduce different pay rates is equally flawed. UNISON wants better pay for all NHS staff, but not by the route of local pay ... these hospitals would be able to poach staff from the rest of the NHS, causing instability in surrounding hospitals and inevitably affecting their performance. (Unison 2002: 6)

Ironically when Foundation Hospitals do emerge, it is likely that those trusts and the top managers within them that championed trust status and local pay will again be in the vanguard of reforms to the pay system.

Finally, one of the difficulties highlighted by local pay was the limited managerial capacity available to formulate and implement complex pay reforms. Uneven investment in the personnel function, an administrative legacy reflecting highly centralized and standardized personnel practice, alongside political constraints has ensured that in the past personnel specialists have often been confined to a narrow operational role with limited influence (Bach 1995; 1999b). As the Department of Health (2002a: 32) has correctly acknowledged, building HR skills among all managers and ensuring the credibility of the HR function are important elements of HR strategy and will be crucial for the success of pay modernization.

Discussion

There has been a long-standing debate about the system of pay determination in the NHS, and many of the problems highlighted in the 1960s and 1970s were not satisfactorily resolved by the 1990s. A striking feature of these earlier debates is the relatively narrow parameters in which they were conducted, to the exclusion of many of the policy concerns of subsequent Conservative and Labour governments. Discussion concentrated on *reforming* the national Whitley system of pay determination. Alternative pay determination mechanisms, such as review bodies and indexation arrangements, were discussed only briefly despite the early establishment of the Doctors' and Dentists' Review Body. Furthermore, the emphasis was on enhancing the effectiveness of a *national* system of pay determination; a system of local pay determination was discounted by trade unionists and managers.

In pay determination as in other areas of health service policy the centralized form of the health service has shaped developments. The experience of the 1970s and 1980s suggests that, despite vigorous efforts, managers had limited success in enhancing their representation in the centralized system of pay determination or influencing its bargaining agenda. Instead the priorities of the Department of Health and the Treasury prevailed. This may not be surprising when account is taken of the size of the NHS pay bill and its implications for public expenditure and government economic policy. These strong centralizing tendencies have inhibited attempts to cede greater influence to health service managers over NHS pay determination matters, as the conduct of the 1995 pay dispute illustrated. An additional consequence of the dominance of prescriptive national agreements for most of the last fifty years has been that the development of the personnel function has been stifled.

The professional character of the workforce has been reflected in trade union practice in the NHS. For the staff side the last forty years have been marked by friction between a multitude of trade unions which found expression in the squabbles over representation in the Whitley councils. During the 1990s there were differences in emphasis between the RCN and Unison in the approaches that they adopted, with the RCN adopting a less oppositional stance towards local pay and opting out of the negotiations that settled the 1995 dispute. In the context of the *Agenda for Change* negotiations, in which all the trade unions anticipate gains for the majority of their membership rather than the losses expected under local pay, there is more scope for common ground. Nonetheless important differences in emphasis remain. Overall these divisions reflect competition for membership, different conceptions of trade union purpose, and the fierce occupational rivalries which have characterized the NHS.

Finally, reforms of pay determination have been an increasingly important component of health service restructuring. The Conservative government viewed local pay as integral to the internal market reforms because they expected it to control the pay bill, reduce trade union influence and alter working practices. These views were not shared by the Treasury, health service managers or trade unions, and this loose coalition of forces arraigned against local pay ensured that it never became embedded within the NHS. Nonetheless, the opposition to local pay couldn't disguise the shortcomings of the national system of pay determination. The reduced regulatory influence of national pay determination, as the Whitley system decayed and national agreements became less prescriptive, encouraged the establishment of a workplace system of employment relations. These developments prepared the ground for more radical changes and opened up the possibility of more local flexibility within a national framework.

The Labour government's *Agenda for Change* proposals represent an attempt to consolidate and extend the workplace reforms of the 1990s. In contrast to local pay the Labour's government's planned changes have been developed with full trade union involvement over a lengthy period. This indicates the importance that the government attaches to pay reform as an integral component of health service modernization. *Agenda for Change* is viewed as pivotal to reforms of working practices, improvements in recruitment and retention, and attempts to demonstrate that the NHS is a model employer (Department of Health 2002a). The degree to which these aspirations will be achieved, however, can be gauged only by assessing current HR practice at trust level.

5 STRATEGY AND STRUCTURE AT THE WORKPLACE

The previous chapters explored the wide-ranging debates surrounding Conservative and Labour government policy towards the NHS, the impact of new public management, and the difficulties associated with the reform of pay determination and work organization. Behind these debates lurks a more fundamental question. In essence what unites these disparate policy concerns is the question: To what extent has there been a transformation of employment relations in the health service over the last two decades?

There are many different methodologies that could be used to address this question. Nonetheless, in the past scholars within an employment relations and sociology of work tradition immersed themselves in researching the conduct of managers, workers and their representative organizations in the workplace (Burawoy 1979; Edwards and Scullion 1982; Scott 1994). These classic studies make sense of workplace behaviour in a manner that cannot be replicated by other research methods, because they are based on the participants' own understandings of management–worker interaction. They have bequeathed an important legacy in illuminating workplace behaviour. As Barley and Kunda (2001) have pointed out, organization theory's efforts to make sense of contemporary organization is hampered by the dearth of detailed studies of the work process.

Within the health service, government reforms initiated at national level have to be implemented at workplace level within NHS trusts that employ most health service workers. Governments, employers and trade unions have invariably highlighted the disjuncture between government policy and workplace practice. This indicates that workplace behaviour needs to be considered in its specific historical context, taking account of internal and external factors and grounded in an examination of management–worker interaction.

This chapter introduces the three case study organizations. To ensure anonymity and safeguard confidentiality they have been given the pseudonyms

Eastern, Northern and Western. This chapter explores a number of the themes introduced in earlier chapters and outlines a number of variables that could be expected to influence employment relations processes and outcomes that are discussed more fully in the following chapters. In each case the role of the trust within the local health economy will be examined. This relates to the location, size and range of services offered and the scope for trust managers to carve out a niche for the trust within the competitive ethos of the internal market and the altered context after the Labour government took office in 1997. The financial position of the trust and the patterns of competition and collaboration developed with other local and national actors are an important part of this picture. These factors enable each trust's particular circumstances to be identified and the impact of the changing policy context under successive Conservative and Labour governments to be gauged in terms of the impact on the overall priorities and policies within each trust.

The second dimension relates to the organization and management of each trust. As noted earlier the principles of new public management have emphasized the development of multi-divisional or M-form structures that link the organization's management structure to its strategy and market conditions. Divisionalized structures are well established among large UK companies and embody a number of organizational principles: the dis-aggregation of the enterprise into semi-autonomous divisions and business units; the devolution of responsibility to these divisions, enabling the head office to focus on strategy; and the establishment by the head office of a framework of performance control of the divisions (Marginson *et al.* 1995: 5). During the internal market period this type of approach was associated with organizing trusts into separate clinical directorates enabling each directorate to focus on its own 'business' requirements. This reflects Chandler's (1962) famous dictum that 'structure follows strategy'. Simulating market processes within trusts may have been an appropriate model for the internal market period, but has the emphasis on networks under the Labour government required alterations in organizational structure? Related aspects of management organization concern the type of involvement of medical and other clinical staff within the management process.

The third dimension concerned the organization and status of the personnel function within each trust. This was influenced strongly by other aspects of management organization in terms of the adoption of M form structures and the degree of devolution of personnel practice. The influence of the personnel function can be gauged by whether it occupies a board level position within each trust, by the size of the department and by less tangible indicators, especially the perspective of the chief executive officer towards personnel. Finally, the overall employment relations climate could be expected to influence the aims and substantive outcomes of the management of employment relations.

Eastern

Eastern was formed in 1993 and has been the least organizationally stable trust of the cases considered. When it gained trust status Eastern comprised a large general hospital and associated hospitals with some specialist services provided on a regional basis, serving a largely urban population. In 1993 Eastern had a total of more than 650 beds, employed nearly 3,000 staff and had an income of £60 million. By 2001 and following a merger with a neighbouring trust it had grown to almost 5,000 staff, contained nearly 1,200 beds and had an income of more than £140 million. During 2002, a further merger occurred and a new chief executive was appointed.

Eastern serves one of the most deprived areas of population in the country, with poor health status and large inequalities. Not surprisingly there is a legacy of high demand for services. For example, Eastern district has the fifth highest admission rate for people over 75 nationally. These workload pressures impact on staff. In the 2000–01 annual report the chief executive comments: 'Once again the demands on staff at all levels were immense with continuously rising activity not matched by adequate resources.'

Role in the local health economy

In comparison to the other two case study trusts (Northern and Western), Eastern occupied an uncertain position within the local health economy. Eastern strove to be more than a standard district general hospital, providing a number of regional services and sub-regional specialities. These services, however, have been in flux due partly to planning decisions and temporary difficulties in recruiting consultants in particular specialities. Managers suggested that it was difficult to sustain strategic initiatives because they were constantly distracted by short-term operational difficulties. For example, during the course of the initial fieldwork one of the regional specialities was relocated to another trust.

Second, in the mid-1990s the relationship with the local health authority was tense because the health authority lacked a coherent strategy for the provision of services, focusing on obtaining the cheapest services available. Eastern exceeded contract levels agreed with its main purchasers, and failure to agree on additional income for this work resulted in arbitration during 1996. An additional source of uncertainty was that by 1996–97 18 per cent of Eastern's income derived from GP fundholders, a higher figure than at Western or Northern. This proved to be destabilizing because fundholders requested the development of new services, but were unwilling to provide any commitment that they would continue to purchase the service once it was established. Relationships with other trusts were also tense because it was widely recognized that there was insufficient funding to sustain all the local trusts, which made collaboration difficult.

Financial problems have plagued Eastern, and from the mid-1990s senior managers were required to implement major cost improvement programmes. In 1995–96 a deteriorating financial situation precipitated a £3 million cost improvement programme, and the departure of the chief executive and other members of the senior management team. In 1996–97 a financial recovery plan was agreed with the NHS Executive, which included an 18 per cent reduction in the trust's management costs.

The financial position remained difficult, however, and the trust ended the financial year 1999–2000 with a deficit of over £2 million. Budgetary pressures arose from the need to meet waiting list targets and increased activity levels and the recurring financial deficit of the health authority.

In April 1997 the trust merged with a smaller neighbouring acute trust whose management was viewed as more effective by the regional office. Following the merger the trust operated from two acute hospitals approximately ten miles apart with services duplicated between the two sites. The merger was a difficult process for staff as the culture of the two hospitals was very different. At the smaller hospital, staff felt that they had been swallowed up. Nonetheless their management team took charge of the merged trust and moved to the other site, confronting suspicions from the larger hospital's staff that alien managers had taken over 'their' hospital. These difficulties were exacerbated by the legacy of the internal market in which the two hospitals had been fierce rivals. Four years later these difficulties had not been fully resolved and were alluded to by the chief executive when he commented in the 2000–01 annual report that: 'continuous progress was made in building stronger links between the two hospitals'.

Management organization

Eastern has been through a series of management reorganizations. Between 1993 and 1997 it was reorganized three times under two different chief executives. When the hospital gained trust status in April 1993 the first chief executive organized the trust into four divisions each headed by a general manager. Jobs were divided into five management tiers with clear identification of the roles and responsibilities of managers at each level. This was intended to ensure that the headquarters management team focused on setting strategic direction, producing policy frameworks and managing overall performance. The emphasis on divisional autonomy was modelled on a multi-divisional company structure with powerful divisional general managers, responsible for divisional performance, reporting directly to the chief executive. This structure, however, resulted in the fragmentation of the organization. There were tensions between the corporate centre and the divisions, and between individual divisions.

The first chief executive was soon replaced, and his successor tried to increase the corporate focus of the organization by bringing clinical services together into a single division. In 1996 further reorganization occurred, with business units encouraged to trade with each other to recognize the interdependent nature of the organization while maintaining their independence to pursue their own business requirements. The M-form structure was viewed as appropriate for the internal market environment because it was assumed that individual divisions' activity levels would be reconciled with their financial allocations through the contracting system. It was also intended to foster entrepreneurial behaviour, with divisional managers encouraged to market their services to GP fundholders to bring in more income. The difficulty with this approach was that it assumed that the internal market was an authentic market environment, in which money followed the patient, rather than a politically created and centrally regulated one, in which resources were constrained. Activity levels rose sharply in the mid-1990s, but this increase was not matched by the requisite level of funding. This exacerbated conflictual relations with the health authority and led to a financial crisis and finally a merger.

The third chief executive since trust status, who remained in post until 2001, aimed to establish a more open organizational culture. Medical involvement was increased, with initially eight and then subsequently eleven clinical service units established, each with its own clinical lead and general manager. The aim was to create integrated structures with closer managerial and clinical relationships. Nonetheless attempts to increase clinical involvement via clinical director roles had their limitations. As the director of nursing argued:

> It's a bit of a sham really. What you end up with is a part-time clinician in a management role. On paper, they are the person responsible, but in reality it is the general manager that gets the stick. People's thinking has moved on from how do we involve docs to how do we focus them on issues they must do. In reality these are not about budgetary control, but about managing the medical politics and about clinical performance of doctors. (Interview notes, July 2001)

HR: structure and influence

The structure of the personnel function reflected the initial organizational design, with personnel specialists devolved to the divisions. This had an important impact on personnel practice as it discouraged a trust-wide approach to staff management, and the turbulent context in the trust led to a focus on short-term operational problems. The intention was that staff remaining at headquarters would be freed from operational pressures to concentrate on strategic issues. In practice there were few signs that this had occurred. The director of personnel was not a member of the trust board, there was no written human resources strategy document and the board rarely concerned itself with personnel matters. Furthermore, the first chief executive was viewed as attaching a low priority to personnel issues, and the second disregarded the advice that he was given.

The devolution of personnel activities to the divisions had some tangible benefits, with line managers suggesting that personnel had become much more visible and accessible. Alongside these benefits problems emerged with devolution which undermined the coherence of personnel activity at Eastern. The divisional personnel managers faced some conflict of interest as they were managerially accountable to the divisional general managers but were also the guardians of corporate policies within the divisions. They did not believe that trust policies were always appropriate for their division; nor did they believe that they had sufficient influence over the content of trust policies, which they argued were imposed by HQ with little consultation.

The policy of devolution created new conflicts between the divisions. There were inconsistencies in the manner in which they handled personnel issues, for example disciplinary cases. The general managers did not view this as a problem, arguing that it was part of moving away from a standardized, Whitley culture towards a more entrepreneurial and dynamic one. For the divisional personnel managers the situation was more difficult as they subscribed to the view that personnel should be fair and consistent in its treatment of staff.

Following the trust merger in 1997 and associated reorganization the HR function (as it became known) broadly mirrored the clinical service unit (CSU) structure. The new director of HR was critical of the devolution model, however, because she argued that it diluted HR influence and made it difficult to enforce central standards. Instead the department was recentralized, accompanied by increased devolution to line managers. Although one HR manager was linked to a number of CSUs, they were located within the HR department and viewed their primary loyalty as to their function rather than to their general manager. Not surprisingly some general managers expressed a preference to have their own dedicated HR presence. As significant was that despite the increase in the size of the trust following the merger, the numbers of HR managers had not increased, with three HR managers covering the CSUs and the director having two deputies. The HR director was not an executive member of the trust board, although she participated in trust board and other senior management forums and the chief executive after the merger was viewed as supportive of HR issues.

Eastern is geographically situated in an area of traditional union strength, and this legacy is reflected in a tradition of militancy. Unison was the dominant trade union within the trust, comprising half the total union membership and providing the chair of the joint consultation committee. Union density was high, fluctuating around 70 per cent of the workforce over the period of the fieldwork. There were a number of prominent local Labour MPs, and Unison had good access to the local media that took a close interest in developments at the trust. Although trade union officials and activists had been weakened by competitive tendering, the closure of a nearby long-stay hospital and a more assertive management style, they retained a capacity to mobilize ancillary workers and to embarrass senior managers via their access to the local media and MPs.

The turbulent environment in which Eastern has been subject to two mergers, confronted continuous financial difficulties and been led by five chief executives over a ten-year period was reflected in the uneven performance of the trust, an adversarial employment relations climate and a more dissatisfied workforce than in the other two case study trusts. As many of the senior managers acknowledged, crisis management typified the management process at Eastern for lengthy periods of time, and there were uncertainties about whether Eastern had sufficient management and staffing capacity to deliver on its targets. This had resulted in regional office intervention to tackle the problem of long waiting times resulting in weekly monitoring meetings with staff from the region. As the director of nursing commented:

> We don't identify problems early enough. We are like part-time lifeboat men. Someone's on the rocks, the flare goes up, we drop everything, rush down together, row out together, sort it, put the boat away, but nobody thinks what about building a light house? (Interview notes, July 2001)

Eastern was awarded a one-star rating in the NHS performance league tables published in 2001. The Commission for Health Improvement (2001a) highlighted areas of progress in the management of waiting lists but raised concerns about poor handling of complaints. In terms of human resource management CHI required the trust to address nurse shortfalls and to be more proactive in its approach to work related stress.

Northern

Northern NHS Trust was established in April 1994. It is unusual in that it provided a full spectrum of hospital and community services, including acute services, community services, services for people with mental health problems and services for people with learning disabilities. During the establishment of NHS trusts the Conservative government discouraged integrated trusts that reflected the existing health authority pattern of care. The government believed that it would inhibit the development of the internal market and the establishment of the purchaser and provider split, but Northern was allowed to gain trust status as a single district trust. It remained stable until the establishment of primary care trusts (PCTs) led to the break-up of Northern in 2002 with its community services forming part of a PCT and its acute services absorbed into a neighbouring acute trust.

The trust was small, employing approximately 1,800 staff, with an income of £50 million in the mid-1990s that had increased to almost £80 million by 2001. The trust faced some financial difficulties in the mid-1990s, but these were less acute than at the other two case study trusts. Northern has consistently met its financial targets. In 2001–02 financial pressures re-emerged, however, mainly as a consequence of achieving the New Deal for junior doctors' hours. It is situated in an area of moderate deprivation.

Role in the local health economy

Within a 15-mile radius there are a number of large acute trusts providing specialized services on a regional basis. Managers therefore pursued a three-pronged strategy to safeguard their position and differentiate Northern from neighbouring providers. First, senior managers emphasized the benefits to the local population of the integrated care that the trust was able to provide. This allowed greater co-ordination between services, straddling the usual division between separate acute, community and mental health trusts. It also provided managers with an established network of community-based staff who were sensitive to the opinions of GPs. The mix of community and acute services also established a more stable financial environment, not least because the non-acute services could be used to cushion the more volatile budgetary position of acute services. Set against these advantages its small size made it vulnerable to relatively high management costs, and managers confronted the constant threat of a hostile takeover from larger neighbouring trusts.

Second, the chief executive was highly regarded and read the political signals effectively. This was confirmed in the Commission for Health Improvement (2002a) clinical governance review that commented several times on the strong leadership that had 'a clear strategic vision' and noted that 'The trust has an excellent record of delivery on targets in activity, waiting lists and finances.' This was reflected in Northern positioning itself as an innovator, gaining additional funding for a variety of projects which later became mainstream government policy (see below). Trust managers placed primary care at the top of its agenda from early on, encouraging the provision of services at GP surgeries and at health centres rather than in hospitals. The use of service level agreements with GP surgeries, which defined the level and range of services provided to GP practices, reinforced the support of local general practitioners. This situation contrasted with the position of many acute trusts, whose managers remain concerned that the shift to primary care has led to a loss of income, as primary care services are provided by rival community trusts and latterly PCTs. It also enabled Northern to be relatively entrepreneurial. As the trust business manager during the internal market period boasted:

> the CEO would say, 'I want to run this service, go and find me some more
> money.' We poached lots of work from other trusts based on access. The first
> three waves of fundholders had more money than they needed to deliver the

> service and that was defunded from their host trusts, so we promised them
> the earth and gave it to them. (Interview notes, July 2001)

Third, trust managers pursued a policy of developing a range of local services, reducing the requirement for patients to travel elsewhere. With the
existence of specialist centres nearby, and with too small a catchment
population to justify the development of comprehensive services, trust
managers developed partnership arrangements with neighbouring specialist
hospitals. Consultants from the specialist hospitals provided in-patient
treatment in their specialist facilities and out-patient appointments and day
surgery treatment in Northern's facilities. This strategy enabled patients to be
seen locally, generated income for the specialist providers and, by developing
co-operative rather than competitive relationships with larger trusts, created
stability, delaying hostile takeovers and ensuring a secure position within the
merged trust when the inevitable merger occurred. It also reflected the
capacity of managers to anticipate government policy. As the chairman noted
in the 1997–98 annual report: 'It was particularly pleasing to note the new
emphasis on collaboration between NHS centres, something which we have
enthusiastically pursued locally for some years.'

Management organization

The chief executive was appointed in 1993 and remained in post until 2002,
when he gained the chief executive role in the newly merged trust, despite
being in charge of an organization that was half the size of its merger partner.
He adopted a clinical directorate model based initially on six directorates
with budgetary responsibility. The rationale for the structure was that:

> It inverts the traditional hierarchical organisational model. Business and
> financial personnel are devolved to Clinical Directorates – in effect virtually all
> employees work to Clinical Directorates. This reduces HQ functions to a
> minimum and requires Clinical Directors and their managers to be responsible
> for the full range of managerial tasks. (Chief executive communication, 1994)

In practice, the emphasis on devolution and autonomy of the directorates
was tempered by the chief executive's wish to ensure that Northern maintained a clear corporate direction and did not become a series of competing
directorates. This was facilitated by its relatively small size, which reduced the
rationale for a highly decentralized management structure. When a conflict

of interest arose within the organization, for example between the directorates, this was resolved at the corporate management group, chaired by the chief executive, which comprised the executive directors and the general managers of the clinical directorates. In contrast to the other two trusts, decision-making was much more centralized and tightly controlled in Northern, although this did result in some clinicians and other staff believing that they had a limited capacity to influence decision-making.

Although less autonomous than in the other case study trusts, the limitations of the directorate model were becoming apparent by the late 1990s, reinforced by policy changes under the Labour government. Directorates had been encouraged to be relatively entrepreneurial and to seek increased activity and income from local GP fundholders. This was successful, but invariably managerial activity was focused on the directorate level and the implications for the organization as a whole became a secondary consideration. This reinforced a vertical structure that made effective cross-directorate working difficult.

Second, the clinical directorate model was premised on the active involvement of clinicians in management, but in practice this had not really occurred. The clinical lead role was underdeveloped (no job description existed), and relatively few clinicians wished to take on the lead clinician role. The small number of committed and relatively 'corporate minded' clinicians were increasingly overloaded as they were encouraged to take on more management responsibilities. As with Eastern, the type of clinical involvement was also seen as increasingly inappropriate. Scarce clinical time, it was suggested, needed to be focused on service planning and achievement of National Service Frameworks rather than day-to-day budgetary and staff management responsibilities. Trust managers recognized that they had to increase the number of clinicians and alter the ways in which they were involved. Because relatively few clinicians were willing to take on managerial roles, selection was relatively informal and highly political with an emphasis on acceptability to senior managers and other clinicians; they did not necessarily have particular management skills or appropriate training for the role.

Third, the policy environment under Labour had shifted from an emphasis on competition between trusts towards one based on collaboration between clinical networks that straddled trust boundaries. Managers argued that forms of competition continued, with trusts competing to provide services to particular populations, competing for earmarked monies (e.g. for waiting list initiatives), and trust managers were rivals in their attempts to gain high star ratings. Nonetheless, the focus on clinical networks that straddled existing organizational boundaries had encouraged clinicians from neighbouring trusts to work together to consider the most effective location of services. As one senior manager commented, 'clinical networking is merging the clinical mind before you merge the managerial mind' (Interview notes, July 2001).

During 2001, these changes, arising from the National Plan and associated National Service Frameworks, led the chief executive to restructure Northern to deliver the National Plan. The new structure adopted a matrix form which was primarily task-orientated and involved the creation of specialist modernization task groups that had responsibility to achieve the National Service Framework requirements in a particular service area (e.g. cancer services, waiting times, coronary heart disease, services for older people, etc.) that cut across the vertical directorate structure. The lead individual for each area (a mixture of clinicians and general managers) was represented on the trust's modernization board.

HR: structure and influence

The organization of the personnel function mirrored these changes in organizational structure. The first director of personnel was supported by a deputy responsible for three personnel managers who provided support to the six directorates. The personnel managers were located within a central personnel department and there was regular contact to ensure consistency of approach. The directorate general managers' preference had been for each directorate to have their own personnel specialist, but the director of personnel argued that this would have proved costly and resulted in less experienced staff being used to fill the posts. Although personnel managers supported individual directorates and were involved in their management boards, they remained accountable to the director of personnel; their primary loyalty was to the personnel function, although they argued that they were advocates for their general managers.

This overall structure remained virtually unchanged over the period of the fieldwork. In comparison to Eastern the HR function was well resourced and the director of personnel (retitled director of human resources in 1998), who had been in the district since 1988, was an executive director of the trust board, a position which she shared with the director of hospital services (they alternated on an annual basis) so as not to exceed the statutory number of executive director positions. With her departure in 1997, the former deputy director became director and subsequently became an executive member of the trust board in 2001, until the merger in 2002 when HR relinquished its board status.

Northern had a less adversarial employment relations climate than that at Eastern. This was partly attributed to the small size, a modern working environment with buildings less than twenty years old and a reputation for being a friendly place to work. For example the 2002 staff survey indicated that almost 80 per cent of staff agreed that 'the trust is a good place to work'. The mixture of community and acute services resulted in a union staff-side that was not dominated by one union. There was substantial membership among RCN, Unison and MSF. MSF provided the chair of the staff side for most of the fieldwork period. Although there were tensions in management–union relations, especially during the period of the national dispute over local pay, the trade unions were less well organized and active than at Eastern, with staff having limited engagement with the trade unions. There were no apparent tensions between the main trade unions.

Although Northern faced the perennial threat of being taken over, its small size, high degree of continuity among senior managers, a far-sighted and respected chief executive and the integrated service provision ensured a less turbulent environment than at Eastern. Northern gained a two star rating during 2001. It also received a very positive report (Commission for Health Improvement 2002a) that highlighted its effective performance in achieving its targets and noted that the hospital was popular with junior doctors. It was viewed as a friendly place to work although in the 2002 staff opinion survey 5 per cent of respondents stated that they were currently being bullied. Concerns about stress, high workloads and low staffing levels in some areas were recurring themes within the survey.

Western

Western is a large acute trust formed in 1993 that has not been subject to merger activity. In 2000–01 Western employed approximately 6,500 staff with an income of approaching £200 million. Western provides a comprehensive range of acute services and some regional specialities to an urban population of approximately 500,000 residents. Poverty figures suggest an average level of deprivation in the health authority, although the city centre forms part of a Health Action Zone in recognition of the challenging social and economic conditions in that particular area. Services are divided between two main sites. This has created difficulties in service provision, and in 2001 a lengthy planning process culminated in government approval of the strategic outline case for a new single-site hospital, financed under the Private Finance Initiative.

Role in the local health economy

The crucial position that Western occupies in the provision of health care in the area made it difficult to reduce services to cope with financial constraints in the mid–late 1990s. In particular, senior managers were unwilling to close the accident and emergency department despite a sharp rise in emergency admissions each winter and the concomitant increase in expenditure. From the mid-1990s a deficit of £1 million grew to a cumulative deficit of almost £2.5 million by the end of the decade. Following regional office intervention a cost reduction plan was put in place. It was agreed that the overspend would be repaid over five years by the sale of land and reduced spending on equipment. By 2002 the trust had addressed its financial difficulties and met all its statutory financial targets, but as the director of nursing suggested:

> If you look at Milburn [Secretary of State for Health] now, saying that the NHS is on target to meet all its targets, things are really good. There is a major financial gap in the service all over the country, however, with major problems in hitting the targets and the modernization agenda. (Interview notes, June 2002)

Consequently Western's financial position had fluctuated over the last decade. During the internal market period the trust was in a relatively monopolistic situation without the immediate threat of a major loss of income to other providers, although it confronted some loss of income arising from the development of GP fundholding. A key source of uncertainty, however, was its strained relationship with the host purchaser, exemplified by increased levels of activity the host purchaser required without adequate financial recompense. Related disagreements concerned the manner in which Western health authority distributed waiting list monies, and its emphasis on market-testing for clinical services which led to work being transferred to other providers.

Management structure

When Western gained trust status in April 1993 the former unit general manager became the first chief executive. He was a very strong advocate of involving clinicians in management, and the management structure was based around eleven clinical directorates. During the 1991–97 period clinical directors were granted considerable autonomy, with 95 per cent of budgets devolved to directorates. Each directorate had a set of objectives, and the clinical director was responsible to the chief executive for meeting them, and for keeping within budget. Each directorate had its own management team with dedicated business, nursing, finance and personnel support. Directorates carried out the main business of the trust, enabling decisions to be made as close to the patient as possible. This ensured a relatively flat management structure and low management costs.

To avoid the inevitable tensions between directorate autonomy and corporate policy, clinical directors were drawn into overall corporate management by their involvement in the management board, which comprised all the clinical directors and the executive directors. Reinforcing the importance of clinicians in management was their lead role in key managerial tasks. For example, the business planning group was chaired by the renal clinical director and the Investors in People initiative was chaired by the locomotor clinical director. Major policy issues were considered at the management board prior to discussion at the trust board. The management board was the key decision-making forum and one in which the clinical directors were numerically dominant. It was intended to ensure that directorate autonomy did not detract from the overall corporate objectives. When an issue had been agreed at the management board all directorates were expected to adhere to the corporate approach.

It was evident, however, that attempts to find an appropriate balance between directorate autonomy, clinical involvement and corporate control were in difficulty by 1997–98. The span of control for the chief executive was too great, with eleven clinical directors and five executive directors reporting directly to him. This led to ambiguous forms of control and accountability and enabled some of the clinical directorates to pursue their own agenda, with little regard for corporate requirements. One manifestation of these problems was poor financial control. This was acknowledged in the 1998–99 annual report:

> For the past two or three years we have been spending more than we received. During this year we have spent time getting to understand our budgets better. We now have a firm timetable to pay back our past debts and a number of schemes designed to prevent us overspending again.

There was also a recognition that the external environment had altered significantly, with a shift from an emphasis on competition, in which directorates were seeking to maximise income for their part of the organization, to collaboration, with an emphasis on clinical networks in which financial resources are more linked to achievement of corporate objectives that straddle individual directorates. In addition the emphasis on the development of clinical governance (i.e. a focus on safeguarding high standards of care) has required a more cohesive organizational approach.

The second chief executive, appointed in 1997, did not immediately restructure the trust but embarked on a period of discussion and consultation. This led to proposals, approved by the trust board in 1998, that a new structure be introduced from April 1999 with three key changes. First, clinical directorates were clustered into six divisions with the responsible officer being the head of division reporting to the chief executive. This change aimed to improve accountability and corporate control. Some responsibilities were devolved to the divisions, with financial accountability and capacity strengthened by placing accountants within each division, although separate support directorates for finance and human resources remained intact. Second, the role of the trust board in setting strategic direction was supplemented by an executive board that was responsible for turning strategy into policy and action. Third, a clinical management forum was established that addressed clinical issues and provided advice to the trust board.

An internal piece of research undertaken two years after the 1999 organizational arrangements had been put in place, based on interviews with managers and clinicians, revealed variable outcomes and highlighted the pressures confronted by staff in the organization. The organizational changes had led to much greater clarity about the roles of the divisions and the divisional managers. An important exception, however, was the role of clinical directors who felt that their contribution to the management process had diminished because they were no longer represented on the executive group. There was a general sense that communications between the divisions needed to be improved. This was reiterated by the CHI review (2002b), which noted 'a general lack of communication across and between the clinical divisions'.

The relations between clinicians and managers were positive and there were no discernible differences in perspective between managerial and clinical respondents. Indeed many clinicians argued that managers were under too much pressure and that more managerial capacity was required. For example, managers were concerned that they spent a lot of time collecting performance information about activity and waiting lists to fulfil central government requirements, but had little opportunity to analyse and act upon the data. This reflected a more general concern about high workloads and the difficulties of dealing with long-term aspects of policy because managers were overwhelmed by short-term problems. These difficulties reflected an overall concern among managers and clinicians that their workloads were not sustainable.

HR: structure and influence

The personnel function initially reflected the highly devolved clinical directorate structure with the director and his deputy supported by five operational personnel managers whose role was to implement the trust HR agenda within the directorates and to take a lead on specific human resource issues. Routine tasks including recruitment and selection were devolved to line managers. This was designed to enable personnel managers to address the corporate agenda, which concentrated on shortages of medical staffing, local pay bargaining and generic support workers, as well as dealing with operational problems.

The director of personnel tried to reconcile the corporate and directorate agenda in two main ways. First, personnel managers reported to the director of personnel rather than being managerially responsible to several clinical directors. He liaised closely with the clinical directors in establishing their objectives and involved the clinical directors when reviewing the performance of his staff to ensure that corporate human resource objectives were delivered through directorate business plans.

Second, there was considerable overlap in the corporate personnel agenda and directorate priorities. The corporate planning process ensured that the trust's personnel agenda was discussed at the management board whose membership included all of the clinical directors and was then delivered through the directorates. Consequently, a personnel manager could be on the trust steering committee for the 'Investors in People' initiative, while leading on the issue within individual directorates. Even for an avowedly corporate issue like the annual trust pay offer, the focus of activity in terms of informing and persuading staff of the merits of the management offer was carried out within the directorates.

The personnel function was well resourced and wielded considerable influence during this period. The director of personnel for the period from 1992 to 1996–97 was considered to be a leading member of the top management team and was later promoted to chief executive in another trust. Although he was not a formal member of the trust board, he was close to the chief executive, who provided him with the necessary support to maintain the momentum on initiatives such as generic working (see Chapter 8).

Against this background managers and union officials acknowledged that there had been a radical shift in the management of employment relations in Western:

> He [director of personnel] revolutionized HR in the Trust – turned it around, nothing is done in the Trust without HR's involvement. (Interview notes, executive director, August 1996)

And:

> They [the chief executive and the director of personnel] have changed the culture of employment law within Western ... he was very influential, one on his own in the Region. (Interview notes, full-time union officer, August 1996)

Following the departure of the director of personnel, the trust had several HR directors between 1997 and 2002, but they did not enjoy the same level of influence as their predecessor.

At Western, trade union membership density was approximately 60 per cent, with RCN and Unison the dominant trade unions in the trust. Trade union members, however, were relatively passive and there was some reluctance by members to take on shop steward roles. Partly for this reason, and because of the relatively large size of the trust, the full-time officers were more heavily involved in the trust's joint consultation arrangements than at Eastern or Northern. The lead full-time officer (unusually elected by the staff side) attended the trust joint consultation meetings, and in the mid-1990s the staff side had chosen to replace the Unison full-time officer with the RCN full-time officer, generating tension between the RCN and Unison. Notwithstanding some conflict over particular issues, trust managers fostered a positive employment relations climate, as noted by CHI (2002b), and the trade unions were relatively quiescent.

The trust was awarded two stars in the 2001 performance tables, and the 2002 CHI review was generally positive. It raised some concerns about levels of supervision of junior doctors in some specialities and identified some other problems (e.g. information management), but suggested that the trust involved patients and the public well, was effectively led, and that staff considered Western to be a good place to work with an open culture that encouraged training and development.

Discussion

This chapter has provided an introduction to the organization and management of the trusts. The three organizations differed substantially in their size and mix of services, and Northern and Western have been evaluated by the government and its regulatory agencies as more effective in managerial and health care terms than Eastern. The implications of these different organizational contexts for staff management are considered in the following chapters.

Despite these differences, the policy context in which managers operated were similar and the same trends were evident in the case study trusts. In the early to mid-1990s, the precepts of new public management influenced organizational design in the case study trusts. The chief executives favoured forms of multi-divisional organization that aspired to devolve authority to clinical directorates linked to clear monitoring of performance. These trends were less marked in Northern because of its smaller size and more heterogeneous mix of services, but in Eastern and Western, directorate managers had a pivotal role. The monitoring of performance and control of resources, however, was not entirely effective, and both Eastern and Western experienced financial difficulties that were linked partly to the devolution of managerial and financial responsibilities to the directorates. The integrated and interdependent character of health care provision highlighted the limitations of a multi-divisional type organizational structure.

The policy environment and the particular regulatory regime adopted by Conservative and Labour governments had a strong bearing on management policy. The multi-divisional organizational form that was geared to the internal market environment was less appropriate for the later emphasis on co-operation within and between trusts. The focus on safeguarding clinical standards and the requirements of the *NHS Plan* necessitated more corporate and horizontal forms of organizational structure within the trusts. These changes in the policy context were reflected also in the language employed by managers to signal their adherence to the new agenda, for example, an emphasis on modernization and partnership working.

Chief executives emerged as powerful figures within their organizations. They had considerable discretion in terms of the organization and management style within each trust, exercised overall control over expenditure, directly appointed or at least had a power of veto over key appointments, such as clinical directors, and ensured that clinicians were responsive to the trust's requirement to fulfil its waiting time targets. Nevertheless, they also recognized that they were far more accountable than in the past and that increased scrutiny of trusts made performance outcomes (however contentious) more transparent. As one of the chief executives commented in comparing his role to that of a unit general manager in the 1980s:

> Accountability and responsibilities are much more explicit. It is the issue of carrying the can, because of the politics [of the NHS]. If things go wrong within a trust it is much more explicit that the CEO goes, not just financial problems, if something goes wrong clinically, I expect to be sacked, because it's part of my remit. (Interview notes, August 2001)

The role of professional staff, especially medical staff, had altered as a result of the establishment of trusts and the evolution of the chief executive role. Chief executives tried to reinforce their authority by incorporating clinicians into the management process. Although managerial and medical staff questioned the effectiveness of the precise manner in which they were involved in management, it was clear that much of the hostility between managerial and medical staff had dissipated and a stronger sense of mutual interdependence had emerged.

Medical staff remained cynical, but towards the end of the fieldwork this was much more likely to be directed at the government than at their own senior managers. For example, one consultant at Northern commented, 'people feel very much that they are puppets being controlled by puppet masters,' because of his feeling that consultants were simply there to fulfil the government's political agenda on waiting times. Moreover, medical staff were much more likely to allude to the pressures that managers confronted than hitherto, in terms of the targets that they were required to achieve. For example, within the internal research conducted at Western during 2001, there was very little difference between medical and managerial staff in terms of their concerns about managerial workload and the shortcomings of the managerial process in the trust. Consequently the new public management reforms seem to have led to some realignment of managerial and medical behaviour at workplace level, although as later chapters indicate, nursing staff in particular remain very concerned about the impact of the new public management ethos on patient care.

6 EMPLOYMENT RELATIONS: PERFORMANCE, UNION INFLUENCE AND EMPLOYEE INVOLVEMENT

This chapter considers the approach towards employment relations in the three case study trusts. A dominant theme of the reform agenda instigated by Conservative governments, and reinforced since 1997 under Labour, has been the importance of reshaping employment practices and adopting a more strategic approach to staff management. It is not clear, however, whether the internal market reforms and the subsequent modernization agenda pursued by the Labour government have overturned traditional patterns of employment relations. To what extent did the emphasis on trust 'freedoms' enable managers to pursue their own employment relations, and was this sustained after 1997? How far have long-standing institutional arrangements that have provided a voice for trade union representatives been sustained? What influence have personnel specialists exercised on the process of change? These issues are addressed by examining why employers adopted particular approaches towards employment practices and the discretion that they were able to exercise at local level, taking account of changes in the policy environment under Conservative and Labour governments.

Each case is structured in a similar fashion. The overall approach towards employment relations is outlined. It was termed by trust managers as 'HR strategy', reflecting a generic approach to HRM rather than signifying a particular high commitment management style. The overall approach to HR is then considered in relation to two issues: absence management and union influence. The focus on absence management reflects the emphasis that it was receiving at the workplace during this period. The management of attendance is used as an indicator of wider changes, providing valuable insights into the changing workplace order (see Edwards and Whitston 1993). The second issue concerns management–union relations and associated attempts to foster involvement and participation.

Eastern: management control and union erosion

The implications of the divisionalized structure of the personnel department, noted in Chapter 5, inhibited the development of a corporate approach to staff management prior to its first merger in 1997. Eastern's approach was essentially pragmatic: there was no formal human resources strategy document; the trust had a relatively small personnel department; and the director of personnel was not a member of the trust board. The first chief executive took a limited interest in human resource issues, while the second disregarded the personnel advice he received. Eastern's financial situation encouraged staffing issues to be subsumed within the need to control expenditure.

In place of a formal human resource strategy, managers emphasized value for money and the need for greater flexibility, particularly in the numbers of staff employed. The guiding principle that informed the work of the workforce steering group was that Eastern would have 'the right person, in the right place, at the right time, doing the right job' (Trust documentation, 1994). The first priority was to examine the workload of nurses with a view to establishing generic workers, termed ward assistants, who would carry out some of the housekeeping duties undertaken by nurses (see Chapter 8). The second area to be examined was the role of junior doctors and envisaged the creation of a clinical support worker to carry out phlebotomy, basic electrocardiograms and clerical work. Third, the workload and demarcations between professional groups in the therapies (physiotherapy, occupational therapy and radiology) was to be investigated with a view to establishing a generic support worker.

In practice, as the financial position deteriorated managers turned more frequently to short-term measures, especially the use of temporary contracts. These contracts took a variety of forms, including 'as and when' contracts (a form of zero-hours contract), particularly among ancillary staff. In 1996–97 the trust had a corporate aim that 20 per cent of staff would be employed in a 'flexible' way. The use of temporary staff was reinforced by the closure of a long-stay hospital within the trust, with temporary staff employed to facilitate the hospital's closure and to reduce staff relocation problems.

The staff side persistently expressed concern about the use of temporary staff, which drew the following response from the chief executive:

> It would always be preferable to employ permanent staff, as this results in a better service, better team working etc. Due to the current uncertainty over contracts and the future of services, however, the Trust was reluctant to

employ staff on permanent contracts where there might be no long term work if purchaser contracts were cut. It might be necessary to look at different types of employment contracts, for example 3 year rolling contracts, to give new staff a degree of security, whilst retaining flexibility for the Trust. (JNCC Minutes, September 1995)

The director of personnel recognized the limitations of this approach. At ward level the use of temporary staff was felt acutely, because as patient activity increased, ward managers experienced recruitment and retention problems and were unable to enrich the skill-mix. In fact the reverse occurred, which put more pressure on ward staff. Ward managers believed that the quality of staff had suffered, which contributed to their own demoralization and high rates of sickness absence among ward staff. In addition, personnel managers argued it was not a conducive environment to introduce further changes in working practices, and the use of temporary staff was sometimes used by line managers as a substitute for effective recruitment and selection practices.

Following the merger in 1997 the incoming chief executive appointed a new personnel director (retitled HR director). In contrast to the previous chief executives, he was more supportive of HR, and his own membership of the Institute of Personnel and Development was viewed as a tangible sign of this commitment, although the HR director was not an executive member of the trust board. The controversial nature of the merger and the traditional rivalries between the merged hospitals meant that working relations were strained. In a letter to all staff on taking up post in May 1997 the chief executive suggested that:

We must develop and use a set of values which ensures that all staff at all levels feel valued, informed and motivated. This philosophy is not just about working towards an 'Investors in People' award but rather how we help staff to achieve their best on a daily basis.

The director of human resources prepared an HR strategy each year that was primarily based on responding to national initiatives. It identified a number of strategic aims that were converted into specific objectives. For 2000–01 the strategy identified nine themes (Table 6.1) linked to 66 separate objectives. The majority of these objectives flowed from national initiatives that were reinforced by monitoring or specific targets from the regional office (e.g. on absence management). There was a trust specific dimension to the strategy, for example its evaluation of the employee relations system, but this was

Table 6.1 *HR strategy at Eastern Trust 1999–2000*

Strategic themes	Indicative objectives
Effective workforce planning and workforce profiling	• Continue to increase the understanding and importance of workforce planning in the trust and the use of data once collected • Integrate business, training, and workforce planning processes within the clinical service units
Appropriate education, training and development both for the individual and to achieve the organization's aims	• Continue to provide development that is multi-sectoral/professional/ organizational wherever possible • Develop clinical directors/managers to increase their HRM capability • Provide training for the trust board on managing equality and diversity by April 2001 (Health Service Circular 2000/014)
Create a workforce that utilizes the performance management process as part of their learning and development, and way of working	• Ensure that appraisal is in place for all members of staff which will provide the annual training plan for the trust and contribute to the Workforce Plan • Work with the medical director on the development of doctors in appraisal, job plan review and other doctor development plans
Agree flexible HR policies through involvement of staff, monitor their implementation and their impact on performance, retention and recruitment	• Agree outstanding and review existing policies, disseminate and provide training within the trust • Assess the national 'Improving Working Lives' strategy and further develop the Trust's approach to implementing family-friendly and flexible policies
Ensure that the current pay and grading system works effectively and contributes to the national discussions on a modern NHS pay system	• Link the discussion on pay and reward with the performance management process and the development of individual appraisal and a personal development plan

Develop a culture that attracts and retains high calibre people committed to providing the best care to patients	• Provide a quality recruitment service that is responsive to users and develop quality standards
Create a culture of involvement that becomes a way of life for everyone in the organization and ensure that systems of communication are honest, two-way and meaningful	• Evaluate the formal employee relations systems jointly with the staff side • Continue to evaluate staff involvement in clinical service units
Benchmark the trust against other health care providers in relation to staff health, safety and welfare and reduce the absence rate showing annual improvements	• Monitor the absence of each CSU and department
Create a culture that has quality and learning as key values	• Develop team-working and leadership programmes and support

Source: Eastern Trust documentation, 1999.

secondary to national priorities, such as reducing the working time of junior doctors. At the end of each year the HR director identified progress. This evaluation comprised a focus on outputs, e.g. the numbers attending training programmes, as much as outcomes.

The extent to which national priorities and local priorities operated in tandem was an issue in Eastern as in the other trusts. CHI (2001a) was concerned about the staffing complement because 'the trust has 1.9 times as many beds as the average trust, 2.0 times as many medical/dental staff but only 1.6 times as many nursing staff'. A review of the nursing workforce in 1999–2000 identified a serious shortfall of nursing staff and proposed that another 100 nurses were recruited. It took almost two years before action was taken with the recruitment of approximately seventy nurses from the Philippines. As the director of nursing explained about the discussion at that time:

> we came up with a requirement for another 114 staff on top of what we've got but we've got no cash. We've raised expectations and the trust board would like to do something but can't; it's in the too difficult box, it's not a priority. (Interview notes, July 2001)

Performance management and attendance

The trust had placed greater emphasis on training and development, a point acknowledged by CHI, with the trust gaining its Investors in People award during 2001. The trust's development activity, however, was increasingly focused towards developing 'customer' orientated skills that formed part of the redefinition of professional roles (see Fairbrother and Poynter 2001). At Eastern during 2001–02, after induction training, the highest number of staff attendances in relation to in-house training concerned: 'Assertive Communication' (147); 'Customer Care' (100); 'Performance Management' (89); 'Recruitment and Selection' (69); 'Leading the Team' (62); with 'Improving Quality' and 'Facilitating Change' also attended by just under 50 staff (Eastern Annual Report, 2001–02).

The main HR priority, however, was that performance management had gained a much higher profile with a willingness to tackle poor performers. This firmer management approach increased the number of employment tribunals and disciplinary hearings, but this reflected a concerted effort to alter the culture of the organization. One HR manager argued that in contrast to her experience in the private sector, the NHS had been very reluctant to tackle poor performance, especially among medical and nursing staff. In the eight years since she had joined the NHS, however, this had altered and a stronger performance culture had been developed. For example, the HR performance framework data indicated that by April 2000 approximately 90 per cent of staff were being appraised, although it was less evident that this process included consultant medical staff.

This overall focus on performance was borne out by the staff survey distributed in February 2000 in which 1,786 forms were returned (38%). Eighty per cent of respondents were female and 62 per cent worked part-time. The largest occupational group that responded were registered nurses and midwives (31%) followed by administrative and clerical staff (21%). Almost 85 per cent of respondents in the staff survey agreed that 'they have a clear understanding about their role in the organization', and almost 90 per cent of staff agreed that they had 'a clear understanding about expected standards of performance', indications of a well developed performance culture. The changing approach to absence management was illustrative of these changes in management style.

The management of absence had been on the HR agenda since the mid-1990s, but at that time within a highly decentralized divisional structure, managers were reluctant to tackle absence issues because they argued that that they lacked adequate data to address the issue. By the end of the 1990s, the HR information produced was more dependable, with both individual and departmental data collected. The trust board received monthly reports about absence data that was fed back through the trust board update and other communication channels. Absence levels were also discussed at clinical service unit meetings. During 2000 a revised management absence policy was introduced that reflected the requirement to meet the national targets. The trust was required to reduce its absence target by 20 per cent by 2001 and by 30 per cent by 2003. The main impetus of the policy was involving managers more in absence management and back to work interviews and greater use of dismissal for employees with a poor sickness record. The impact on staff was evident, as data from the staff hotline illustrates:

Question: I am a member of staff who has been sent a letter about sickness absence and I feel that I am being victimized. There are many occasions when staff turn up for work when they feel unwell or return to work after an illness early. These matters should be dealt with sensitively at ward level, as nurses do not take time off unless absolutely necessary. Poor handling of these matters leads to low morale so why is this happening?

Answer: Ward and Departmental managers are required to monitor, and where appropriate, take action in relation to sickness absence. Where staff have had four or more periods of absence in a twelve-month period, a manager has the option of referring the member of staff to Occupational Health to determine whether or not there is an underlying cause, which may affect or be affected by employment.

Effective management of sickness absence by the Trust will help to meet its sickness absence target of 4 per cent, to ensure that undue stress is not placed on staff who continue to provide the service while colleagues are absent on sick leave, and also, to identify if anything in the workplace is contributing to the sickness absence. (Staff hotline feedback, March 2001)

HR managers expressed ambivalent feelings about the 4 per cent target because the overriding objective became the requirement to achieve the target rather than to address the underlying problems causing staff absence. One suggested that directors were under a lot of pressure:

Our directors are sometimes given very clear messages from the people that come from Region. The conversations they have are often about targets. Our directors feed that through, as they want those that can deliver for them to understand the pressure they feel under. However, when we go back and say 'yes, but', they'll say 'yes we understand the difficulties that you are working with but you still need to try and deliver'. (Interview notes, July 2001)

The emphasis on meeting the target encouraged more intensive scrutiny of the absence figures and created incentives to rework the existing data. Absence reports to the board differentiated between non-work-related and work-related sickness, but staff side representatives were unclear about how managers allocated sickness to each category. They expressed concern that the global statistics could give a false impression of work-related sickness by excluding, for example, back pain that could have arisen as the result of cumulative stresses at work rather than being 'non-work' related. In addition the target culture was viewed as a crude indicator for a complex series of problems that were related to low staffing levels, issues about management style and perceptions among staff that the trust had a problem with bullying and harassment.

This latter point was investigated by Unison in a survey of staff at Eastern during 1999. The results provide no indication of the number of staff that replied to the survey or whether responses were confined to Unison members, but it found that 26 per cent of respondents considered bullying to be a very serious problem, the main source being from colleagues, with 50 per cent attributing it to staff shortages and 43 per cent to 'stressed colleagues'. The director of HR was sufficiently concerned about the perception of bullying among staff to include a question in the staff opinion survey. The results were inconclusive, but the director of HR gave a high profile to developing an anti-bullying and harassment policy.

Employee relations: communications and union influence

The trust had a legacy of adversarial employment relations, reflected in the industrial action over the introduction of ward assistants (see Chapter 8). Against a background of uncertainty within the trust, and the government emphasis on staff involvement, the director of human resources had tried to refashion employment relations. This had a number of dimensions. First, since 1993 and especially since the merger in 1997, the trust had radically altered its approach to communicating with staff. In the early years of trust status, managers relied primarily on the formal joint consultation and negotiating committee (JCNC) between staff side representatives and management. There was an intermittent written team brief, and on particular occasions (e.g. during the dispute on local pay in 1995) the chief executive wrote to all staff.

After the merger a communications group was established which included the trust chair, HR staff and staff side representatives. By 2001, the formal trade unions channels were viewed as only one among many forms of communication with staff. As the director of human resources commented:

> We communicate through the intranet, through team brief and through clinical service unit meetings – our HR managers go to that. We've got the shared governance group and we pull people together for certain things. For example we pulled together a group of ward sisters to look at recruitment and retention. It is a range of different mechanisms and involvement of people. I prefer to involve the staff rather than the unions, but I have to involve the unions. (Interview notes, April 2001)

Table 6.2 *Employer-led forms of communication at Eastern Trust*

Written communication
Chief executive letter (e.g new year message to all staff)
E-mail and trust intranet
Feedback on annual staff survey
Minutes of joint consultative and negotiating committee meetings (placed on noticeboards)
Nursing and midwifery directorate newsletter
Staff information (telephone) hotline – feedback (approximately every fortnight)
Staff magazine (monthly)
Trust board update (issued after each trust board meeting)
Trust business plan/annual report

Direct communication
Chief executive information exchanges
Diagonal slice groups
Service unit and department meetings
Team briefings

Indirect communication
Employment relations institutions – staff side machinery
Shared governance structures (in nursing)

Source: Eastern Trust documentation, 2001.

These comments indicate the number of channels that trust managers had established with the workforce. It had increased from virtually nothing in 1993, with a reliance on the formal staff side institutions, to a dense system of *top-down* communication channels (Table 6.2).

The data is striking in terms of the expansion of channels over the eight-year period. These increased channels of communication contributed to the diminution in importance of joint management–union consultation structures, eroding staff side representative roles. An illustration of these trends emerges from the staff survey. In response to the question 'I am made aware of what is happening in the trust by …' staff were offered eleven main choices reflecting the communication channels outlined in Table 6.2. Only 14 per cent of staff ticked the box 'my staff side representative' which placed it 10/11 in rank order with only the staff information hotline lower (it had just started at the time of the survey). By contrast 82 per cent of respondents cited team brief, as the channel most used by staff.

Trade union activities are obviously not confined to communicating with members, but their ability to convey an independent perspective on developments within the trust was important for their visibility and credibility. A joint union newsletter did exist, but it was brief and appeared irregularly. Some staff side representatives contested this interpretation of diminished influence, suggesting that trade unions were able to use managerial information sources to their advantage, for example through seeking information from management by putting questions on the telephone hotline. They argued also that union membership levels were holding up, but other evidence painted a less sanguine picture.

Senior managers were dissatisfied with the employment relations climate, especially the adversarial relationship with Unison, which represented the interests of ancillary staff. Trade unions had the capacity to embarrass senior managers by high profile demonstrations and petitions (e.g. against the private finance initiative) that were widely reported in the local newspaper and sometimes led to questions in Parliament. For example, during May 2000, at the JCNC, the day before the trust board, the staff side were informed that a broad range of support services were to be market tested, subject to board approval the next day. Unison immediately lodged a dispute and contacted the press and local MPs to support their case.

This prompted the HR director to approach the Advisory, Conciliation and Arbitration Service (ACAS) to develop partnership working with the staff side and to reduce the antagonism of the JCNC meetings. The staff side were sceptical of the initiative, but a series of workshops were held with ACAS and several reforms were made. The JCNC continued to meet monthly, but corporate directors and the chief executive were expected to attend quarterly. The quarterly meeting was termed the Trust Employee Relations Forum (TERF).

The HR director argued that the relationship with the staff side had become less difficult and that ACAS involvement had been very helpful in addressing bullying and harassment issues. Staff side representatives valued the ACAS input on bullying issues, but felt that senior managers had not adhered to the commitments that they made to staff. The CEO had not attended a TERF meeting for eighteen months since January 2000 and a similar picture emerged for other directors, with the exception of the finance director. Staff side representatives complained also that they were not always consulted on staffing policies prior to approval at the trust board.

The director of nursing established a separate system of employee involvement to increase the role of nurses and midwives in decisions affecting clinical practice and working practices. The system involved three nursing policy councils – clinical practice, education and research. Each council has 15 elected members from a broad spectrum of grades who meet monthly to discuss issues, such as a new dress code for staff, or the administration of drugs by newly qualified staff. The chairs of each council meet with the director and assistant director of nursing, which provides a link to the top management team and the trust board. The director of nursing argued that it formed an essential part of corporate governance at Eastern and provided development and leadership opportunities for nurses. Moreover, because the director of nursing does not manage nurses directly, there was a gap between the ward managers and the director, and this structure allowed that gap to be bridged. The initiative cost Eastern about £45,000 per annum.

The opportunity to become more involved in decision-making was welcomed by nursing staff involved in the councils. Some ward managers, however, were guarded about the initiative. An important consideration they highlighted was pressure on them to release staff for the meetings, but they argued that shared governance had a limited impact on nursing practice at ward level. Staff side representatives expressed more scepticism. As the Unison branch chair commented:

> They let them talk about uniforms but when it comes to staffing levels it's [the] unions. They are not an independent voice. It's just another way of undermining unions. (Interview notes, July 2001)

Staff representatives were particularly concerned about the differential treatment of staff side representatives in comparison to the shared governance representatives. Each council member was allocated one day a month for their council duties, and this was covered by the nursing budget. By contrast staff side representatives struggled to attend JCNC meetings:

> while the attendance of the staff side representatives may seem small, this reflected the difficulties caused by work pressures. The staff side representatives were under pressure to forgo attendance at meetings which form part of their union representative role, as backfilling is not provided for most union duties. (JCNC minutes, October 2000)

These comments were backed up by staff representatives who acknowledged that workload pressures were making it very difficult for them to fulfil their role as staff side representatives. In the August 2000 JCNC minutes it was recorded that a particular representative 'was unable to support JCNC activities for 2 months due to work pressures'. In a context of staff shortages and increased workloads, managers were often reluctant to allow staff to undertake their union duties, despite good formal time-off policies, and clinical staff were ambivalent about 'letting down' colleagues to attend JCNC meetings. This had led to the staff side failing to meet quorum requirements on several occasions, although the meetings had proceeded as 'updating' forums. These initiatives, taken together, indicated a diminution of trade union voice and influence with important implications for trade union practice.

Northern: from managerialism to partnership

The financial context and employment relations context was less volatile than in Eastern and the chief executive attached importance to the personnel role. The director of personnel (retitled director of human resources in 1998), who had been in the district since 1988, was an executive director of the trust board, a position which she shared with the director of hospital services (they alternated on an annual basis) so as not to exceed the statutory number of executive director positions. With her departure in 1997, the former deputy director became director and subsequently became an executive member of the trust board in 2001, until the merger in 2002.

In the first year of trust status, the personnel directorate's business plan (Table 6.3) emphasized that the human resources strategy should support the delivery of the corporate business plan. A variety of initiatives aimed to develop the organization to ensure the delivery of high quality patient care.

Table 6.3 *Personnel directorate business plan at Northern Trust 1994–95*

---

1. Development of the clinical directorates within a corporate context.

2. Effective use of staff through reprofiling and effective workforce planning.

3. Delivery of Investors in People targets for action and of the management/staff development strategy.

4. Development of pay/rewards/benefits packages for the Trust.

5. Development of Health at Work initiatives for staff.

6. Implementation of an effective communications strategy.

7. Development of a strategy for equality of opportunity.

8. Development of corporate identity project.

9. Ensure that risk management issues receive high priority within the organization.

Source: Northern Health Care Business Plan, 1994–95.

This included: an emphasis on communicating more effectively with staff through the use of team briefings; roadshows and written communications; encouraging staff to feel that the organization valued them by seeking 'Investors in People' status and developing a range of training and development activities, particularly customer care courses for all staff. Training and development activities were also marked by a sensitivity to the gender and ethnic composition of the workforce.

In a similar manner to the policies in Eastern, managers made widespread use of fixed-term contracts in the mid-1990s, particularly for ancillary and nursing staff. Their use reflected some deterioration in the trust's financial position and uncertainty over contract income. During this period managers had to obtain special dispensation to place a new staff member on a permanent contract. Fixed-term contracts were usually of three to six months' duration, but were generally renewed.

Personnel managers expressed concerns that line managers were too eager to put staff on fixed-term contracts because line managers believed, probably erroneously, that it would be easier to dismiss staff. Senior management disenchantment with fixed-term contracts was reflected in the chief executive's comments:

> The Trust wishes to move away from the use of temporary contracts although this will not be the end of the use of fixed-term contracts. Bank staff will also be shed to redeploy staff into permanent contracts. (Joint Consultative Committee (JCC) Minutes, December 1996)

During the spring of 1997 a meeting was held to encourage managers to convert posts from a fixed-term to a permanent basis. Nonetheless, the staff side continued to complain that a high proportion of posts continued to be offered on a fixed-term basis.

The election of the Labour government in 1997 shifted the HR agenda towards fulfilling the requirements of the national HR framework, the National Plan and dealing with the consequences of continuing NHS reorganization. In April 2002 Northern was restructured, with the community and primary care services moved into a primary care trust (PCT) and the acute services absorbed into a neighbouring acute trust. Managers argued that staff were having to come to terms with changes that had happened in other locations in the early 1990s, when separate acute and community trusts were established in many parts of the country.

Staff were confident about their employment status (they were protected by the Transfer of Undertakings Protection of Employment (TUPE) regulations), but were uncertain about whether the PCT could address their professional development and training needs. These concerns stemmed from their transfer from an established organization with a well developed human resources infrastructure to a new organization that was developing its management capacity. The gap between the responsibilities assigned to PCTs and the managerial capacity to undertake their responsibilities has been identified as a national problem (Dowling *et al.* 2002). For staff transferring to the PCT, appraisal arrangements, access to training and development opportunities, and the role of GPs in the management of PCTs were all sources of concern. The director of HR invested a considerable amount of time in meeting with staff to allay their fears during 2001–02.

The management of absence

The human resources agenda reflected the priorities established by the national HR strategy in terms of performance management including the management of absenteeism. Since the mid-1990s absence management had been a high priority at Northern, with information systems established that calculated an individual absence figure for each member of staff. This figure was weighted to highlight frequent short periods of absence. A trust-wide performance target of 4 per cent was introduced, and this target became, for the first time, a key performance indicator for managers.

To enable managers to achieve their targets a mandatory training programme was introduced during 1995. Whether because of these initiatives or other aspects of working at Northern, in general absenteeism was viewed as less of an issue than at the other two trusts. There were some concerns expressed, however, that managers interpreted the policy in different ways, leading to inconsistencies in the management of attendance.

By 2001 the monthly absence figure was usually just above or below 4 per cent. This figure compared relatively favourably to many other trusts but created difficulties because managers felt penalized by the national target reductions. The director of HR commented:

> As far as targets are concerned, no matter how low or high, you get the same improvement target which is a bit soul destroying really when we have been working hard to achieve a low level. The target is 20 per cent. No way are we going to achieve a 20 per cent reduction. I have informed the regional office of this, but the response is 'well that's the target'. That's difficult. (Interview notes, April 2001)

There was also uncertainty as to the ultimate goal that the government was trying to achieve, in terms of what the government considered to be an acceptable level of absence. The criticism that the HR objectives were not always sufficiently attuned to local needs also arose in relationship to the requirement to undertake an annual staff survey and the obligation to introduce personal development plans. For some job roles, for example hotel services staff, a departmental development plan was viewed as more appropriate than an individual one. Nonetheless, the HR framework did provide a catalyst for managerial action, and this was viewed as especially important in encouraging middle managers to consider HR issues. There were also some additional resources available linked to achieving the *Pledge* stage of the Improving Working Lives initiative (£25,000).

Employee relations: communication and union influence

A key decision for managers was the type of local consultation and negotiating machinery that was to be established and the type of recognition granted to the trade unions. This was especially important during the mid-1990s when Conservative government policy emphasized the importance of local decision-making over pay and rewards (Chapter 7). Trust managers aimed to maintain a good relationship with staff side representatives while developing more direct forms of communication with the workforce.

Managers had reviewed the existing consultation and negotiation agreements that had been established prior to trust status, and a decision had been made not to replicate the national arrangements, but to recognize only those organizations that had members within Northern. Trust managers decided that all unions would be recognized for consultation purposes, but not all of them would be recognized for bargaining purposes. The involvement of non-union staff in the trust's systems of representation was also considered, but managers decided not to proceed on this basis because it was viewed as too contentious. A trust joint negotiating committee (JNC) was established in anticipation of a shift towards local pay and conditions of employment. Trust managers insisted that the JNC limit staff side representation to six members that had to include the three largest trade unions (RCN, Unison, MSF). The staff side requested more places over several years, concerned about the representation of smaller organizations, but this request was declined.

The approach of trust managers towards the relationship they wished to develop with the workforce had two dimensions which focused, first, on the role of the trade unions and, second, on the wider communications strategy. Managers were committed to consulting with the trade unions over a range of issues, using the JCC structure, but they reserved the right to impose changes if the consultation process had been exhausted and no agreement could be reached. This had occurred on several occasions. From the mid-1990s the NHS Executive replaced detailed national agreements with framework agreements that allowed greater scope for trusts to shape local policy. For example, during 1995 the protection of earnings arrangements (Section 47 of the Whitley Council handbook) was removed. Trust managers consulted the staff side on their proposals, which limited protection to two years. This arrangement was rejected by the staff side, but managers notified them that it would be imposed at the start of 1996. An appeal that was heard by three members of the trust board was rejected. Senior managers were willing to consult with staff representatives, but they were not prepared to allow opposition to their plans to alter their position.

Second, managers assigned a high priority to communicating effectively with the whole workforce to ensure that they understood the competitive position and budgetary constraints that Northern faced arising from the internal market reforms. Finance staff attended the meetings with the staff side to provide information on finance and contracts. A communications sub-group was established with a series of communications goals identified (e.g. promote the corporate identity and a sense of belonging among staff).

For the workforce as a whole, managers used a variety of communication methods, including team briefings, a staff newsletter, roadshows and departmental meetings. Nonetheless, separate surveys of staff highlighted communication problems and indicated that team briefing operated in a patchy manner. A discussion at the JCC noted:

> A communications survey of 200 staff had been undertaken in the Trust. The results of this exercise were mixed and again it seemed to emphasize the quality of communications was not good. This communications questionnaire in addition to the Investors in People pre-assessment suggests that communication is not right in the organization. (JCC Minutes, October 1995)

When the former deputy director became HR director during 1998 she placed emphasis on reshaping employee relations in the trust, following a deterioration in the climate of employee relations during the mid–late 1990s. This had arisen from the national dispute over local pay, the commitment of the former director of personnel to develop trust terms and conditions of employment, and disagreements with the staff side over the recognition agreement.

A series of workshops were held from 1998, facilitated by ACAS, to improve employee relations. This led to the establishment of sub-groups of the JCC, for example to take forward the Improved Working Lives initiative, and the JCC meetings were reorganized to make them less formal so that there was less of an 'us' and 'them' culture. Trust managers were also interested in establishing a partnership agreement with the trade unions.

The ability of trade unions to shape developments remained uncertain. First, the primary forum in which they could influence management policy was the JCC, but the agenda of the JCC remained narrow. It focused on discussing trust policies (for example, disciplinary and grievance policies) and traditional issues, such as car park charges for staff. In recent years the HR director had tried to improve JCC representatives' awareness of trust developments with more information provided, for example, on the financial position of the trust. Although it was viewed as valuable information, the former chair of the staff side acknowledged that:

> At the meetings there is a lot of information coming down, so you do tend to feel when you are getting lots of information that you haven't had a lot of input to, that there is a little bit of 'alright we are being told things here'. But I think that's unavoidable with all the change that is going on at the moment. (Interview notes, July 2001)

Senior managers, even if involved in the JCC, attached limited importance to its deliberations, as one general manager commented: 'I'll talk to staff direct.

The JCC is about organizational policies and I sometimes feel that we talk to the JCC just to keep them informed. The JCC is not the key forum' (Interview notes, July 2001). More generally the staff opinion survey suggested that the JCC scarcely registered as a means of finding out what was going on at Northern (Table 6.4).

Table 6.4 *Staff use of communication mechanisms at Northern Trust*

Responses to the question 'I am made aware of what is happening in the Trust by' (tick all that apply)	
Trust newsletter	65%
Noticeboards	15%
Briefings by line managers	56%
Word of mouth/grapevine	78%
My staff/trade union representative	17%
Joint Consultative Committee	3%
Attachments to payslip	66%
E-mail	15%

Source: Northern staff opinion survey 1999–2000. The staff opinion survey obtained a 38 per cent response rate. 86 per cent of respondents were female and 40 per cent worked part-time. The largest group of respondents (31 per cent) were among qualified nursing and midwifery staff.

Finally, some of the same difficulties that were evident in Eastern also confronted staff representatives. Managers confronted with staff shortages and workload pressures were sometimes reluctant to allow staff time off for their union duties, and staff side representatives also expressed concern about their exclusion from HR decision-making. These dual concerns were reflected in the JCC minutes:

> Staff confirmed their commitment [to the HR performance framework] but needed reassurance of their manager's support regarding time off and replacement costs. Staff side members are primarily clinicians and are not always able to devote time to such issues ... [the staff side chair] expressed concern on behalf of staff representatives at their exclusion from various groups over the last 12–18 months which she felt did not support the principle of partnership working. (JCC Minutes, January 2001)

In summary, employees consistently expressed more satisfaction in the interviews about staff management and working at Northern than at Eastern,

Table 6.5 *Staff opinion survey responses at Eastern and Northern Trusts 1999–2000*

Question	Northern		Eastern	
	Agree (%)	Disagree (%)	Agree (%)	Disagree (%)
I have a clear understanding about expected standards of performance	91	5	88	6
My line manager/team leader deals with poor performance effectively	39	32	44	38
The Trust provides me with enough information to do my job well	80	18	65	32
I feel my experience is valued by the Trust	50	49	39	59
I feel my employment security at the Trust is good	71	25	57	39
I believe that the Trust provides me with good information about the training and development available to me	65	28	54	40
The Trust is a good place to work, I would recommend it	63	26	44	43
I am confident that my ideas and suggestions will be listened to	54	40	44	51
I am confident that I would get feedback on my ideas and suggestions	49	47	41	52
I feel the Trust Board is interested in staff's well being*	43	50	30	65
I feel the Trust Board is interested in staff's views*	36	55	25	65
In my department there are enough staff	30	68	30	69
Have you ever been harassed or bullied?	25 yes	75 no	24 yes	71 no
I feel the Trust deals effectively with stress	25	60	16	66
I feel the Trust deals effectively with excessive workload	20	70	9	79
I feel the Trust provides good support to help me balance work and home responsibilities	63	37	54	39
I feel everyone is treated equally with regard to their domestic commitments	42	38	45	47

*In the Eastern questionnaire for both these questions the question referred to directors rather than the trust board.

Source: Eastern and Northern staff opinion surveys 1999–2000 (data from Western was not comparable). Responses do not equal 100% due to figures being rounded and non-responses being excluded.

a view borne out by the staff opinion survey. At Northern staff had consistently more positive perceptions about their employer in relation to employment security, training and development opportunities and a range of other issues than at Eastern (Table 6.5). Nonetheless, the survey results also confirmed a sense among employees, reflected in the erosion of traditional institutional structures of employment relations, that they had limited scope to shape the human resource management agenda at the trust. Senior managers were viewed as too busy and too orientated towards achieving their targets to take a meaningful interest in staff perspectives. For example, in the orthopaedics review, the management consultant undertaking the initial review noted in her (2000) report that 'staff have enthusiasm, energy and motivation but lack a consistent mechanism through which to channel their innovative ideas'. The inability of staff to contribute effectively led the CHI Review to comment that the trust's management style 'has not always empowered staff in the organization and has resulted in disenchantment in some areas, particularly amongst some consultants'. For clinical staff, the ability to contribute to improvements in service standards remains integral to their professional identity.

Western: between strategic intent and the survival of tradition

In Western, successive trust chief executives were supportive of a high profile for human resource management issues. The first director of personnel, who was appointed in 1992 as the unit was preparing for trust status, believed that personnel specialists needed to break with the administrative tradition in the NHS, which was essentially reactive and concentrated on maintenance tasks. His approach was articulated in the human resource strategy which identified three strategic themes. The first priority was more effective labour utilization. In the first instance this approach was to be addressed by developing generic working. A second theme concerned pay and reward; taking advantage of the freedoms offered by trust status, to review pay and conditions of service with a view to developing more innovative employment practices. Third, staff involvement and development was required to ensure that changes in the human resource agenda were understood and effectively implemented. Developing a communications strategy and streamlining the bargaining process to develop single table bargaining were central to this approach. The director of personnel emphasized that his approach to these three key areas would be underpinned by an emphasis on incorporating human resource issues into the directorate business planning process. This philosophy had clear implications for the personnel department, which had to balance meeting the needs of the individual directorates and ensuring an overall corporate approach to employment issues.

These aims were incorporated in Western's strategy for the period 1996–2001, which set out two critical success factors related to staffing issues. The first was a corporate aim to reduce staffing costs by 5 per cent over five years, reflecting finance-led pressures rather than the priorities arising from the HR agenda. The second objective was to achieve 80 per cent staff satisfaction with communications, based on independent assessment. Both objectives appeared to have been quietly dropped as managerial personnel and national policy altered.

Many of the key challenges facing Western during that period were personnel related issues. In particular, its relative geographical isolation ensured that managers had to be vigilant about recruiting and retaining medical staff. This difficult situation was exacerbated by the reductions in junior doctors' hours associated with the 1991 'New Deal'. The introduction of generic working gained a high profile as did the attempt to gain Investors in People accreditation, the establishment of local pay bargaining and a more systematic approach to communications, with senior managers holding 'road-shows', explaining their position on key issues to staff.

Between 1997 and 2002, the overall approach towards human resources was set by the national agenda, supplemented by workforce planning for the new single-site hospital. The HR strategy outlined the main priorities at Western, but the key document was the trust HR performance management framework that followed national priorities based on the *Improving Working Lives* standard. The HR performance framework recommended that 'hard' measures of HR performance should be presented to the executive board, HR sub-committee and trust board on a monthly basis. The measures would be: retention rates; sickness absence and reasons for sickness absence; workplace accidents and incidents of violence against staff; locum, agency and bank spend; and vacancy levels. It was acknowledged that 'softer' measures of HR performance would also need consideration (e.g. staff training and development plans). The HR performance management framework ran to 26 pages divided between five standards: securing a quality workforce; quality of working life – equality; quality of working life – creating a healthy workforce; staff involvement; and HR management and capability. In total these standards were linked to 60 targets related to HR issues, although they varied in how specific they were.

Managing absence

A key priority was the management of absence. In one sense this was not a new concern. In the mid-1990s a District Audit report had drawn attention to absence levels, concluding that:

> The Trust's average sickness level is gradually falling, though at 10.6 days per employee it is higher than that experienced in the private sector, and by the best performing trusts. There is considerable variation between directorates within the Trust and also opportunity to reduce costs if nursing sickness was reduced to that of the lowest 25% of trusts.

It was among nursing staff that absence levels were highest. The District Audit report commented that staff were not always replaced (even in the case of nursing staff) and this contributed to work intensification and role overload. As the director of nursing acknowledged with reference to ward managers:

> They are under pressure, and getting mixed messages from the trust; want you to be a ward manager, want you to be a clinical nurse, want you to reskill the workforce, too much to do – I am really worried about the ward sisters. (Interview notes, July 1996)

Between 1996 and 2002 a concerted effort was made to reduce sickness absence, with a target of 4.9 per cent that was subsequently revised downwards to 4.2 per cent in 2001. Considerable efforts had been placed on the training of line managers, improvements in corporate reporting and greater involvement of the occupational health department. Nonetheless, managers argued that staff shortages were increasing workloads, contributing to high levels of sickness. This was borne out by the 2000–01 staff survey, in which high levels of concern were recorded in relation to the section on working arrangements and job demands. The most marked levels of dissatisfaction among staff were in response to three questions: 'My workload is rarely unreasonably high,' 'Sometimes my work makes me feel anxious and distressed' and 'I am rarely required to work extra hours.' Managers therefore argued that they would not be able to achieve their absence targets, and in the national NHS performance targets published in February 2002, the national trust figure cited was 4.5 per cent, and Western had a figure of 5.5 per cent, which placed it in the lowest (worst) national band.

Employee relations: communications and extended involvement

In preparation for trust status senior managers commenced negotiations on recognition and collective bargaining arrangements. Prominent directors shared a belief in the value of a good relationship with the trade unions. The chief executive had managed hospitals during the 1970s which had been beset by industrial relations difficulties. This convinced him of the need to develop dialogue with the staff side and to avoid the imposition of change. An indication of this philosophy was that the chief executive chaired the trust joint consultative and negotiating committee (JCNC) and attended most of the meetings. Other senior managers attended on a regular basis, which represented an unusually high level of representation by senior managers in a trust consultative forum.

The recognition procedure was agreed with the existing eleven trade unions shortly after Western became a trust (Table 6.6). It covered consultation and negotiation on all pay and non-pay matters and conditions of service for all staff with the exception of training grades and senior managers. The agreement made provision for the attendance of full-time officers and

Table 6.6 *Recognized trade unions at Western Trust*

Amalgamated Engineering and Electrical Union
British Association of Occupational Therapists
British Dietetic Association
British Medical Association
British Orthoptist Society
Chartered Society of Physiotherapy
Manufacturing, Science and Finance Union
Royal College of Midwives
Royal College of Nursing
Society of Radiographers
Transport and General Workers Union
UNISON

Source: Western Recognition and Local Collective Bargaining Arrangements Agreement, 1993.

the co-option of one of these to be the union lead officer who would be the main point of contact between trust management and the full-time officials.

At Western the employment relations context was less adversarial than at Eastern. There were some similarities with Northern in that staff appeared to respect senior managers. The two chief executives that steered Western between 1992 and 2001 gave a high profile to staff management and communication issues, and this was noted by the Commission for Health Improvement team (2002b):

> Staff informed CHI that they liked and respected the senior management team. We were told that the open management style was improving communications and that a positive, listening culture was developing.

This was reflected in a willingness to consult with trade unions, and in the 2000–01 trust annual report the staff side secretary commented:

> Staff, human resources and all the trust management have 'worked in partnership' long before it became the buzz word. All policies and procedures currently in use have been written jointly, the majority based around legislation and good practice. It is no surprise that some of our policies are being used as a model elsewhere.

Despite the willingness of senior management to engage with staff side representatives, they also sought to develop communication and involvement strategies for the whole workforce. The HR function remained the custodian of the joint management–union structures with the staff side consulted over policy issues, for example the development of *Improving Working Lives*. Nonetheless the main focus of involvement activities in the post-1997 period resided outside the HR function and encompassed the whole workforce.

The most notable example of this approach concerned the 'Extended Involvement' initiative that had been established within nursing and subsequently expanded to the remainder of the organization. This initiative reflected the personal management style of the director of nursing, who was highly visible and respected within Western, a point noted by the CHI reviewers. In a similar manner to the director of nursing at Eastern, he had been influenced by the shared governance movement in the USA and suggested that the initiative was:

> a way of engaging with staff. The other by-product, as nurse director in a very large trust with 2,400 nurses and midwives, is that it is a good way of making

sure that I got a lot of contact (with nurses) either in meetings with them, in workshops, or they would phone me up, stop me in the corridor. It's about maintaining the visibility of the director. (Interview notes, June 2002)

The extended involvement initiative did not use the model of elected councils (as at Eastern) because of concerns that it would become too bureaucratic and elitist. Instead, within an established set of ground rules relating to finance, and maintaining the reputation of the trust, staff were relatively free to establish ad hoc working groups to examine issues that were of concern to them. Outcomes included raising the profile and confidence of nursing staff in the trust, for example by developing a directory of nurse expertise, in a similar way to that which existed for medical staff. Other outcomes included improvements in information provided to patients; the development of a shadowing programme with approximately 40 nurses per annum shadowing the director of nursing for a week; and open space events for 300 staff that communicated their perspectives on how the trust should work in the future. CHI commented positively on the initiative and the separate establishment of a staff charter noting that 'CHI found evidence that these had a positive effect on the working environment.'

For a traditionally hierarchical profession like nursing, however, nurse managers found the initiative threatening and a culture shock, because nursing staff were being encouraged to question existing practice and managers had to respond to a variety of suggestions. As with all staff involvement initiatives, the early champions began to tire after about two years and little consideration had been given to succession planning to maintain its momentum. The impact on the staff side was more ambiguous and some tensions were acknowledged. As the director of human resources commented with particular reference to the open space events:

We struggled with the staff side. They want to play a representative role, they are there, but they are struggling with how they play into that because it's very much about what the *individual* wants and how they feel. (Interview notes, September 2001)

Second, managers argued that even if they wished to involve staff side representatives more fully, this was impractical. This arose because of the difficulties that the unions faced in recruiting representatives, and increased staff workloads made it difficult for them to participate fully in the employment relations agenda at Western. These difficulties were not entirely novel: in an earlier phase of fieldwork in 1996, both the chair and staff side secretary

Table 6.7 *Western Trust staff satisfaction survey 2000–01: staff priorities for change*

1. Fair pay and conditions of work.
2. Staff participation in decision-making.
3. Regular appraisal and feedback about job performance.
4. Staff involvement in improving working practice.
5. Working relationships between staff and management.
6. Open discussion about work issues between staff and management.
7. Clear aims and objectives for all staff.
8. Equal opportunities with respect to training, development and promotion.
9. A work environment free from aggression, harassment or bullying.
10. The physical safety of staff in the Trust.

Source: Western Trust, staff opinion survey, 2000.

commented that they had reluctantly taken on the roles because no-one else was prepared to undertake these roles. By 2002, increased workload pressure had made this problem more acute.

The overall state of employee relations in Western was reflected in the staff satisfaction survey that was administered in autumn 2000 and received almost 2,000 staff responses. The questions asked, and the data analysis undertaken, differed from the Eastern and Northern cases making direct comparisons difficult. The top ten priorities for change are identified in Table 6.7. Taking into account that the trust has been praised in the NHS as a leading example of staff involvement, it is especially notable that three out of the five priorities of staff relate to increased voice and participation issues.

Discussion

This chapter has examined the approach towards employment relations in the three trusts. In all three cases, and particularly since the election of the Labour government in 1997, the employment relations agenda has been dominated by the national HR framework and the targets that have been established by the Labour government.

This has raised the importance of the HR agenda in recent years, but to a lesser extent than is usually assumed. It is important to distinguish between the higher profile assigned to specific HR issues in the trusts and the role and influence of the HR function. In the main the HR agenda was being driven by Conservative and Labour government policy priorities – local pay in the mid-1990s and performance targets after 1997 – alongside severe operational difficulties, especially staff shortages. In the sense that the HR agenda was expected to contribute to this overall agenda by meeting government targets in terms of absence and vacancy levels, HR had the opportunity to become more integral to the trust to support the corporate agenda. In all three cases, however, this proved difficult. It partly related to the workload associated with organizational changes including trust mergers (Eastern), the establishment of the PCT (Northern), or internal reorganization (Western) exacerbated by complex time-consuming operational issues such as medical or nursing staff disciplinary cases.

This led to other directors taking a lead role in addressing HR issues. In both Eastern and Western efforts to bolster staff involvement in recent years had been initiated and led by the directors of nursing. With the exception of Western in the 1992–96 period, there was limited evidence that the HR director and the HR function had a pivotal *and visible* impact on developments within the trusts. The point about visibility is significant. It was striking from the fieldwork and the CHI reports that staff often spoke favourably about senior managers that they had seen at ward and departmental level. This seemed to be interpreted as a proxy for the commitment of these managers to the values and concerns of staff, and it aided staff in understanding senior manager roles more effectively. HR directors and managers, however, often referred to their perception that staff did not know what HR staff did, reinforcing the negative perceptions of 'management' noted in Chapter 2.

In all cases HR directors argued that they were woefully under-resourced and driven by short-term operational problems that resulted in a reactive human resources function. This difficulty was most acute at Eastern, which was not surprising considering the turbulent organizational context. Ward managers argued that HR had devolved issues such as maternity leave to them with insufficient support, but there was uncertainty as to whether this had enabled HR to develop a more strategic role. The director of nursing suggested that the trust had ended up:

> with an HR administrative function rather than an HR strategic function. Lots of strategic principles – want to be a good employer, want to retain our staff, not the same as operationally managing it. (Interview notes, July 2001)

Opinions were less polarized at Northern and Western; nonetheless, there was little sense that HR made a central contribution to trust management. As one general manager at Northern commented:

> The type of HR support that managers need is quite different from what HR managers think they need, although most HR departments would claim to be quite sensitive to the HR needs of the service departments. Where we do need support is more an HR consultancy role, facilitating processes; that needs new skills for HR people, restructuring the way services are provided to directorates or modernization task groups, and it needs a leap of faith that GMs can deal with routine stuff. (Interview notes, April 2001)

Instead, the emphasis that was being placed on achieving the government's service targets (waiting times) and HR targets in terms of absence and vacancy targets raised two issues for trust HR managers. First, they were concerned about the balance between national requirements and their local priorities, with the latter often being marginalized. One director suggested that she had 'space around the edges' and used the language of national priorities, for example involvement and partnership, as a catalyst to alter employment relations practices. Second, as managers were under pressure to achieve short-term results they focused on achieving the target, even if they acknowledged that this might prove detrimental to staff management in the longer term. Consequently HR managers adopted a 'harder' approach to absence management, focusing on reducing absence levels rather than addressing the underlying problems that stemmed from a more demanding performance agenda imposed by central government, making staff feel that they had little control or ownership of their work priorities.

The perceptions of staff about the degree that the HR agenda signified that they were valued by the organization was variable. As Table 6.5 indicates, at Northern almost two-thirds of staff viewed it as a good place to work compared to under half at Eastern. The scores were much lower in terms of staff perception about whether the trust board/directors were interested in staff well-being. Staff welcomed some of the initiatives relating to *Improving Working Lives*, but their priorities were not always addressed by national initiatives. In the fieldwork research, the immediate concerns of staff related to high workloads and stress, which they acknowledged would take some time to resolve. Nonetheless, staff frequently mentioned a sense that they had little control over their working lives and aspects of ward life that compromised service standards. This was expressed most forcibly at Eastern as one ward manager commented:

I have talked to lots of people in the trust, but nothing changes. I don't feel that anything can change. I would like to provide a quality service, but can't do that. (Interview notes, July 2001)

More generally, however, as managers focused on achieving their waiting list targets, the scope for staff to shape workplace developments was heavily constrained. At Western the Extended Involvement initiative provided some counter-weight to these trends for nursing staff, but overall the staff opinion survey indicated that increased employee involvement to shape development at the trust remained a key demand. Similarly at Eastern, despite staff involvement initiatives in nursing, the staff opinion survey indicated high levels of scepticism among staff about senior management's interest in staff views and their ability to gain feedback on their suggestions. Similar results emerged at Northern.

A traditional source of employee voice and counter-balance to managerial perspectives has resided with trade unions. Union density in the trusts remained high. Nonetheless, there were indications that trade union influence had diminished. Trust managers had invested considerable efforts in developing alternative channels of communication. Thus, the traditional institutional structures of union–management consultation were becoming less central to employment relations practice and, for a variety of reasons including increased workloads, trade unions confronted difficulties in recruiting and retaining staff representatives.

There was little evidence that HR managers were deliberately trying to marginalize trade unions, with the possible exception of Eastern that stemmed from the long-standing adversarial relations in the trust. In general HR managers saw benefits in working with trade unions to help them achieve their HR agenda. Nonetheless, HR directors seemed uncertain about whether trade unions could fulfil such a role, and for much of the last decade little priority was attached to union–management relations. This was particularly the case for other managers, such as the directors of nursing that had championed other forms of employee involvement in Eastern and Western. In contrast to the trust-wide orientation of the staff-side–management consultation arrangements, these initiatives reflected the professional character of the workforce. Because they were grounded in the particular occupational concerns and aspirations of nurses, especially at Western, they were of greater direct relevance to these staff and they were more engaged in 'extended involvement' than other more traditional forms of joint consultation.

7 THE MANAGEMENT OF PAY

The shortcomings of the Whitley system of pay determination have been a continuous preoccupation of government ministers, employers and trade unions. In the last two decades the shift towards decentralized pay determination in the private sector provided the impetus for Conservative and subsequently Labour governments to endorse a shift towards more locally determined pay and conditions. This policy approach dovetailed with Conservative rhetoric of trust freedoms and was compatible also with the Labour government's commitment to a modernized pay system that would provide trust managers with increased scope for local flexibility within a revamped national framework. The potential significance of a shift towards trust based pay determination was the opportunity it presented to move away from rigid national occupational boundaries towards more flexible work organization. Local pay, by emphasizing the distinctiveness of each trust's pay system, was also conceived as a means to strengthen loyalty to the trust and could be used to reinforce the link between pay and performance.

This chapter examines the degree to which trust managers have reformed their payment systems to pursue these objectives. It focuses on the reform of payment systems while the next chapter explores the degree to which more trust based employment systems produced changes in work organization. It examines the main influences that fostered or hindered workplace change and goes on to explore what the experience of local pay indicates about the prospects for pay modernization. The response of managers, employees and trade unions to other forms of pay flexibility, especially discretionary points for nursing staff, indicates the type of issues that will need to be addressed at workplace level during the implementation of *Agenda for Change*.

Pay determination in Eastern

The budgetary difficulties and changes in top management personnel within Eastern produced an uncertain context that shaped the approach towards local pay determination. It was recognized even before trust status had been attained in 1993 that the prospects for the introduction of local pay and trust terms and conditions of employment were not propitious. The hospital had experienced a major scandal and the first trust chief executive had been brought in with a brief to stem the political furore surrounding the hospital and to ensure that the trust got off to a smooth start. Consequently, local pay did not feature as a management priority. This stance was reinforced because it was anticipated that the staff side would vigorously oppose local pay. Unison was the dominant union within Eastern, and the senior lay officers were viewed as 'militant'. Unison had strong links with the local Labour council and the local media, which managers expected to support the Unison position. In addition, managers argued that the resources to pay for change were not available. In these circumstances managers adopted a pragmatic approach with the reorganization of working practices by staff group, and the introduction of trust terms and conditions of employment on a block-by-block basis as opportunities arose.

As part of their preparations for local pay managers made some use of the Medequate system of job evaluation, and during 1995 a number of senior management jobs were analysed. However, managers found it difficult to apply the human resources and finance factors to finance staff who had an indirect impact on operational budgets. The director of personnel was ambivalent about the value of job evaluation because she suggested it did not inspire staff confidence, not least because non-managerial jobs appeared to come out too low in the hierarchy, and the strength of the trade unions locally would make it difficult to implement. The trade unions were formally involved in pay matters in the JCNC, whose composition did not substantially alter after Eastern became a trust. Ten trade unions were recognized for bargaining purposes, with a separate sub-committee established to handle local pay negotiations.

The most contentious developments in local pay occurred in 1995–96 reflecting the national pay dispute. This dispute stemmed from the recommendation of the Nurses' Pay Review Body for a 1 per cent national increase, with a further 0.5 per cent to 2 per cent to be decided at trust level (termed the x + y formula). Trust managers delayed making a local offer, but irrespective of the local position, union representatives followed national union guidance and refused to enter into trust negotiations pending an outcome to the national dispute. In addition, Eastern's Unison branch held a vote on local pay, resulting in a 96 per cent vote against local pay and supporting a national ballot on the issue.

With no sign of a resolution at national level, and under pressure from the NHS Executive to make a payment on account, in August the trust board sanctioned a 3 per cent offer to all staff. However, the offer included a condition that 0.5 per cent of the sum was dependent on management and unions working together with a view to negotiating local pay for 1996–97.

The staff side vociferously opposed the payment on account approach that was viewed as an imposition of the pay deal, and they were especially incensed by the conditions attached to the offer. Staff who wished to reject the 'payment on account' had a maximum of ten days to reply to the payroll department, otherwise a payment of 3 per cent (incorporating basic pay and allowances) was to be added to their October salary. Despite the inherent bias in this procedure towards acquiescence in management plans, nearly 20 per cent of staff initially refused the payment on account. It was only with the resolution of the national dispute that a 3 per cent settlement was reached at Eastern.

In a paper to the chief executive in November 1995 the director of personnel noted the constraints:

> The events which took place during the current pay round constrained our ability to access the 'freedom' of local pay because:
> - resources were not available to work on pay issues
> - the timetable was set by the centre
> - the ability to negotiate a deal was diminished by the centre's position
> - as we approach the end of the calendar year the position of many staff groups particularly the PAMs group is not resolved.

Although in subsequent years local pay negotiations were somewhat less conflictual, managers focused on work reorganization, using local terms and conditions as a means to support alterations in job roles (see Chapter 8).

The election of a Labour government formally ended this phase of the local pay experiment, although it was clear that there could be no return to the position prior to local pay. Instead, with the distraction of negotiating the local element of a national settlement removed, employers focused on other aspects of their employment relations agenda. Moreover, the publication of *Agenda for Change* in 1999 ushered in a long period of uncertainty as managers awaited the outcome of the pay reform negotiations. Reward policy remained on the agenda to the extent that trust managers needed to respond to national developments, with discretionary points the most prominent national pay initiative.

Discretionary points

The Nurses' Pay Review Body Report (1998) recommended that within the existing pay structure three discretionary increments to the value of £375–£400 at the top of the existing F, G, H and I grade pay scales were to be introduced during 1998–99. Discretionary points were not intended for staff that had just reached the top of the scale. The Office of Manpower Economics earnings data indicated that 49 per cent of Grade F nursing staff and 75 per cent of Grades G, H and I were at the top of their Whitley scales (cited in MSF 2000b: 6). These increments were anticipated to provide some immediate relief to the career development problems of these grades while the longer term structure of the NHS pay system was being considered. The government guidance stated that

> Discretionary points are not individual performance related pay nor should they be regarded as part of automatic incremental progression. Payments should be targeted to those who have demonstrated a significant contribution to service priorities by undertaking additional tasks and responsibilities. (NHS Executive 1998: para. 5.46)

Increments were not automatically transferable when an individual moved between trusts or when they changed posts within a trust. Funding was to be provided locally because there was no central allocation.

At national level, the staff side expressed reservations about the scheme because it only applied to senior staff and did not support good equal pay practice, but it 'felt uncomfortable about rejecting an agreement which held out the prospect of some staff earning more' (Nursing and Midwifery Staffs Negotiating Council Staff Side 1998: 2). Consequently all the trade unions, with the exception of MSF/CPHVA, voted in favour of the scheme. MSF/CPHVA, however, argued that the scheme would be divisive, unfairly excluded staff below F grade and could waste time with appeals and become a scaled down version of clinical grading appeals (MSF 2000b). The staff side recommended that as the value of discretionary points was low, eligible staff should receive all three discretionary points together.

At Eastern a formal trust policy was agreed that followed closely the national guidance. Eligible staff were informed and had to apply within two months, making out a written case based on the agreed criteria (Table 7.1). A committee was established to consider applicants, chaired by a trust director and senior nursing staff and three representatives drawn from the shared governance structures. Each applicant was scored against the criteria, and it was rare for any applicant to be awarded more than one point. A similar arrangement was used for para-medical staff. An appeal process allowed applicants to appeal to the committee in writing, and if still dissatisfied to appeal to the director of HR, who would reconvene the panel.

Table 7.1 *National criteria for the award of a discretionary increment*

Contribution to professional and multi-disciplinary team working;

Training and education of other staff, and/or participating in the training of staff from other professions;

Demonstrating a wider contribution to the work of the Trust;

Demonstration of research, innovation and/or responsibility for improvements in service delivery;

Demonstration of advances in knowledge and skills to the benefit of patient care;

Demonstration of significant contribution to service priorities.

Source: Eastern policy on discretionary points (based on Advanced Letter (NM) 2/98).

For managers and staff the experience of discretionary points highlighted many of the shortcomings of existing forms of local pay flexibility in the NHS. First, managers argued that local flexibility, like local pay, was in practice highly constrained by national policy. Discretionary points combined a system of national rules on eligibility, the overall criteria to be used and the process that was to be followed, with local flexibility on implementation. Managers argued that they had been given the responsibility to implement a national scheme at local level without any of the necessary prerequisites for effective implementation. This created frustration for managers, who argued that discretionary points had been imposed on them, with their main responsibilities being to establish funding for them and to make difficult choices about awards, using a laborious and divisive process.

Second, trust managers argued that discretionary points were an imposed form of 'flexibility' that was not linked to the needs of the organization. It encouraged staff to view discretionary points as an entitlement, raising expectations that could not always be met. As one of the HR managers commented:

That isn't flexibility. It's about a nurse coming in and saying I have done x, y, z before 31st March, therefore I deserve another increment. That to me isn't flexibility; to me flexibility is about us saying 'I want you to carry on working for this trust, therefore I'll give you another increment', but we haven't got that power. (Interview notes, July 2001)

The imposition of national criteria was therefore unwelcome because managers viewed the criteria as generic *professional* criteria rather than enabling managers to link pay to *managerially* defined needs to fit local circumstances. For staff, however, it was the managerial interpretation of the national criteria that was a source of dissatisfaction. Staff expressed concern that discretionary points enabled subjective managerial interpretation of national criteria to be used in the allocation of pay increases. This widespread view has wider implications for the *Agenda for Change* proposals because it highlights the difficulties that arise when crude forms of competency-based pay are used that rely on managerial interpretation of staff contribution.

Third, there was criticism that discretionary points had been established without consideration of how it linked to other aspects of the pay agenda or its effect on relativities. Staff could not keep their discretionary points if they were promoted internally or left the organization, but this did not act positively in a managerial sense as a form of 'golden handcuffs'. The awards were too small to discourage staff from seeking promotion and career advancement, but it meant that staff lost their discretionary points when they were promoted. Discretionary points therefore eroded the impact of a pay increase associated with career progression, but fostered a sense of injustice because of the loss of discretionary points when individuals changed jobs.

Finally, the Nurses' Pay Review Body's targeting of pay increases at particular grades undermined the potential motivational impact of discretionary points. In 2001 the Nurses' Pay Review Body (2001: 63) consolidated the first of three discretionary points for grades F to I, leaving two discretionary points available at the top of the scale, but this was perceived negatively by staff that had applied for a discretionary point that they would have been awarded automatically in 2001.

Ward managers were highly critical of the scheme. They argued that it was a time-consuming process that rewarded assertive and confident staff rather than those who made the most important contribution. Reflecting similar concerns as those raised about other forms of discretionary pay in the public services (for example, Marsden and French 1998), they suggested that given the severe financial problems confronting Eastern, it was difficult to make resources available for the initiative. Consequently, many staff were sceptical about the utility of applying because their perception was that they were unlikely to be awarded a discretionary point. At a time when workloads were rising, nurses expressed resentment that they had to apply for increments to prove that they were making a 'significant contribution'.

Trust managers expressed concern that in a period when many staff felt under enormous stress, a concern highlighted by the CHI review, discretionary points sent the wrong message to staff. As one HR manager commented, because 'people believe that their boss just wants more and more out of them [rather] than is genuinely concerned about them' (Interview notes, July 2001), discretionary points reinforced instrumental low-trust behaviour and undermined the team ethic. For example, it was suggested that discretionary points had created an incentive for some responsibilities to be excluded from ward manager job descriptions in order to facilitate claims for discretionary points.

Reward policy in Northern

The rewards strategy had been stated briefly in the personnel directorate's business plan for 1994–95. The initial focus of the reward strategy had been an examination of senior managers' pay and their removal from the NHS-wide performance related pay scheme. This scheme had proved costly for Northern, as the performance related element was recurring up to a maximum of 20 per cent. Discussions with senior managers revealed that the scheme was viewed as divisive and perceived to be unfair as each band was limited to a certain proportion of staff. Because of the use of a forced distribution system, managers believed that the band that they were placed in did not necessarily reflect their individual performance. They expressed a preference for a bonus linked to the overall performance of the trust, but concerns about its affordability had prevented such a scheme being introduced at local level.

Trust managers also examined the development of trust terms and conditions of employment, viewed as a catalyst to enhance flexibility, by linking terms and conditions to the acceptance of altered working practices. Between 1995 and 1997 a pay and rewards sub-group, comprised primarily of HR managers, met regularly to consider the trust's approach. The director of personnel developed an action plan in 1995 that outlined key issues including: identifying current position; aims and values; establishing local pay machinery; management arrangements and capacity; tools (job evaluation); and approaches (performance pay and skill enhancement).

One mechanism to develop this agenda was the use of job evaluation. Northern adopted Klynveld Peat Marwick Goerdeler (KPMG)'s Medequate system of job evaluation to measure and compare the size of different jobs. It was viewed as a defence against claims for equal pay for work of equal value. However, the director of personnel was cautious about attaching a pay spine to the existing job structure as measured by the job evaluation exercise because of the danger that attaching a monetary value to existing jobs would make it more difficult to alter working practices. The importance attached to job evaluation declined as the trust rewards strategy developed, reflecting a general disenchantment within the NHS about the value of job evaluation, a view shared by the chief executive. The pilot of the Medequate system at the Central Manchester NHS Trust had experienced numerous difficulties, and these types of problems encouraged the government, employers and trade unions to develop their own NHS-specific job evaluation scheme as part of the *Agenda for Change* reforms. At Northern a number of posts had been evaluated and validated in the mid-1990s, particularly those of senior managers. It was envisaged that job evaluation would aid the development of a new pay and grading structure for these managers, but its overall contribution to the design of future pay and conditions strategy was limited.

Management aspirations were clear from the deliberations of the sub-group. The overall objective was to reduce the complexity of the reward structure in which separate Whitley councils had established different pay and conditions for each occupational grouping. This aim was linked to harmonization of conditions of service, including annual leave and hours of work, to simplify staff management and facilitate cross-functional working. Other managerial aims included the removal of many allowances, which were viewed as outdated, and:

> the removal of overtime in favour of fully flexible working. As the Trust is a 7 day/24 hour service, a standard rate for whatever hours worked would seem the key objective. (Minutes of Pay and Rewards sub-group, April 1997)

In practice the difficulties of implementing local trust terms and conditions of employment were universally acknowledged and many of the same issues are likely to arise in relation to the *Agenda for Change* proposals. First, managers were concerned that there was forceful staff side opposition to trust terms and conditions that reflected broader employee opposition to local pay because local trust contracts were invariably equated with low pay or deteriorating conditions of employment. In order to overcome this opposition incentives would have been needed 'to pay for change'. This option was not feasible, however, with the exercise intended to be cost neutral. Managers were also concerned that if only those staff that would benefit moved over to trust contracts this could be costly and would bring further managerial complications with two sets of pay arrangements existing within Northern. Relatively low staff turnover could ensure this position continued for a long time, fostering inequities and diminishing rather than enhancing forms of flexibility.

Second, there was a recognition that managerial aspirations could not necessarily be translated into practice, not only because of existing employee expectations about rewards, but also because of the uncertainty about whether other trusts would adopt similar policies. This created a risk that if Northern went it alone other trusts would be the beneficiaries:

> The group felt that the NHS sick pay entitlements were generous but there was a general expectation of this level of payment throughout the NHS. The group felt that sick pay entitlement could be reduced and it was noted that this may lead to savings. However, it was noted that effective management of sickness was more effective than reducing the entitlement and to do so may have an adverse effect on the Trust's image and ability to recruit to certain posts. (Minutes of Pay and Reward Sub-Group, 1995)

Third, during the 1980s and 1990s many national agreements had become more flexible and the scope for local agreements increased. Trust managers suggested that this was a less risky approach that was more in tune with local requirements than a radical, trust-wide, shift to local pay and conditions. Although, as noted above, managers were dissatisfied with aspects of the national arrangements, the stereotype of a rigid, unchanging, national system was wide of the mark. Northern implemented a series of local agreements that were linked to managerial requirements (Table 7.2). Alongside the scope to alter working time arrangements, cumulatively these local agreements were the most important source of trust discretion, that are frequently overlooked in the debate about local pay flexibility. Nonetheless, as in the other trusts, Northern managers were caught up in the workplace implementation of the national policy on local pay.

The adversarial nature of local pay determination in Eastern was replicated at Northern in its implementation of the 1995–96 pay award. The infamous x + y formula appeared to offer managers genuine scope to establish the annual uplift at local level for the first time. In practice, the discretion available to trust managers remained severely circumscribed. At Northern, staff had been offered 1.5 per cent in addition to the 1 per cent national

Table 7.2 *Local agreements at Northern Trust*

Occupational group	Main points of the agreement
Dental surgery assistants	Rates of pay per session (out of hours)
Medical secretaries	Additional payments for work involving clinical information systems
Occupational therapy – student training allowance	Linked to the number of students placed each year, assessed on a team basis
Operating department assistants (ODAs)	Rates of pay per session (out of hours)
Pathology	Rates of pay per session (out of hours) for each laboratory. Allows for time off in lieu
Pharmacy	Rates of pay per session (out of hours) linked to individual's spine point
Radiographers	Fixed rate of pay per session (out of hours) which varies according to the day
Estates	Reduction of the working week from 39 hours over 5 days to 37 hours over 4 days
Nursing on call (community and midwifery)	Additional time-off
Health care support workers	Trust terms and conditions [see Chapter 8]
Clinical psychology counsellors	New terms and conditions of pay linked to administrative and clerical pay-scale
Annualized hours	Available as appropriate
HSDU performance agreement	Linked to individual attendance
Day care nurses and assistants	Trust terms and conditions linked to competency based job descriptions and progression

Source: Northern documentation, July 1995.

award. A number of conditions were attached to the award, including a commitment to more flexible working practices, cross-cover between professions, the buying out of bank holidays and the harmonization of entitlements, such as annual leave. This offer was rejected by the staff side, and as the trade unions nationally campaigned for the retention of a system of national pay bargaining, managers became reluctant to force through their lower offer in the face of forceful opposition. This view was held strongly by the chief executive, who argued that staff had worked hard to raise productivity and should be granted an overall 3 per cent rise without strings. This became the revised trust offer.

Trust managers were constrained also by the conflicting signals that they received from the NHS Executive. At first, managers believed that the national recommendations allowed them to negotiate locally on conditions of employment which managers regarded as important as the annual pay uplift, but subsequently they were advised not to alter conditions of service. Similarly trusts were told that they would be expected to offer a 3 per cent pay rise, irrespective of the local financial conditions within their organization.

As the dispute continued the trust board, following national guidance, agreed in August that a 3 per cent pay offer 'on account' should be made to staff. Employees were given the opportunity to refuse to accept the pay award and to await the outcome of the national dispute. Few staff declined to accept the payment on account and the national dispute was settled in September.

During 1996–97 the Nurses' Pay Review Body recommended a national award of 2 per cent and did not specify the anticipated range of local top-ups. Despite a less conflictual context nationally, at Northern local negotiations proved to be more intractable than during 1995–96. The staff side followed the national lead and put in a claim for a 6.5 per cent pay increase. Managers concerned about the trust's financial position were acutely aware that of the trust's £56 million income, £34 million comprised the pay bill. They realized, however, that they could not offer only the 2 per cent national award; this would be viewed as inflammatory and could exacerbate the trust's recruitment and retention problems. In an internal management briefing paper the director of personnel suggested that:

> The Trust would therefore wish to make a local offer ranging from 0.25 per cent with no strings to 0.5 per cent with strings. Within this range depending on acceptability the Trust can offer a local element of pay whilst not accelerating its financial problem. (Trust documentation, June 1996)

During the summer and autumn of 1996 negotiations continued with a number of permutations offered by management, but none of them exceeded a 0.5 per cent local element and they were all rejected by the staff side. In October the director of personnel reiterated that the trust's offer could exceed 0.5 per cent only if strings were attached and staffing levels reduced. Managers raised their offer fractionally to 0.6 per cent but this pay offer did not apply to local agreements (Table 7.2) and excluded some national allowances (e.g. geriatric leads). This was justified by the argument that the allowances had not been increased nationally for many years, so the local pay offer should exclude them as well. With no prospect of agreement in sight the director of personnel wrote directly to staff in November reiterating the 2.6 per cent pay award:

> Any higher percentage would have to come from staff savings over and above those already identified by the Trust to achieve its financial targets.
> Unfortunately the JNC have not been able to reach agreement and a 'failure to agree' has been lodged as negotiations have ended.
>
> The Trust Board at its November meeting agreed, that if the JNC could not agree, staff would be contacted individually with the offer. This letter therefore offers you an additional 0.6% to the 2% already paid, applied on the same basis as the 2% for 1996–97. (Letter to Northern staff, November 1996)

Staff were required to write to the director of personnel if they did not wish to accept the offer, which few did, as 82 per cent of staff accepted the pay increase that was implemented in January 1997.

Two issues can be highlighted about the local bargaining process. First, local pay negotiations consumed large amounts of managerial and staff time for little result. Negotiations were conducted over fractions of one per cent, reflecting Northern's limited scope for financial manoeuvre and the requirement placed on trusts that their pay offer did not exceed a defined proportion of their pay bill. Staff side representatives also had little genuine autonomy as they were constrained by the policy of their unions that were in a national dispute with the government. Second, the effective imposition of the pay award soured the relationship between the staff side and management at Northern. Moreover, by diverting managers from their personnel priorities, local pay delayed the development of more far-reaching trust terms and conditions of employment.

In the period since 1997, limited attention had been focused on reward issues as managers and staff side representatives awaited the outcomes of the *Agenda for Change* negotiations. This was reflected in the trust's response to discretionary points that was viewed very much as 'only a stopgap to addressing the whole issue of NHS pay' (JCC Minutes, January 1999). The implementation of discretionary points at Northern raised many of the same issues as had occurred in Eastern because: 'All present felt that this was a divisive recommendation as it did not address the pay for junior grades of staff' (JCC Minutes, January 1999). The staff side requested that the appeals panel be chaired by a non-executive director because Unison, in particular, raised concerns about the objectivity of an appeals panel chaired by the director of HR, but the request was turned down. During 1999–2000, of the 64 nursing and midwifery staff and 29 para-medical staff that applied, very few were awarded discretionary points. This led to 25 appeals being lodged, but only one additional point was awarded in the case of one nurse.

The management of pay in Western

The underlying premise of the trust's reward strategy in the early 1990s was that the priority for Western should be an examination of existing working practices and conditions of service. It was anticipated that such a review would lead to changes in work organization, particularly the introduction of generic working, which would then require new terms and conditions of employment to be attached to these new roles. The director of personnel believed strongly that many trusts were putting the cart before the horse in developing elaborate local pay structures, using proprietary systems of job evaluation, based on *existing* working practices.

Anticipated developments in the national system of pay determination were another crucial consideration in shaping the trust's reward strategy. In a 1993 paper to the trust board, the director of personnel reviewed the future of the Whitley system, arguing that:

> In light of the experience of the past 2–3 years, and the reluctance of the Department of Health to serve notice on the Whitley system, it would appear unrealistic to expect anything other than slow, incremental change at a national level.

This analysis suggested that the development of a new holistic local pay framework was unnecessary as the Whitley system was unlikely to be dissolved, and the consequent need rapidly to develop local systems of pay determination was reduced. The cost of developing a new local pay determination system for all staff usually involved the purchase of a proprietary system of job evaluation. This was rejected as being time-consuming and costly (estimated at 5 per cent of the pay bill) and 'at the end of the exercise staff are still doing the same jobs, but are rewarded on a local rather than a national basis'. Moreover, the director of personnel's experience with job evaluation in his previous post, had made him sceptical about the effectiveness of job evaluation systems in measuring accurately between, and within, the range of occupational groups found within the NHS.

One alternative approach would have been to maintain the status quo and keep the existing national conditions of service framework. This would have been a safe approach but was rejected because it would have prevented the development of a range of more flexible and cost-effective locally determined employment initiatives. Instead the trust continued to use the Whitley framework, but in a structured manner. This had a number of strands: reviewing the existing Whitley framework and identifying areas where the trust wished to make changes; pilot work on 're-profiling' initiatives (i.e. developing locally determined jobs on locally determined conditions of service); and attaching a local pay framework to these jobs.

The advantages of this approach were seen to be the ability to maintain a degree of stability in pay determination arrangements. At the same time it provided scope to introduce targeted changes in a controlled manner without precluding the option of responding positively to the evolving national situation.

The Trust's pay strategy incorporated an assumption that the national system of pay determination would remain dominant, leaving limited scope for local pay settlements. It was not until 1995 that the possibility of local pay settlements became more likely. Nonetheless, the ability of trust managers to devise an affordable local pay settlement which reflected its contract income remained severely circumscribed by national developments. First, the trade unions were explicitly waging a campaign to maintain a system of national pay determination. The national pay dispute led the staff side at Western, as in other trusts, to refuse to enter into discussions on the local pay offer. Similarly, the tensions between the staff organizations at national level were reinforced by differences between the staff side organizations at local level.

Second, managers were receiving mixed signals from the NHS Executive about the stance that they were expected to adopt, but at the same time were coming under considerable pressure from the centre to make a pay offer. The chief executive alluded to this pressure at a JCNC meeting when he commented:

> Management have been held back in making this offer for approximately two months and, in doing so, have come under considerable pressure. (JCNC minutes, May 1995)

The Trust offered all staff a 3 per cent increase without strings. This reflected a 1 per cent national component and a 2 per cent local addition. The only exception was medical staff, who received a 2.5 per cent award reflecting the recommendation of their review body. Trust managers indicated that they wished to address the issue of low pay in future pay rounds and wanted to discuss possible changes to the clinical nurse grading structure. Ultimately, reflecting developments at national level and guidance from the NHS Executive, a payment on account was made to staff in December 1995.

The 1996–97 pay round commenced in earnest with the publication of the review body reports in February 1996 at a time when trusts had scarcely resolved the previous year's pay negotiations and were assessing the implications of the September 1995 national agreement, 'Local Pay in a National Framework'. The Nurses' Pay Review Body recommended a 2 per cent increase in pay with any further increases to be decided at trust level. The trade unions' response was to put in a joint national pay claim for 6.5 per cent.

In March 1996 the trust board considered the options for the 1996–97 pay award. It discounted the option to settle above 3 per cent as being prohibitively expensive, particularly as Western had been assured by the NHS Executive that there would be no 'going rate' in excess of 3 per cent. A second option was to offer 3 per cent, but this would not enable the pay settlement to make a contribution to its overall cost improvement programme. Consequently, the director of personnel recommended a pay offer of 2.5 per cent, because

> There will inevitably be a staff side perception of a higher going rate – however, local affordability must balance these factors. The message is uncomfortable, but any higher award will inevitably lead to job losses, which in turn may compromise our ability to deliver contracts, which in turn leads to loss of income and job losses, and so the spiral of decline could continue. (Paper to the management board, March 1996)

The structure of the pay award took account of the commitment made in the 1995–96 pay round to address the issue of low pay with an additional 0.5 per cent offered to hotel support workers that were on trust terms and conditions (see Chapter 8). Managers also offered the staff side an 'in-year' review in December 1996 which indicated that additional monies could be forthcoming, depending on corporate performance.

The staff side expressed disappointment with the pay offer considering the amount of change that staff had accepted in recent years and the emphasis that managers placed on the value of staff. The manner in which managers presented the offer to staff was a further cause for concern. Prior to reaching agreement on the offer and while the staff side assumed that negotiations were ongoing, managers had written to all staff about the offer and had engaged in a vigorous attempt to sell the deal to staff directly through roadshows. This was not the only occasion that managers had adopted this strategy, which the unions argued undermined the local bargaining process. However, for managers the strategy was effective as employees accepted Western's pay offer without damaging industrial relations consequences.

As in Eastern and Northern the election of a Labour government and the lengthy evolution of *Agenda for Change* led to a period in which the management of pay was less prominent. Trust managers implemented the discretionary points scheme for nurses, midwives and para-medical staff but with the same lack of enthusiasm as at the other case study trusts As the director of human resources argued:

> For the 30k that we paid out it was the biggest load of hassle that we've had; bureaucratic, long-winded, a total disaster and not linked to an overall pay strategy, a cop-out to shut up the nurses and midwives.' (Interview notes, September 2001)

Discussion

Although this chapter has focused on the pay determination process, the evidence that staff were dissatisfied with their reward package was less marked than other aspects of working conditions (see Table 6.7). This finding could have been expected to have strengthened as public sector pay increases have outstripped those in the private sector in recent years (Industrial Relations Services 2001c). At Eastern and Northern where comparable data was available, there was limited evidence that staff felt dissatisfied in comparison to staff doing similar jobs for other local employers, but staff felt more strongly about the effort–reward bargain (Table 7.3). In general ancillary staff were the least satisfied and executive directors the most content. One caveat is that neither trust was located in an area of high living cost, especially the South-East, in which dissatisfaction with pay could be expected to be more pronounced within trust staff opinion surveys and the issue of local labour market supplements a more important issue for recruitment and retention.

In all the case study trusts managers expressed dissatisfaction with aspects of the national Whitley system and had aspirations to alter terms and conditions of employment. The priority of managers, as discussed more fully in Chapter 8, was to alter job roles and break down demarcations between occupational groups. They were also seeking to simplify and harmonize the existing Whitley system, with local pay viewed as a mechanism to achieve these changes. In all three cases, however, trust managers recognized the

Table 7.3 *Staff opinion survey responses at Eastern and Northern Trusts 1999–2000*

Question	Northern		Eastern	
	Agree (%)	Disagree (%)	Agree (%)	Disagree (%)
I feel fairly paid in relation to people doing similar jobs for other local employers in the area	46	51	40	55
I feel fairly paid in relation to other staff at the Trust	50	46	45	51
I feel fairly paid for the work I do	38	60	30	65
I feel terms and conditions within the Trust are fairly and consistently applied	62	31	55	37

Source: Eastern and Northern staff opinion surveys. Non-responses are excluded.

danger of preventing more flexible working practices by attaching a new pay spine to existing jobs. Managers focused on using the flexibility within the national agreements to develop local agreements and to use local pay flexibilities as opportunities arose. Behind the 'failure' of local pay, considerable managerial efforts were being made to adjust payment systems, as national agreements ceded greater discretion to trust level. Nonetheless these local agreements, because they derived from separate Whitley council agreements, were determined on the basis of existing occupational groups. It was only trust specific pay systems, discussed in the next chapter, that presented opportunities to break down occupational demarcations.

Managers were disenchanted with the manner in which national policy on local pay developed with a focus on the annual pay settlement. Local pay settlements in the case study trusts were in line with national developments. Trust managers had very little discretion to decide their own local settlement, undermining trust managers' ability to use the local pay element to control the pay bill. The national dispute over local pay soured relations with trade unions in all the trusts, making other workplace reforms more difficult. It also led to the issues of local pay (i.e. trust terms and conditions of employment) and local flexibility (i.e. local interpretation of national agreements) being conflated, stifling attempts at trust based reform. Moreover, there were strong isomorphic pressures between trusts following the national dispute. Trust managers were reluctant to risk becoming an outlier on pay and conditions, because of the implications for recruitment and retention. As the Eastern director of human resources commented:

If we had pushed it and reduced sick pay we'd have lost staff to other trusts, you are going to get resistance, but even if you give notice and impose it you are going to lose people. (Interview notes, April 2001)

Other nationally instigated forms of pay flexibility, notably discretionary points, were viewed as time-consuming, prescriptive and largely unworkable without additional central government resources. The experience of discretionary points also has implications for *Agenda for Change* because it provides a warning about the requirement to move beyond crude forms of competency pay as a basis for pay increases that rely on managerial interpretation of national criteria. The experience of discretionary points also reiterates the crucial importance of central funding to make new pay systems work effectively. The problems with discretionary points at the three trusts mirrored the difficulties elsewhere, leading the Nurses' Pay Review Body (2001: 61) to conclude that the system is held to be: 'burdensome to implement, to have brought few benefits for staff, and to have had a demotivating effect'. It also expressed concern that the inability of the NHS to operate the scheme effectively 'hardly bodes well, in our opinion, for the development of local approaches to pay and grading envisaged in *Agenda for Change*' (Nurses' Pay Review Body 2001: 62).

Finally, the uneven moves towards a more trust-specific system of employment relations presented trade unions with a number of challenges. In a similar way to management, staff side representatives took their lead from, and were constrained by, the national position of their trade unions. This undermined the scope to develop local expertise and inhibited the establishment of distinctive trust-based patterns of management–union relations that continued to bear the imprint of national developments. The bargaining criteria used placed further constraints on trade union representatives because the emphasis on affordability within all the trusts left little scope to develop a wider bargaining agenda, for example based on giving priority to the needs of the low paid. Representatives also commented on the time-consuming and stressful nature of the local pay bargaining process that scarcely lent itself to encouraging more involvement and activism among a wider cross-section of the membership.

8 THE MANAGEMENT OF WORK

This chapter examines the degree to which trust managers have reorganized working practices in pursuit of more effective labour utilization. As discussed in Chapter 2, a long-standing preoccupation has been the degree to which the division of labour between occupational groups in the NHS has militated against flexible labour utilization. The attempt by the Conservative government to promote local pay, and the Labour government's *Agenda for Change* proposals, share an assumption that pay reform is a necessary prerequisite for changes in work organization. Are these assumptions borne out by the case study evidence, and what does this experience indicate about the prospects for further alterations in work organization in the NHS?

An important component of the trusts' labour utilization strategies focused on developing forms of generic working that aimed to redistribute tasks between occupational groups, reinforcing the reform of working practices encouraged by compulsory competitive tendering (CCT) (Foster and Scott 1998; Munro 1999). In contrast to CCT, which focused almost exclusively on cost reductions, generic working was underpinned by the emphasis on a 'customer ethic' that was reflected in the job titles used (e.g. hotel support workers). In addition, changes in work organization are examined to establish whether they have fulfilled managerial expectations of greater 'flexibility' and the implications for the workforce, including more recent attempts to develop 'family-friendly' working conditions.

Eastern

With the uneven development of local pay, work reorganization initiatives became the focal point of changes in employment practices. The first attempt to quantify the amount of time that nurses were spending on housekeeping duties took place on a medical ward during 1993 (Table 8.1) using a workforce planning tool (Nursing Information System for Change Management – NISCM). The results produced by the exercise demonstrated that nursing staff, whether qualified or unqualified, spent a considerable amount of their time on housekeeping duties. On the early shift this amounted to 23 per cent of their time, in comparison with 20 per cent and 10 per cent for the late and night shifts respectively.

Managers calculated that approximately three whole time equivalents (WTEs) of qualified nursing time were being used inappropriately on ward housekeeping duties. This result reinforced the view among managers that work organization should be altered.

Table 8.1 *Housekeeping duties performed by nurses at Eastern Trust*

Collecting and delivering items to and from departments
Taking patients to other departments
Ordering, receiving, checking and storing supplies
Menus – distribute, help to complete, collect and send to catering department
Serving meals and drinks
Prepare snacks
Make empty beds
Wash lockers and beds
Care for flowers
Safety checks – fire exits, call bells, etc.
Reporting maintenance jobs
Remove rubbish and dirty linen, store clean linen
Replenish soap and towels
Tidying up, e.g. day room

Source: Eastern documentation, 1994.

These results were significant for two reasons. First, nursing staff had generated the data which was used to calculate the time spent on housekeeping duties. It was therefore difficult for nurses to challenge the findings of the pilot project or the NISCM methodology. Senior managers took the decision to adopt the NISCM methodology to assess workload across all the areas identified for re-profiling. Second, senior managers confronted with a difficult financial position needed to control staff expenditure. The results of the NISCM exercises indicated that re-profiling could generate significant savings and improve the service for patients. This approach was endorsed by the chief executive, who wanted the rapid introduction of ward assistants by 1995.

Ward assistants were piloted on two wards using domestic staff, who remained on national terms and conditions of employment but received an extra 25 pence per hour for their participation. A job description was developed, based mainly on the housekeeping tasks identified from the NISCM studies, and ward assistants received training in basic food-handling skills. One WTE ward assistant covered the ward from 7.30 to 21.00 hours supported by a domestic assistant in the morning, and there was extra support over mealtimes.

Evaluation was carried out using activity analysis and by surveying staff and patients. The project manager summarized her findings:

> There was a dramatic rise in the amount of time nurses were spending with patients. It was noted especially that activity of greatest concern, i.e. communication and involvement of patients in the planning of their care had increased. The staff felt that they were spending more time with the patients and valued not having to serve meals and drinks and carry out office duties. It was recognised that the preparation for patient discharges had improved, reducing the time patients were delayed at the point of going home. No disadvantages were identified in the feedback from patients. (Eastern documentation, 1994)

Feedback on the pilot project from the staff questionnaires included many positive comments, for example, 'More interesting job, variety of work, never bored, shift work. Meeting more people, helping patients and staff' (Ward assistant, 1994). Conversely there were concerns among catering staff and nursing auxiliaries that their own roles were jeopardized. As one of the management progress reports acknowledged: 'Nursing auxiliaries feel that some of their jobs have been taken over.' It was the opposition of domestic staff, however, to the proposed terms and conditions of employment that proved to be the most intractable.

Negotiating terms and conditions for ward assistants

Senior managers viewed the establishment of a new group within the workforce as an opportunity to break away from existing national terms and conditions of employment, providing a bridgehead for the development of trust terms and conditions, as a means to alter working practices. For this reason the negotiations on ward assistants were significant as they would provide an important precedent for other trust negotiations.

Managers expressed dissatisfaction with a number of features of the existing Whitley conditions for ancillary staff. First, they were critical of the composition of the ancillary wage packet. This consisted of a relatively low basic wage with enhancements linked to the shifts worked (e.g. rotating shift allowance, weekend enhancements) and a range of allowances (e.g. foul linen allowances). One hotel services manager commented bluntly:

> where in the world would you pay a domestic £8 per hour on a Sunday to do exactly the same job that they are doing Monday–Friday for less than £4? (Interview notes, February 1996)

Managers wanted to simplify pay arrangements and instigate a rate for the job which was paid irrespective of when the work was performed.

Second, managers were critical of the conditions of employment that applied under Whitley council regulations. They argued that these were too generous and reflected labour market conditions in the South of England. Instead trust terms and conditions of employment needed to reflect what Eastern could afford. A particular concern were Whitley Council sickness arrangements that managers argued exacerbated high levels of absence. Domestic staff were entitled to sick pay even if they were absent for one day, and when absent received the same pay as when at work (including premium rates). In addition, domestic staff that had been employed by Eastern for more than five years were entitled when sick to a maximum of six months' full pay and six months' half pay.

Third, managers sought greater flexibility in the organization of the workforce. Domestic staff were divided between staff who worked during the week and those that worked exclusively at weekends. Managers viewed this system as inflexible and expensive because neither group had contracts that required them to work outside of their usual hours. Similarly managers wanted to increase geographical flexibility, requiring staff to work at other hospitals if necessary.

The attempt to gain agreement for this approach took over six months of negotiation, brought Eastern to the brink of industrial action and generated bad publicity. The central feature of the trust's proposals tabled in early 1995 was an increase in the basic rate of pay from £3.20 an hour to £3.90 an hour, but this was coupled with the removal of any premium payments for working on a Saturday and a reduced premium for working on a Sunday, moving away from the Whitley condition of double time for Sunday working. Overtime hours were to be worked at basic rates. Additional elements included proposals to reduce the maximum paid absence from six months to three months; to end the division between weekday and weekend staff, with all ward assistants required to work 5 out of any 7 days; and staff were to be required to work at any location within a twenty mile radius of the main hospital site.

Unison, which represented the staff concerned, suggested the weekend staff would face a 43 per cent reduction in their pay while the impact on the weekday staff was less stark. Staff side representatives were vehemently opposed to the establishment of trust terms and conditions of employment because they believed that trust contracts strengthened management control and inevitably resulted in worse terms and conditions of employment. Nationally, the trade unions were effective in inculcating a fear of trust contracts into their membership, and some managers admitted that employees were reluctant to accept promotion if it required acceptance of a trust contract. Opposition to this movement away from Whitley conditions crystallized around the principle of a flat rate payment and the removal of enhancements.

There was also opposition to the manner in which the negotiations were conducted, reinforcing Unison's belief that managers sought to reduce union influence. Managers' strategy was to try to divide the workforce with the gains offered to the weekday staff in terms of increased basic pay designed to entice them to accept the offer at the expense of the weekend staff. This would have resulted in agreement for their proposals as there were fewer weekend than weekday staff. Managers tried to impose changes without consulting the unions, which Unison representatives argued was symptomatic of the macho management that was spreading throughout the NHS.

With discussions deadlocked Unison officials informed trust management that they would be balloting the staff on industrial action. The result of the ballot indicated a majority vote in favour of industrial action (Table 8.2) and Unison informed managers that their membership would be reverting to

Table 8.2 *Outcome of industrial action ballot at Eastern Trust*

In favour of working to contract	142
Against working to contract	35
In favour of strike action	150
Against strike action	20
Total votes cast	190
(13 spoilt ballot papers)	

Source: Eastern Trust documentation, April 1995.

their domestic roles. Managers were dismayed with the outcome of the ballot, which they had not expected.

The chief executive wrote to all ward assistants in May:

> I recognise the strength of feeling behind the ballot result and I have invited your representatives to continue our discussions in order to try to resolve our differences … I feel obliged to point out that, by accepting an appointment as a Ward Assistant with a specific job description, you have accepted a change to your terms and condition of employment with the Trust. You do not have a legal right to go back to working as a Domestic Assistant. If you were to attend for work prepared to work only as a Domestic Assistant, your actions would be in breach of your contract of employment and beyond the industrial action notified by UNISON. Such action would therefore put me in an extremely difficult position and could ultimately result in an action I wish to avoid.

On the same day the chief executive and hotel services managers met with the Unison regional officer and representatives from the staff side and reached a settlement (the personnel director had no direct role in these discussions). This provided for a basic rate of £3.71 with a premium of £1.50 for Saturday working and £3.00 per hour for Sunday working. Protection arrangements were to apply for an indefinite time period, but sickness entitlement was reduced.

At the time managers argued that although they made concessions they achieved most of their objectives. First, the principle of local pay and trust contracts was established, and all overtime was to be worked at plain time rates. Although premium payments for weekend working were not removed, the Whitley regulation of double time for a Sunday and time and a half for a Saturday were eliminated. Managers believed that this would provide them with much greater flexibility in the future. This proved to be the case, as when Eastern made its 1995 pay award it increased the ward assistant pay scales by three per cent but left the premium payments unchanged.

Second, managers suggested that they had achieved important changes in sickness management by cutting in half the entitlement to sick leave and by removing payment for absence for the first three days. It was calculated that this latter change would reduce the cost of sickness absence from £60,000 per annum to £34,000 per annum. The ward assistant supervisors commented that by not paying for the first three days of absence it allowed them to bring in a replacement without incurring additional budgetary costs and enabled a consistent service to be maintained.

Third, although not an explicit objective of the negotiations, the dispute eroded the credibility of Unison. The emphasis that the Unison representatives placed on the interests of the weekend staff, focusing on retaining premium weekend rates, led to a reduction in the basic hourly rate of pay from the £3.90 an hour initially offered. Managers claimed this situation led to dissatisfaction with the staff representatives among the membership and taught them a lesson about raising expectations that could not be met. One personnel manager commented 'Weekday staff felt sold down the river; where's my £3.90 gone?' (Interview notes, February 1996).

Unison disputed this interpretation. They argued that managers had tried to impose changes on staff and that it had only been through the balloting of the membership that senior management had been forced to enter formal negotiations. Union credibility had increased with the domestic staff and was reflected in increased membership levels. Although premium rates had been reduced the union had obtained concessions, not least an agreement to maintain the remainder of the domestic service in-house (on similar conditions as the ward assistants) and recognition rights for Unison. Reductions in sickness benefit had been difficult to counter as the membership themselves were sympathetic to management aims, believing that some employees took advantage of existing arrangements.

Managers argued that the struggle to implement the ward assistant scheme had proved worthwhile because patient feedback recorded that the quality of service provided had improved (e.g. food was served hot). Nonetheless the most capable and conscientious domestic staff chose to become ward assistants, leaving a residue of staff as domestic assistants, resulting in a poorer quality of domestic service. One hotel services manager summarized the situation bluntly: 'one of the reasons that we have such high sickness in domestics is that we would not let those duffers be ward assistants' (Interview notes, February 1996).

Ward managers shared the generally positive evaluation of the scheme, although this was tinged with cynicism: 'they were not going to give us any more nurses so this is better than nothing' (Interview notes, March 1996). They felt that there was an imbalance between ward assistants and nursing staff, with insufficient nursing staff. On some wards, managers had to restrain ward managers who were tempted to use them for more extensive duties than contained within their job description, for example recording the precise amount of fluid a patient consumed in a day. The personnel manager viewed such behaviour as an abuse of the role of ward assistants and posing significant legal risks. A simple rule of thumb that demarcated ward assistant duties from those of nurses was that ward assistants were to have no hands on patients.

For the staff the transfer from domestic staff to ward assistant jobs represented a potentially major change in their role. They were required to complete additional tasks and needed to work more flexibly to fit in with the ward routine. Cleaning duties were scheduled less rigidly, and ward assistants were required to work as part of the ward team and to prioritize their work in conjunction with the other members of staff. The new roles represented a considerable intensification of work as the greater range of tasks reduced the periods of slack that had existed for domestic assistants. It also brought a number of benefits. Ward assistants gained an enhanced role within the hospital, they were no longer 'just domestics' and became more accepted as part of the ward team by nursing staff. Ward assistants had more variety in their work and increased contact with patients, which they viewed as a source of job satisfaction. They gained more formal training and qualifications (e.g. food handling certificates) with the possibility of progression into health care assistant roles.

Ward assistants, nursing work and shifting occupational boundaries

Since 1995 ward assistants have become embedded at Eastern. By 2001 managers were more candid in acknowledging that ward assistants had been viewed as being in the vanguard of developing trust terms and conditions of employment. It was envisaged that these changes would have formed the basis of a trust contract that incorporated a range of alterations, but this failed to transpire. According to the hotel services general manager:

> We were far too draconian in our terms and conditions of ward assistants when we brought them in initially, which would have been fine if the rest of the service had moved in the way it intended to move, but it didn't. We were in the vanguard with better basic rate, less sick pay, less frills, and every other service was supposed to follow in line. In terms of terms and conditions I have got a disenfranchised group, in unique and splendid isolation treated completely differently from everyone else in the trust ... we've done something a little bit nasty as an employer there, with good intentions at the time, to save money, but also to march at the same pace as the rest of the NHS. The rest of the NHS decided not to get on that boat. (Interview notes, July 2001)

Over time this had led to some improvement in terms and conditions. The struggle to instigate arrangements in which sick pay was not paid for the first three days of absence had simply encouraged ward assistants to be absent for more than three days in order to be eligible for sick pay. This quickly reverted to the old practice of paying staff sick pay from the first day that they were absent. Ward assistants still had inferior sick pay arrangements from other staff in the trust, however, and were eligible for half the length of sick pay as other long-serving staff. This was a source of dissatisfaction, but the general manager argued that it would be too costly to reverse these arrangements. Instead, improvements in terms and conditions were sanctioned at the margins, for example reduced working hours for supervisors. Staff side representatives argued that the poorer terms and conditions, especially the absence of enhancements, discouraged ward assistants from remaining in post, and many became health care assistants. In addition it raised questions about equal pay for work of equal value issues as the ward assistants were predominantly women.

Nursing staff valued the ward assistants' contribution and there was consensus that they enjoyed their role, took pride in their work and often worked beyond their job description, incorporating health care assistant functions into their role. One interpretation was that this reflected a positive attempt to develop a career ladder for ward assistants in which they could migrate from ward assistants to health care assistants and in some cases continue into registered nurse training. Another interpretation, however, was that the increased role of ward assistants reflected chronic staff shortages and enormous pressure on qualified nursing staff, not least from the reduction in junior doctors' working hours.

These pressures were felt acutely by ward managers. They had to reconcile a range of contradictory demands on their time, of which the greatest tension arose between their management activities and their clinical activities. Ward managers reported directly to general managers, many of whom did not have a nursing background, and they argued that over time they had been expected to become 'mini' general managers, and that was drawing them away from their clinical duties. The director of nursing had become concerned about the role conflict and role overload experienced by ward managers and the implications for clinical care standards. Consequently much greater emphasis had been placed on clinical standards in line with *Making a Difference* (Department of Health 1999b). This included establishing a nursing charter with specific quality standards. The clinical indicators were identified by a survey of all registered nurses in the trust, via the shared governance network, and through the use of focus groups. Fourteen clinical performance standards were established (e.g. pressure sore prevalence and incidence, effective record-keeping, prevention of hospital acquired infections) and audits are conducted throughout the trust. These initiatives reflect a deliberate attempt to re-balance ward managers' responsibilities, and since 2000–01 a formal expectation had been placed on them that they would spend 2–2.5 days per week working clinically. This represented a reversal of policy from the mid-1980s onwards when ward managers were being encouraged to take on more managerial responsibilities.

Although this shift was welcomed by ward managers they still had to confront a range of other pressures. A key source of stress derived from what Isobel Allen has termed the presence of 'inappropriate patients' (Allen 2001). This situation arose when patients from other areas, for example elderly medical patients, were placed on other wards. Ward managers found this stressful because it not only increased the number of consultants with whom they had to liaise, but the complex case mix, including specialisms outside their primary area of expertise, increased their levels of anxiety about providing high standards of care. They also argued that it discouraged job seekers because when applicants visited the ward informally, the large numbers of elderly medical sleepovers discouraged them from applying for the vacancy.

Ward managers' responses to more flexible working practices that were designed to improve recruitment and retention need to be interpreted in relation to workload pressures and high levels of stress, documented by the staff opinion survey and the CHI team (Chapter 6). The trust had a series of policies that enabled staff to work flexibly (e.g. part-time working), but these policies were more of an indication of what was available to staff rather than a centrally endorsed agenda that was being actively pursued by HR managers. This led to a high degree of informality at ward and departmental level because the decision to grant a more flexible work schedule rested with the departmental manager or ward sister. Although ward managers acknowledged that adjusting to staff requirements was necessary, to cover staff shortages, nonetheless they viewed it as an additional source of stress within their managerial responsibilities:

> For me to put them into practice as a ward sister is a constant struggle. At the end of the day, I need someone to work nights, I need someone to work lates. I can't fulfil all the requests that staff want. I can tweak them, but I am trying to provide a 24-hour service. I struggle to cover nights. Some staff feel that you are actually favouring staff with children. (Interview notes, July 2001)

As staffing the ward fell to ward managers, the pressure to square the circle resulted in flexible working policies not being viewed in an especially positive light. This reflected their concern that staff negotiated on an individual basis and viewed the existence of a trust policy as confirmation that they were entitled to 'flexible' working practices. The decision, however, rested with the ward manager, limiting the degree to which HR was necessarily aware of the problem or able to embed corporate polices within the organization, inhibiting their capacity to support managers in implementing flexible working practices effectively.

Finally, tensions emerged within the ward environment, because staff with children were viewed as gaining favourable working arrangements in comparison to other staff. In response to these difficulties the HR director had relabelled policies as 'employee-friendly' rather than 'family-friendly'; and because she suggested it was not always possible to grant staff the working hours they wished for, greater emphasis was placed on providing alternatives (e.g. crèche facilities). Whether these measures met staff aspirations was unclear because in the staff opinion survey just over half of staff felt that the trust provided good support to balance work and home responsibilities (see Table 6.5).

Northern

The cautious approach to local pay and grading systems in Northern was not matched by managerial attitudes towards work reorganization. The immediate catalyst for the consideration of generic working was the expiry of the contracts for the domestic and catering services in the mid-1990s. This approach had a broader appeal to other managers who were interested in developing generic working across specialities such as Pathology, Radiology and Pharmacy. The trust board stipulated that if any of the support services were provided externally the contractor would be required to introduce generic working within six months of the contract starting.

The market-testing exercises led to the portering and domestic service being retained in-house and the catering service being contracted out, but with a commitment to introduce generic working. The aim of the project that started in support services was to improve labour utilization by developing a multi-tasked worker (termed a ward steward/stewardess) that would amalgamate existing support staff duties to include domestic duties, portering tasks and some tasks undertaken by nurses such as bed-making. It was necessary to establish the time spent on the wards by nurses undertaking the type of duties that were being transferred to the ward stewards, using a nursing workforce planning tool.

The results were a mixed blessing because they indicated that previous re-profiling exercises undertaken as the hospital prepared for trust status in the early 1990s had ensured that nursing staff were undertaking 'appropriate' duties, but it left limited scope for generating further savings. There was little justification for transferring resources from the nursing budget to fund the ward steward service as its staff would not be carrying out duties transferred from nursing staff.

Implementing ward stewards

Three wards were chosen for a pilot project scheme. Support services staff were approached to act as volunteers on their existing terms and conditions of employment, with the option to return to their existing jobs at the end of the pilot scheme. They were offered a one off payment of £100 for their participation, training in specific competencies, and the opportunity to take on a new role with more patient contact. Managers needed to reconcile the cost neutral principles of the project with the extra work that the ward stewards were expected to perform.

Some of these unresolved tensions emerged in the pilot scheme despite ward staff acknowledging some benefits of the proposed changes. New job descriptions had not been issued and there was uncertainty about the role that the ward stewards were expected to perform. The domestic supervisors' requirements had not altered, but the ward managers expected the ward stewards to undertake additional housekeeping duties, which squeezed out the time available for domestic duties. A related concern was that some of the ward stewards were undertaking direct patient care tasks without prior training that had significant legal implications. It became increasingly apparent that the scheme could not be implemented and, over time, managers abandoned the ward steward project. Four main reasons were cited for its failure.

First, nursing staff unease about ward stewards crystallized around the movement of 'nursing monies' into the ward steward project. Managers argued that the budgets were to be devolved to nurses increasing their control of the ward environment, in an initiative that pre-empted the Labour government's housekeeper initiative. By taking an element of the nursing auxiliary role and incorporating it into the cheaper ward steward service, nursing staff would obtain more staffing hours to undertake the same type of work. In practice, however, ward managers viewed the initiative as an incursion into the nursing budget. Staffing levels were already viewed as very tight given the legacy of re-profiling and staff shortages within the trust. Without the cooperation and support of the ward managers the scheme was never likely to succeed.

Second, managers had discussions with Unison representatives, who they believed would not oppose the scheme. At the local Unison branch meeting, however, a decision was taken to oppose the ward assistant scheme. The Unison full-time officer was involved and a formal grievance was lodged. Managers agreed not to extend the project, although they refused to revoke the contracts that had already been issued to ward stewards. In effect a status quo position was agreed which confined the project to a couple of wards.

Third, although not an explicit objective, the attempt to break down gender demarcations between occupational roles was unsuccessful. None of the portering staff were prepared to undertake generic worker roles, and this was not an isolated incident. It had been proposed that the night porters who were usually not busy after 2.00am should undertake some additional duties that were best undertaken when the hospital was quiet, for example, corridor cleaning. This had met with vociferous opposition from the portering staff supported by their Unison representatives, although the shop stewards' stance had differed. The female Unison representative argued that her role was to represent her members and they would not accept it, in contrast to the more fundamental opposition of the male Unison representative.

Fourth, managers concluded that for a variety of reasons, including the combined nursing staff and union opposition, the anticipated benefits of ward stewards were unlikely to be realized. In particular, because the catering service was contracted out, it restricted the scope to restructure hotel services to establish an integrated housekeeping service. For hotel services managers the broad character of the job description also proved to be a difficulty. In the pilots the ward managers encouraged ward stewards to undertake more patient-orientated work that they enjoyed, which led to less time being available for domestic duties, and cleaning standards deteriorated. As the hotel services general manager acknowledged about the ward steward role:

> There's a natural drift to being 'it's the patient'. Direct patient stuff is always the priority, it eats away at the rest of the work and we found that standards particularly on the cleaning side deteriorated in the pilots. We then found that we had to put in and bolster that up both in terms of the monitoring to make sure that it maintained a good standard for that work, but also picking up where there were problems and gaps. (Interview notes, April 2001)

Notwithstanding the difficulties with the ward steward project, managers had altered working practices on an incremental basis to improve labour utilization and reduce expenditure, despite union opposition. A key concern had been the reduction in levels of overtime worked, and the requirement to comply with the working time directive (that established maximum working hours), enabling changes to be implemented. A system of relief porters was established which increased numerical flexibility but guaranteed porters a set number of hours and ensured that there was a degree of stability in the workforce. In addition a bank of porters had been established that worked on an 'as and when' basis, but they did not attract the premium rates associated with overtime working. Some staff members that customarily worked high levels of overtime had left Northern, and new recruits did not have the same expectations about supplementing their income through high levels of overtime working. Although portering staff wages had declined, the trust had continued to attract applicants because other conditions of employment compared favourably to local employers (e.g. sick leave, annual leave) and because the intrinsic worth of the work attracted applicants. The management style of the department was also viewed as more open than in the past. Employees participated in working groups that considered service priorities, for example recruitment and retention of domestic staff, with management commitment to act on suggestions.

Workplace flexibility and the model employer tradition

Northern had pursued other forms of flexibility, not least to address recruitment and retention difficulties, with managers recruiting nurses from the Philippines in 2000. In addition to recruitment difficulties the implementation of the working time directive had a significant impact on staffing patterns; this is an important area of managerial flexibility, as patterns of working time are excluded from the Whitley council agreements. For example, many nursing staff preferred to compress their working time into three long days, working a 12-hour shift on each day, but trust managers were concerned about their compliance with the working time directive and about the impact on the quality of care. This led to some tension with staff and staff side representatives who wished to maintain 12-hour shifts.

Doctors in training were excluded from the original working time directive, but the 1991 'New Deal' for junior doctors limited their hours of work to 72 hours on duty and 56 hours of actual work. When the working time directive was revised in 2000 a timetable was established for including the exempt groups, and the UK government introduced new measures in December 2000 to reinforce the New Deal. From August 2001 it became unlawful for newly qualified junior doctors to work more than 56 hours a week. Trusts faced large financial penalties if their staff were on non-compliant rotas. At Northern a shift system was introduced from August 2001 because the on-call system could not be made to operate in a manner that was compatible with the new working hours requirements. This had required an increase in the use of non-training grade medical staff. The reaction of the consultants varied. Although they acknowledged that the training and working hours of junior medical staff had to change, and that the 'see one, do one, teach one' medical training culture was 'not very safe', they expressed reservations. As one consultant commented:

> It had to change but it may have gone too far the other way; junior doctors are being deskilled, for example in terms of taking bloods and putting drips in. It may be mundane but people need to be able to do it . . . the bleep free teaching culture people [i.e. consultants] find hard to accept, it's almost like being a proper student! Shifts come in from August; it's going to be hard to give them the teaching they need. (Interview notes, July 2001)

This type of ambivalence among clinical staff about the improvement of working lives was not confined to medical staff. Northern exemplified the model employer tradition with numerous long-standing policies (e.g. job share, annualized hours) and other staff facilities including a workplace nursery (it was over-subscribed) designed to facilitate flexible working practices as part of a corporate strategy to ensure effective recruitment and retention. Nonetheless, the HR department did not actively promote flexible working, rather a request was triggered by an individual member of staff that wanted to alter their working arrangements, and the outcome depended greatly on the attitude of the individual manager. According to the staff side secretary:

> A lot of policies put in place at trust level are very open to managers' discretion. They get interpreted at departmental level, and may vary depending on which department you are in. In fact it does. (Interview notes, July 2001)

Requests were not always viewed favourably, although managers had become more accommodating because of the tighter labour market context. As the director of HR commented, 'A few years ago managers were very sceptical even about job shares. Managers are more flexible now' (Interview notes, April 2001). Nonetheless there appeared to be some presumption that full-time working was more appropriate for many *professional* jobs and there was some ignorance among staff about trust policies. In the 2000 staff survey, only 37 per cent of staff were aware of Northern's policy on job-sharing, and this figure fell to 32 per cent for flexible working. In response to the question 'In the past 12 months I have felt discriminated against because of my part-time working', 18 per cent of part-time staff agreed, a much higher figure than for discrimination on grounds of age, gender or race (the workforce is predominantly white). This discrimination had taken the form of being excluded from communications mechanisms and opportunities for training. This latter point was also highlighted by the Audit Commission (2001a: 42). They reported that part-time staff undertook less training than full-time staff, despite similar skill requirements, and that trusts appeared to invest less per person when they employed a higher proportion of part-time staff. Consequently, although policies promoting forms of flexible working existed, this was not promoted by HR as a key corporate initiative, but left up to individuals to utilize as best they could, dependent on the response of their manager.

Work reorganization in Western

The potential to examine critically existing working practices and devise new roles with local pay and conditions of service formed the core of Western's reward strategy. In preparing his reward strategy, published in July 1993, the director of personnel had conducted discussions with the clinical directors about the development of medical support workers who would carry out tasks undertaken by qualified staff. It was envisaged that this would be the first stage of a process that would impact on most qualified and unqualified groups, by developing generic roles that would challenge the existing division of labour between occupational groups.

The most pressing requirement arose from the 'new deal' for medical staff which required the reduction of junior doctors' hours in stages. The trust achieved the first national target of 83 hours per week, but was required to meet the second target of 72 hours per week by 1995. This placed considerable pressure on the way in which the trust used its medical staff and provided the opportunity to establish a group of support workers who would carry out some of the routine tasks ('chasing' laboratory results, routine form-filling, etc.) currently performed by junior doctors.

Linked to the reduction in junior doctors' hours was the development of highly trained nurses termed the 'advanced nurse practitioner'. They would be an integral part of the medical team, taking on tasks relinquished by junior doctors. This in turn required better trained support staff to undertake the more basic duties delegated to them by registered nurses and junior medical staff. This was the role envisaged for the medical support workers, subsequently retitled clinical support workers. The final element concerned developing a hotel support worker (HSW) role to straddle domestic, portering, distribution, clerical and security duties.

The government's emphasis on market-testing for support services posed difficulties for managers as the development of generic working for groups such as domestics, porters and catering staff was viewed as incompatible with market-testing undertaken on a functional basis. Senior managers wanted to bring the domestic service back in-house when the contract ended in summer 1995. Managers argued that the market-testing initiative had become an end in itself and had lost sight of its stated objective of obtaining value for money, not least because of the transaction costs of specifying, letting and monitoring tenders. Contracting-out of services ran counter to the management philosophy of valuing its staff, so bringing the domestic service back in-house would enable Western to project itself as a good employer. It provided managers with a powerful bargaining lever in discussions with the trade unions, who were anxious to see the domestic service return in-house and were willing to make concessions to achieve this end.

The plans to introduce generic working reflected an attempt to improve the quality of service provided, by developing support workers who would be an integral part of the ward team. By providing more structured competency based training linked to an NVQ accredited framework, scope would exist for support workers to progress into more patient-orientated roles. To reinforce the ward based philosophy it was anticipated that responsibility for these staff would be devolved to the ward manager.

The final rationale for generic working stemmed from the opportunities it provided to review existing working practices to yield financial savings and enhance managerial control. Managers expressed the same grievances as managers at Eastern and Northern in terms of the cost and inflexibility of the existing Whitley terms and conditions of employment in relation to enhancements and sick pay arrangements. Substantial differences existed in the take home pay of different occupational groups, with male dominated portering staff earning substantially more than the predominantly female domestic and catering staff.

Negotiating the generic worker initiative

In contrast to Eastern, a great deal of importance was attached to gaining support for the project from the staff side and the existing contractors. The imposition of generic working would have appeared to staff as equivalent to market-testing services, jeopardizing any good will gained from the decision not to market-test. However, managers were confident that the threat of market-testing which loomed over the generic support worker negotiations was a sufficient threat to achieve an accord with the staff side. Unison was supportive of the principle and was attracted to the prospect that the domestic service would be returned in-house. Royal College of Nursing officials, reflecting its professional orientation, were wary of the concept, concerned that it could create a 'jack of all trades', leading to the erosion of the qualified nurses' role. These fears were allayed as detailed job profiles emerged and coherent training arrangements developed.

A sensitive issue for senior managers, despite trust 'freedoms', concerned their decision not to market-test support services, which could have been interpreted as being in breach of central NHS Executive guidance. Trust managers campaigned to persuade civil servants in the market-testing unit of the merits of their position:

> It is felt strongly that to attempt to combine market-testing with such a radical devolution of responsibilities to ward teams, and introduction of more generic flexible roles, would not be manageable given the change agenda involved. However, the Trust recognises the value of market-testing in accordance with the appropriate NHS guidelines and has agreed to formally evaluate the introduction of Generic Working after a 12 month period and, at this stage, take stock of all options. (Letter from the director of personnel, March 1995)

Linked to these developments was the aim to ensure that the contractors at each hospital site accepted the development of generic working (see Table 8.3). This was difficult as each contractor faced a significant loss of income when the contracts were terminated and managers feared that the contractors would challenge their decision and involve the NHS Executive. Managers cultivated the impression that they were keeping the contractors appraised of their plans and invited them to participate in a formal evaluation, after the project had started, while keeping them at arm's length. Job profiles for the generic support workers were developed and discussed in detail with the trust's joint staff side. Two broad support worker job profiles had emerged: a Clinical Support Worker (CSW) and a Hotel Support Worker (HSW). The clinical support worker role incorporated a range of patient care (e.g. assisting patients to maintain personal hygiene), clinical support (e.g. undertaking routine ECG and other procedures), housekeeping (e.g. cleaning equipment), clerical (e.g. maintenance of computerized

Table 8.3 *Options for maintaining contractors' co-operation*

1. Contractor 1 and 2 invited to compete for provision of Hotel Support Workers at one of the pilot sites.
2. As above except each contractor awarded one ward each.
3. Share all information on pay and conditions with both contractors.
4. Initial evaluation after 6 months, if not successful move to market test the services.
5. Invite both contractors to compete as managing agents for the project for 12 months.
6. As (5) but the trust split into two between each contractor.

Source: Strategy for Maintaining an Element of Support from the Contractors, Western NHS Trust, 1994.

information systems) and therapeutic roles, with the posts being tailored to the particular requirements of each directorate. The HSW was designed to carry out a range of domestic, portering, distribution, clerical and security duties.

A sub-group of the JCNC conducted the negotiations on local terms and conditions in secret, reporting back to the full JCNC for approval. The secretive approach caused difficulties for Unison among portering staff members, who were dismayed with the agreement reached. The proposed local pay and conditions for HSWs and CSWs established a slightly higher maximum possible level of earnings, incorporated nursing conditions of service and included a productivity element based on attendance. The full salary for the HSW and CSW would only be available to individuals who achieved 100 per cent attendance each month, with sharp reductions in basic pay for absence (Table 8.4).

Domestic staff who transferred to HSW roles from the private contractors stood to gain significantly in terms of basic pay; although portering staff might receive modest increases in basic pay, their overall earnings would depend crucially on the future of their overtime arrangements. Ward clerks, however, would almost certainly have their basic pay reduced. The package also included proposals to increase flexible working practices, not only in terms of task flexibility, but also hours flexibility, by establishing an 'annual hours' system with an indicative range of hours each week and overtime paid only when the weekly maximum had been exceeded.

It was suggested that the project would release approximately £0.5 million in savings from the £7–8 million per annum spent on these staff groups. The staff side rejected the proposals on the grounds that they took no account of the loss of increments, or the increases in duties and responsibilities of the post-holders, and no compensation was provided for the greater flexibility

Table 8.4 *Management proposals for attendance bonuses and weekly hours at Western Trust*

	CSW	HSW
100% attendance (basic salary)	£9,135	£7,125
In any month, one day's absence	−£50	−£40
In any month, over one day's absence	−£100	−£80
Weekly hours band	32.5–42.5	34–44

Figures refer to May 1994 levels. The figures are maxima, new starters were to be placed on 90 per cent of total basic pay. Overtime was to be paid above 42.5/44 hours per week at time and a half and double time (as nursing Whitley conditions).

Source: Western NHS Trust, 1994.

associated with the new roles. Unison viewed the attendance proposals as totally unacceptable, particularly on a monthly basis, arguing that staff would be coerced into coming to work even when they were unwell. The principle of annual hours was rejected also.

Management revamped their proposals, abandoning the contentious link between pay and attendance. In hindsight managers suggested that if the attendance proposals had been accepted, and had reduced absence, it would have proved a costly solution. Attendance problems were more cheaply and effectively tackled by rigorous monitoring procedures. In the final package all that remained of the proposed link between attendance and rewards was that an extra day's annual leave could be earned (on a non-recurring basis) if an employee had only one episode (of seven days maximum) or less of sickness absence.

Flexible working arrangements remained a high priority for management, but a minor concession was made to the staff side by rostering work over a one month rather than a twelve month period. This achieved management's main objective, which was to reduce the high levels of overtime worked, particularly among portering staff. The proposals did not specify the shift patterns that staff would be expected to work, allowing maximum flexibility to allocate and rotate staff between different shift patterns.

The sub-committee of the staff side considered that the benefits of bringing the domestic service back in-house and preventing the competitive tendering of portering services outweighed any disadvantages within management's proposals. They had vetoed the proposals to link rewards to attendance and had obtained some modifications to the proposals for annualized hours. For domestic staff and health care support workers, the proposals ensured modest rises in their earnings potential and access to more rewarding jobs. However, the proposals allowed managers a free hand in devising trust specific flexible working arrangements, removed costly overtime and enhancement arrangements and eliminated the ward clerk role.

The implementation of generic working

The human resources directorate orchestrated a comprehensive communications strategy to brief staff and to gain their support for the agreement, prior to discussion at the JCNC. A briefing pack was prepared and senior managers were expected to brief all their staff within a two-week period. Workshops were conducted for middle and first line managers to provide a common understanding of the proposals. The chief executive wrote to all staff explaining the project.

The most vocal opposition to the proposals, and Unison's conduct of the negotiations, came from the portering staff, who expected sharp reductions in earnings on transferring to the hotel support worker role, arising from a reduction in the amount of overtime they worked. Their anger was exacerbated by the range of duties that they could be required to undertake as HSWs. The new role combined aspects of portering, cleaning and clerical work. A typical comment from the almost exclusively male portering workforce about taking on domestic duties was 'I don't do it at home so I am not going to do it here. It's woman's work' (Interview notes, July 1996).

Staff side representatives on the full JCNC felt obliged to accept the views of the negotiating committee representatives that it was an acceptable package, despite their misgivings. In July 1995 about 900 workers, of whom almost 200 had been employed by the private contractors, moved over to HSW and CSW roles. The transfer of staff into the new job roles ensured that staff became contractually committed to more flexible working practices, but the full benefits of generic working would not be achieved until ward managers made full use of the flexibilities available and the planned devolution of HSWs to ward level occurred.

The majority of the clinical support workers had transferred from health care support worker roles and had no familiarity with inputting patient details into Western's information management system. A large training requirement existed for these staff, who expected a full training programme to NVQ level to enhance their career prospects and increase job satisfaction. This training and assessment requirement fell to over-stretched ward managers, who were irritated that the requirements for assessing the CSWs were more onerous than for assessing the qualified nursing staff. Many of the CSWs did not receive the training that they required and ward managers had to undertake the clerical tasks themselves.

Nursing staff had an ambivalent attitude to the generic support working project. Many senior nurses had strong reservations, believing that it could undermine the role of the registered nurse by reinventing the former enrolled nurse position by another route. This was viewed as leading to a process of deprofessionalization, with HSWs gaining NVQs which might ultimately lead to full registration. These concerns were reinforced by a belief that the initiative was essentially an HR project and that senior nurses had not been encouraged to participate in the project. The absence of an adequate nursing input led to an underestimation of the practical implications of the project at ward level. These comments were reiterated by the director of nursing, who argued that the CSW project was unsuccessful because although generic working sounded positive:

> The practice is that the most demanding work on a ward is looking after patients, so the threshold is always not to do the things that are not patient focused, so whereas you have protected time for a ward clerk to manage the notes, phone, and all the rest, suddenly the demand is to take the patient to the toilet and all the rest of it, so the ward clerking never gets done. The notes have become a mess in the trust, now we have slowly put ward clerks back. (Interview notes, June 2002)

The plan to devolve fully a range of tasks to ward level, which had been managed on a central basis or by external contractors, had not been implemented. The unwillingess of the directorates to take on this responsibility stemmed from a lack of confidence about their ability to manage relatively large numbers of staff that had the reputation for being difficult. Managers felt that they were already overloaded, making them reluctant to tackle a further item of organizational restructuring. This stance was reinforced when the staff employed by the contractors were returned in-house. Trust managers were shocked by the low levels of training and poor skill levels among these staff, which required an intensive effort to raise standards that was most appropriately undertaken by the specialist hotel services staff.

For the hotel support workers the degree of flexibility gained was uneven. The main benefit identified by managers was that staff were required to work across all three sites, and that proved useful in covering for absence. This geographical flexibility was not mirrored in terms of the tasks undertaken because of the reluctance of existing portering staff to undertake domestic duties, although this was less of an issue among new staff. The use of monthly rather than weekly hours had brought few changes. As the two managers responsible for HSWs commented:

> It looked really good when we put it in, but in practice it has meant three-fifths of not a lot. The theory was that you reduce the amount of overtime. To a degree that has worked. Where it hasn't been as successful is that we actually know quite accurately how many hours we need and how much relief we need. (Business Manager, July 1996)

And:

> It is used as an advantage for the staff. I still operate on a weekly roster – 39 hours a week, but what I use it for is to give flexibility to the staff themselves. If they have to go early today, they don't have to lose pay, whereas they did have to before. They can do it tomorrow. (Hotel Services Manager, July 1996)

Senior managers accepted that the aspirations of flexible working had only been partially achieved, but argued that the crucial development was that managers had introduced local trust terms and conditions of employment for a significant number of staff with increased flexibility. The generic working project indicated to staff that managers would develop local packages, more attuned to trust requirements, and it broke the logjam where staff were unwilling to give up their Whitley terms and conditions and transfer to trust contracts. The initiative signalled to line managers that innovative employment packages could be developed, and a similar package for catering staff had been developed subsequently with few difficulties. As acceptance grew that the existing pay and working arrangements of all occupational groups would be scrutinized, so more politically sensitive areas such as revising the clinical grading structure for nurses might be addressed.

Discussion

In all three trusts, managers placed considerable emphasis on work reorganization, and there were many similarities in the initiatives pursued. In all cases the approach was centred around the development of generic working, usually bringing back in-house groups of staff that had been contracted out, attaching local terms and conditions to these new roles, and communicating these changes directly to staff, alongside negotiations with the trade unions about proposed terms and conditions and new roles.

The priority that managers placed on developing generic working reflected their view that financial savings and improvements in services were most likely to arise from re-profiling the workforce and increasing its flexibility. These measures accompanied attempts to tighten up on the performance of staff, by soft measures such as improved training and development, and by harder means including more rigorous absence management. A feature of the generic worker project was the attempt to reverse the rigid demarcations between groups of workers associated with competitive tendering for support staff. For example, hotel support workers at Western represented a return to the era of the ward orderly when support staff worked under the direction of the ward sister and carried out a range of duties.

Although managers in all three trusts had not pursued the development of trust terms and conditions for all staff using proprietary systems of job evaluation, they saw positive gains in using local trust freedoms to reshape work roles and to attach trust specific terms and conditions to these roles. Managerial aims included simplifying and harmonizing Whitley conditions between occupational groups and reducing overtime premia and other enhanced rates of pay. There were also attempts to link wage levels more closely to those prevailing in local labour markets. Despite vociferous trade union opposition among the well organized male portering staff, their capacity to resist reductions in their terms and conditions was limited. This provides further evidence of limited union influence, albeit for groups of manual staff with relatively little labour market power. Management's strategy, especially at Western, was facilitated by the threat of contracting out services and negotiating with full-time union officers that were less inclined than in the past to support the sectional interests of the portering staff.

In all three cases managers expressed disappointment that contractual forms of flexibility had not always been translated into more effective labour utilization, and that there had been some retreat from forms of generic working. This partly reflected the reservations that some professional staff, especially nurses, expressed about forms of generic working, although there were important differences between the trusts. The response of nursing staff was shaped in part by whether they perceived generic workers to be a substitute for nursing staff, or an addition to ward resources. In addition, although most discussions of labour utilization focus on managerial requirements for flexibility, generic working highlighted the requirement for a degree of rigidity in order for managers to plan effectively and to ensure that all aspects of ward work were covered. It would be wrong to conclude, however, that managers viewed the existing division of labour between health professionals as the most effective way of organizing work, or that managers were disenchanted with forms of generic working. Instead managers suggested that generic working could not be introduced in isolation for one group of staff without considering the implications for other staff groups.

Although each trust pursued a broadly similar approach there were important differences in the process. In keeping with the management style at Eastern and its turbulent industrial relations and financial environment, generic working was viewed primarily in terms of its contribution to generating financial savings, and the director of personnel had little scope to shape this agenda. In order to achieve budgetary reductions, ward assistant terms and conditions were pared back, and with little HR input, senior managers showed little commitment to negotiating change. Although the negotiations soured industrial relations, the ward assistant project was implemented more fully than at the other two trusts, because managers were more prepared to impose change.

At Western the HR director was responsible for generic working and a sophisticated management strategy was adopted. This was evident in the time spent persuading managers and employees of the benefits of generic working before proceeding. Detailed advanced planning was undertaken on issues ranging from ensuring that the NHS Executive allowed the trust not to market-test to the maintenance of support from the private contractors. One consequence was the length of time that it took to develop and implement generic workers. From its origins in late 1993 it took almost two years before generic support workers were appointed, and this proved to be the first stage, as devolution to the directorates did not occur. It is hardly surprising that managers confronted with heavy workloads and targets to achieve in a short time period, linked to the electoral cycle, are more inclined to impose change than engage in meaningful consultation and negotiation.

These developments indicate that, despite the constraints that managers faced in using their personnel discretion, by the mid-1990s they started to use their trust freedoms to develop core trust terms and conditions of employment that they anticipated would be extended to other groups of staff. This was the real significance of local pay, rather than the cul-de-sac of local pay settlements that dominated the national debate in the 1990s. With the prospect of the Conservative government's electoral defeat, however, and the Labour government's commitment to a national framework for terms and conditions, managers were discouraged from continuing to develop local trust terms and conditions linked to altered roles. Nonetheless managers' interest in pursuing such an agenda was evident from the case study trusts, and in areas where managers could exercise greater discretion (e.g. over working time) significant reforms occurred. Consequently *Agenda for Change*, by establishing a more fluid pay and grading structure and legitimating local flexibility, may provide a platform for more radical changes in working practices. At the same time, as the case studies illustrated, clinical staff remain wary of reforms of professional roles, and uncertainties remain about whether HR has the resources and influence to develop and implement far-reaching changes in working practices.

9 CONCLUSIONS

In the last two decades the health service has been swept along in a continuous process of reform that has reshaped its organization and management. Conservative government ministers developed a more assertive tier of senior managers and market-style reforms that created incentives for change. The Labour government elected in 1997 accepted most of the radical organizational restructuring of the health service while extending the scrutiny of organizational performance. Although not all of the reforms were intended to alter employment practices, cumulatively they have uprooted traditional patterns of employment relations.

This chapter draws together the main findings of the study, explores the utility of the analytical frameworks used in the research, and draws out the policy implications of the findings. It starts by examining the main themes that emerge from the research, drawing on the workplace case studies and the wider national interview sample. These findings shed light on the utility of strategic choice and new public management frameworks that have become dominant in the examination of public sector employment relations reform. It is argued that by directing their attention at managerial decisions at the level of the employer unit, insufficient attention is given to the key characteristics of the health sector that shape management practice and workplace employment relations. Finally, the policy implications of the findings are drawn out.

Employment relations under health care reform

In the last two decades the state has been highly interventionist in reshaping the health service. The implementation of general management, the establishment of the internal market and the development of the audit culture has increased the extent of central government control and monitoring of health service staff. Rather than 'rolling back the state' successive governments have extended state intervention, a process that is not confined to the UK health system (Bach 2001). The contrast between the anticipated autonomy of trust status and the experience of detailed intervention by central government undermined managerial support for Conservative government health reforms.

Initially high expectations among health service staff about the prospects for the Labour government's reforms have not been fulfilled. Instead of emphasizing trust freedoms the Labour government indicated that they would halt the permanent revolution and avoid structural reform (Webster 2002: 212). In practice this has not been the case, and a series of reorganizations have followed in rapid succession, none of which has been fully implemented. This has resulted in a workforce weary of constant organizational change and the pressure to achieve performance targets.

Management reform

Trust managers were encouraged to mimic private sector practice in the way that they structured their internal management processes. The devolution of management responsibilities to clinical directorates was intended to increase the independence of operational units and ensure that they were more orientated to the needs of their 'customers', while remaining within an overall financial and corporate framework. In all of the case study trusts authority was devolved to clinical directorates linked to the monitoring of performance. These directorate structures, however, had a number of shortcomings because they fostered internal competition. The underlying assumption that different directorates would serve different 'product' markets and would therefore benefit from distinct management and employment practices was ill-suited to highly integrated and interdependent organizations covered by a national framework of terms and conditions. This was most visible at Eastern, with directorate structures fostering inconsistencies in personnel practice across the trust. This was a source of dissatisfaction among the workforce that remains acutely sensitive to issues of internal equity.

Despite these limitations, chief executives viewed directorate structures as an important mechanism to incorporate senior medical staff into the managerial process to support and legitimate managerial decisions. Tensions remained between managerial and medical staff priorities and there was a widespread sense that medical staff involvement in trust management was not effective, although the principle that medical staff should be involved in management was no longer contested.

The phasing out of the internal market and the competitive ethos it generated led to changes in organizational structures. There were attempts to exert much greater corporate control over all trust activities. This was linked to an increased focus on monitoring standards of care that derived from the systematic development of clinical governance, including a greater emphasis on risk management. Structural change reflected also a much greater focus on networks involving collaboration between trusts and a series of other actors. As Rhodes (1996) has argued, service delivery is increasingly focused on inter-organizational networks rather than confined to hierarchical intra-organizational relationships. Trust managers, by directing their attention towards the management of networks, in addition to managing their existing internal hierarchies, are anticipating the more diverse and pluralistic health system that the Labour government is increasingly committed to developing.

The outright hostility towards senior managers that used to characterize medical staff responses had dissipated, and the legitimacy of the chief executive role was accepted. This was reflected in another trust (not one of the case studies) by the decision not to develop clinical directorate structures because medical staff expected managers to allocate resources more fairly than their medical colleagues. Bottery (1998: 48) noted similar sentiments among consultants in traditionally lower prestige specialities that welcomed a stronger management culture because it curbed the allocation of resources based on prestige rather than need. Senior medical staff ambivalence towards 'management' had not disappeared, but they accepted the need to become engaged in the management process to protect their interests. Among non-consultant medical staff there was a strong sense that gaining some management training was a prerequisite to gaining a consultant post, an implicit acknowledgement of the shift in organizational values within the health service.

Management of employment relations

A dominant concern underpinning the restructuring of the management and organization of the health service by successive governments has been the importance of reshaping employment practices and adopting a more strategic approach to staff management. Senior managers expressed a strong commitment to reshape employment relations, and there was a strong sectoral effect with similar initiatives adopted across the trusts. This reform agenda had its origins in the altered managerial and organizational context within the health service rather than stemming from specific employment relations reforms pursued by the HR function. A major change in employment relations involved a shift towards a performance management culture.

The pressure on managers to achieve efficiency and other performance targets had a major impact on the workforce. Managers aimed to increase employee awareness of financial and other service outcomes, encouraging employees to internalize corporate requirements and work more intensively to achieve them. More information was communicated to the workforce about contract performance and waiting list targets, and managers emphasized the performance requirements demanded by external bodies. At Northern, for example, in early 2002 the written team-brief posed the rhetorical question, 'Are you personally prepared for the CHI visit?' and exhorted all staff to attend a briefing prior to the Commission for Health Improvement visit. The increase in audit activity arising from CHI and other types of inspection has ensured that performance management issues and the expectations placed on staff are much more transparent than in the past.

Although clinical directorate structures had drawbacks, devolving responsibility to clinical staff had a powerful effect on staff behaviour. Directorates were grouped into divisions that prepared annual business plans with key objectives established for the year. Objectives were cascaded downwards and ward managers in particular confronted severe role conflict between their managerial and clinical responsibilities and the need to juggle different consultant requirements and conflicting national priorities. Although clinical staff did not fully accept the legitimacy of managerial requirements, ward managers were acutely aware of these targets, indicating that performance measurement in terms of quantifiable outcomes had become the accepted yardstick of performance. Medical staff were likely to direct their frustration at external parties, such as the purchaser or the government, as much as at their own senior managers, because they acknowledged the difficulty of the task that managers were expected to perform. Overall the aim of Roy Griffiths to persuade doctors to 'accept management responsibility that goes with clinical freedom' (Griffiths 1983: para. 8.2) has, to an extent that would have been unthinkable at the time that Griffiths was writing, been achieved.

Required standards of performance were widely understood by staff. As Table 6.5 indicated, approximately 90 per cent of staff at Eastern and Northern agreed that they had a clear understanding of expected standards of performance. One of the most visible changes in management approach to performance management related to staff absence. Its high profile in every trust was reinforced by the Labour government's HR targets, although the emphasis on absence management pre-dated them. There was a concerted effort to reduce absence levels and much more willingness among senior managers to discipline and ultimately terminate employment among staff with poor attendance records.

Nevertheless it would be misleading to view this performance culture as all-encompassing. In particular the approach towards the management of consultant medical staff continued to differ, with medical staff questioning the legitimacy of aspects of the management process. There was considerable uncertainty about the degree that performance appraisal was being implemented. At Western, CHI (2002b) noted that 'some consultants were not willing to implement performance appraisal, as they do not agree with the principles'. The disciplining of medical staff remained a highly sensitive issue, as was illustrated by one case at Northern that occupied almost 50 per cent of the director of human resources time in her first year in post. In addition, the commitment of middle managers to performance manage their own staff, especially those from their own professional background, was much more variable. This led to poor performance not always being addressed (see Table 6.5).

The second major change in employment relations concerned the approach towards employee involvement and collective relations with trade unions. In comparison with other aspects of employment relations there was more variation between the trusts. The values of the chief executive and other senior managers had an important bearing on the degree that reforms in employment relations represented a marked break with past practice, or a more incremental and evolutionary process.

At Eastern, a sense of frustration with existing adversarial management–workforce relations and continuing financial crises propelled managers to seek a break with past patterns of employment relations. At the same time these turbulent circumstances placed a powerful brake on change. At the other two trusts it was recognized that many managerial objectives, including the development of generic working, could be achieved without wholesale reform of traditional patterns of management–union relations. At both trusts managers were largely indifferent towards trade unions, while recognizing that on certain issues, and among certain groups of staff, it remained important to be seen to be consulting the trade unions.

Not surprisingly HR managers tended to attach more importance to maintaining good relations with trade unions, and there was widespread interest in developing partnership working. This stemmed from central government encouragement and because managers sought trade union support to implement their own agenda on issues such as *Improving Working Lives.* HR specialists increasingly viewed trade unions as an adjunct to the management process rather than as an important source of independent employee voice. This view was related to their misgivings about how representative staff side members were of wider staff opinion.

Trust managers were prepared to tolerate trade unions as institutions, but they became more marginal to management–workforce relations. In all the trusts senior managers greatly increased the amount of direct communication with employees that eroded trade union influence. Employees were much less likely to look towards trade union representatives and trade union forums for information. A related development was the reduced importance of traditional institutions of joint management–union relations.

A tangible expression of the reduced importance of joint consultation arrangements concerned the establishment of alternative approaches to staff involvement. These initiatives originated outside of the HR function and were championed in two of the trusts by the directors of nursing. In contrast to managerial encouragement to participate in these initiatives, increased workloads made it difficult for trade union representatives to undertake their functions. Invariably there were relatively few trade union members that were prepared to be active members, increasing the burden on already overstretched union activists.

The changing role of trade unions also had major consequences for the human resources function. Organizational restructuring and devolution of responsibility for employment practices to NHS trusts was viewed as an opportunity for human resource specialists to move centre-stage and gain board-level status. With the possible exception of the director of personnel at Western during the mid-1990s, at the other two case study trusts this did not occur to any great extent and the establishment of new forms of employee involvement, the introduction of generic working, and strengthened forms of performance management were not primarily HR led initiatives. By the end of the fieldwork period none of the HR directors were executive members of their trust boards, reflecting the continuing difficulties that the HR function confronts in gaining recognition from trust chief executives.

In keeping with broader developments in human resource management the HR function was attempting to shift from an administrative function towards a more corporate orientated function. Without the support of each trust's chief executive, however, it was difficult for the HR function to prove its worth. HR practice was insufficiently embedded within organizational practice, with limited interaction between service priorities and HR initiatives. The directors of HR expressed some frustration at the difficulty in pursuing a longer-term agenda, a concern that was partly related to limited investment in the HR function. Finally, the diminished role of trade unions may also have eroded its influence because a symbiotic relationship often exists between workplace trade unions and personnel specialists.

The HR function was frequently the repository of a range of disparate central government requirements. Since the Labour government has been elected the increasing number of employment related targets has dissipated the HR agenda because there are too many diverse national initiatives. This led the HR function to focus on fulfilling the requirements of the audit culture: undertaking an annual staff survey, finding ways of driving down absence and ensuring that the trust had various policies as stipulated by central government. There was some scope for HR initiatives at the edges but these were relatively few and far between.

Pay determination and work reorganization

NHS trusts were established in the expectation that they would use their increased discretion to reshape the way that pay was determined and labour utilized. The Conservative government encouraged trust managers to develop local pay and conditions while the Labour government has favoured the establishment of more local flexibility within a national framework. Pay arrangements at trust level exhibited the strongest element of continuity in comparison to other aspects of the employment relations agenda. Pay determination was also the aspect of employment practice that was shaped most forcibly by external influences. The reasons why local pay determination failed to develop are closely related to the characteristics of the sub-sector identified in Chapter 2. These include: fiscal constraints and a reluctance by the Treasury to ease control over the pay bill; the centralized structure of the health service that was reflected in continued use of pay review body arrangements, a form of national pay determination; and the presence of a professional workforce and their representative organizations that resisted local pay because it was equated with lower pay and increased managerial control.

These influences were apparent at the case study trusts. The development of local pay was a low priority for senior managers, and HR directors were wary of provoking staff opposition for few tangible gains. They sensed little commitment among their managerial colleagues for a major drive to implement trust terms and conditions of employment. This overall stance towards local pay did not prevent managers developing some local agreements to meet particular trust requirements. These agreements, however, were facilitated by the establishment of less prescriptive national agreements during the 1990s rather than the rhetorical freedoms associated with trust status.

An important consequence of the failed attempt to develop local pay and conditions has been that there remains very limited expertise among management or trade union representatives in the implementation of complex payment systems. As the fieldwork illustrated, the 'bargaining' over the annual pay settlement in the mid-1990s was largely symbolic, with the key variables in terms of the resources available for local settlements and the acceptability of trust offers decided by management and union officials beyond the individual workplace. The *Agenda for Change* proposals represent a different order of magnitude in terms of their complexity, coverage and scope. Human resource specialists forcibly expressed their concerns about the preparedness of NHS trusts for implementing *Agenda for Change* in a survey conducted at the 2002 NHS national HR conference (Department of Health 2002f). The tone of the 285 responses expressed a high level of anxiety about the lack of trust board interest and ownership of the reforms, fears about the workload involved, and concerns that the process could repeat the problems associated with clinical re-grading in the late 1980s.

In contrast to the limited developments in pay determination, some of the most significant changes in employment practices related to alterations in labour utilization. The most widespread initiative was the attempt to reduce the demarcations between different occupational groups by combining jobs into generic worker roles with trust-specific terms and conditions. Trust managers initially concentrated on the boundaries between different ancillary occupations and the interface between these groups and nursing staff. In tandem with these 're-profiling' exercises respondents noted alterations in the composition of the workforce and more intensive working patterns. Although there were some distinctions between the trusts in the scope and outcomes associated with generic working, these differences were outweighed by the similarity of approach.

For managers, 'flexibility' was a mantra which encompassed several different forms linked to a number of managerial objectives. First, managers wanted to reduce their overall pay bill and to convert it from a totally fixed cost to a quasi-variable cost. The breaking down of demarcations between occupational groups, with the establishment of new roles, provided the opportunity to increase the intensity of work and alter the balance between qualified nursing staff and other support staff. When this process encompassed also the attachment of trust terms and conditions to these roles, further trimming of the pay bill could be achieved. Invariably trust terms and conditions were less generous in respect of overtime working and enhancements. New starters were usually placed on lower basic starting salaries and consequently, as the proportion of new starters increased, significant pay bill savings could be generated.

The second management objective was to improve the quality of service provision. It pervaded management documents, but was less well articulated in practice. It encompassed attempts to improve communications both between management and the workforce and between staff and patients. It was linked to a managerial concern to decentralize decision-making, making the ward the focus of the hospital team, and thus facilitate cross-functional working. An important dimension of this customer orientation required staff to acquire new competencies and extend their role beyond the deployment of traditional professional skills towards the servicing of internal and external 'customers'. This orientation was explicit in the job titles used (e.g. hotel support worker, ward hostess). This development of customer orientated skills altered professional roles away from an exclusive focus on professionally defined norms of competence, a process that has wider implications for professional autonomy (see Fairbrother and Poynter 2001: 319). The knowledge and skills framework that underpins the proposed NHS pay system also places an emphasis on softer interactive competencies. Oral communication, for example, is defined as a core skill for all NHS staff (Department of Health 2002g), foreshadowing major shifts in professional roles.

Managerial attempts to link quality and flexibility had an ideological purpose, because it made staff opposition to flexibility seem less reasonable and was intended to alter staff behaviour. Staff placed a different construction on flexibility, which they viewed as a euphemism for work intensification and less predictable working patterns. Staff representatives tried to develop an alternative conception of quality linked to overall staffing levels and the mix of staff.

A third management objective was linked to the effective use of working time, ensuring that labour was productively deployed and staffing levels were linked more closely to workload requirements. At all the trusts, managers had investigated (and sometimes rejected) the use of annualized hours and forms of self-rostering for nursing staff. The use of bank working arrangements became more prominent and was extended from nursing to other occupational groups (e.g. porters). Other attempts to match working time more closely to demand involved the use of NHS Professionals (the in-house NHS nursing agency) to reduce the cost of temporary agency nurses. This, however, proved to have mixed results. At Eastern the use of NHS Professionals reduced the number of agency hours booked by 20 per cent in the first few months of 2000, but this was more than compensated for by a nearly 30 per cent increase in the use of NHS Professionals staff, generating a suspicion that a somewhat cheaper and easier source of supply created additional demand.

Finally, as recruitment and retention difficulties became more severe from the end of the 1990s, alterations in working time were increasingly linked to attempts to improve working lives and ensure staff retention. In all the trusts well developed policies on a variety of flexible working arrangements existed, but staff awareness of them was patchy. It was more common for individual employees to negotiate with their own managers about working arrangements. This resulted in key staffing decisions being managed relatively informally and with little consistency, linked to the preferences of individual managers rather than the corporate requirements of the trust. It has also been suggested in other trusts that the decentralization of working time decisions potentially reinforces the remoteness of managers from staffing decisions. Ward staffing problems are not filtered upwards and voiced at higher levels, preventing remedial action being taken (Grimshaw *et al.* 2000: 333–4).

In all the fieldwork trusts managers concluded, albeit with differing degrees of conviction, that competitive tendering for ancillary services and contracting-out did not provide value for money and impeded the development of more flexible working practices. The contracting-out of a particular service, such as cleaning, cut across managerial attempts to develop generic, ward-based working arrangements that eroded the traditional boundaries between ancillary services. Managers were reluctant to cede control for parts of their workforce to an outside organization, and the employment of staff on different terms and conditions of employment impeded team-working.

Strategy and structure

During the last two decades there has been an increased focus on the behaviour of public sector managers. A common feature of the new public management frameworks and strategic choice models is an emphasis on the opportunities presented to senior managers to reshape organizational structures and employment practices, arising from the devolution of responsibilities to NHS trusts. The fieldwork indicated a number of influences on management actions, many of which lay beyond the boundaries of the workplace.

A number of *internal* factors were central to managers' capacity to act strategically. An important influence was the degree of internal stability within the trusts in terms of senior management personnel and the scope of reorganization. The starkest difference was between Northern, which had one chief executive for almost a decade and no merger activity until 2002, and Eastern, which had five chief executives and went through two mergers. These differences had a marked effect on the management process. Not only did it take time for chief executives and other senior managers to gain the trust of their staff, but the willingness of long-serving medical staff to commit themselves to proposed changes was inevitably influenced by judgements about how long they expected the chief executive to remain in post. The current short tenure of health service chief executives reflected in turnover of about 20 per cent per annum does not bode well for effective longer-term staff management (Cole 2002).

A difficulty with many new public management and strategic choice accounts remains a tendency to exaggerate the discretion available to managers: agency is elevated to the neglect of structure, notably the constraints that inhibit managerial actions in a variety of ways. In some cases these contextual constraints are recognized; for example, Kessler *et al.* (2000: 19) emphasize the importance of constraints and choice within a public service context that leaves scope for a 'residual degree of choice'. In general, however, constraints are analysed as external influences that have to be reluctantly accepted or circumvented rather than as integral features of management in the public domain.

From the fieldwork a particular constraint arose from problems of short-termism. During the internal market period each trust was heavily dependent on the funding made available to its local purchasers. Contracts were agreed on an annual basis and disagreements invariably arose between purchasers and providers, leaving aside the financial uncertainties created by GP fund-holders. Moreover, the relationship between pay, finance and contracting in the NHS was complex, with pay increases largely excluded from contract negotiations. This situation reinforced the restrictive budgetary context faced by managers that made it difficult to plan systematic long-term changes in employment practices.

The Labour government indicated that it would move towards longer-term service agreements, but after five years in office this has not happened, with the replacement to contracts, Service and Financial Framework agreements (SaFFs), remaining annual agreements. Other sources of financial uncertainty are related to the Labour government's continuous reorganization of the NHS. For example, senior managers expressed concern that the allocation of 75 per cent of the NHS budget to PCTs could destabilize acute trusts. Similarly, it has been suggested that the plans to reinstate forms of contracting that mirror some of the internal market reforms will create further financial instability (Appleby *et al.* 2002).

Trust managers had to obtain the agreement of a number of interest groups for their corporate plans and capital investment decisions. The Regional Offices of the NHS Executive audited their business plans and monitored their financial performance. The support of the host health authority was essential for capital project approval. In terms of workforce issues managers were wary of antagonizing professional trade union representatives, who frequently took their lead from national policies. The support of the medical royal colleges was crucial in gaining and keeping accreditation for specialist medical training. Thus, although greater discretion over employment matters was formally ceded to NHS managers, central government and other statutory bodies (e.g. the Health and Safety Executive) had unprecedented scope to scrutinize performance and intervene in the management of nominally independent service providers. The Labour government has increased this complexity and interdependence, with trust managers required to collaborate with other organizations in a series of clinical networks, with the need to co-operate a prerequisite for the achievement of a series of centrally defined targets.

The terminology of 'strategic choice' does not do justice to the complex management process within the health service. It suggests that managerial decisions are essentially technical, but this does not capture the dynamics of workplace relations or the intrinsic political dimension of managing in the public domain. Strategic choice perspectives, by directing attention to clearly articulated managerial *actions*, are in danger of ignoring purposeful *inaction*. Managers sometimes decided not to implement government policies (e.g. local pay, the national menu) because they judged that particular policy initiatives were likely to be short-lived or were essentially symbolic and that the impending organizational upheaval would detract from other priorities. A related response was when managers superficially implemented a policy initiative with judicious use of government jargon (e.g. the appointment of directors of modernization) to signal adherence to government policy.

Finally the emphasis within strategic choice frameworks and the new public management directs attention towards the establishment of formal strategies and pays too little attention to strategy implementation and operational issues. The concentration on particular strategic choices is insufficiently sensitive to incremental change that over a sustained period of time can bring about substantial changes in workplace relations that are not reducible to a concentration on strategic choices. Within the health service in general, and the case study trusts in particular, there is no shortage of 'strategy' documents and business plans. The difficulty is that these strategies do not sufficiently inform managerial practice, with poor links between strategic and operational practice, a point that has been noted by the CHI (Commission for Health Improvement 2001b: 13–14). The frustrations that staff often expressed stemmed from operational problems in terms of staffing requirements, equipment problems and the flow of patients through the hospital.

The characteristics of the health service

The concentration on the strategic choices undertaken by managers at workplace level needs to be extended by frameworks that provide a fuller understanding of developments beyond the workplace. In Chapter 2 it was proposed that management reforms and their outcomes at the workplace are shaped more by the distinctive characteristics of the health sector than by the actions of senior managers within individual trusts. To what extent does this provide a more adequate basis for understanding health service employment relations reform?

Expenditure constraints

Since its establishment in 1948 a priority for all governments has been to keep a tight rein on health service expenditure. For much of the post-war period the relatively low levels of UK expenditure on health care in comparison to other OECD countries (Table 2.1) was interpreted as a sign of the cost effectiveness of the NHS. In the last decade a different interpretation of these trends has emerged; namely, that cost constraints have been accompanied by chronic capital under-investment and short-termism, an analysis that is increasingly endorsed by neo-liberal policy analysts (Blackwell and Kruger 2002: 8–13).

Fiscal constraints and the requirements of the accounting regime introduced as part of the internal market reforms have continued to exert a strong influence over workplace relations. An additional dimension of this accounting regime that is becoming increasingly important is the Labour government's endorsement of the Private Finance Initiative as the main source of new primary hospital facilities. During the lifespan of these contracts (25–30 years) the revenue consequences for trusts are substantial in servicing PFI contracts. These expenditure flows will have a major impact on trust expenditure, and for critics of PFI these revenue payments can only be achieved by pay bill reductions and reduced capacity (for an overview see Health Committee 2002).

The extent of financial difficulties varied between the trusts, but in all three cases similar responses to budgetary constraints emerged, with financial difficulties impacting on staffing policies. Vacancy freezes and the widespread use of temporary contracts were the most common responses during the internal market period. At Eastern, the trust had a corporate aim that 20 per cent of staff would be employed in a 'flexible' manner, and at Northern fixed-term contracts were also widespread and often of only three to six months' duration, although they were often renewed. At Western senior managers established a corporate objective to reduce staffing costs by 5 per cent over a five-year period.

Low levels of health service expenditure in comparison to other OECD countries impacted on staffing levels because the pay bill accounted for approximately two-thirds of current trust expenditure. At Eastern, CHI (2001a) commented on low staffing complements in nursing alongside substantial increases in workload. Similar comments were made at Northern, with concerns that low staffing levels compromised standards of care in several areas of the trust (CHI 2002a). These concerns were reflected in the staff opinion survey, with only 30 per cent of staff at Eastern and Northern agreeing with the statement 'In my department there are enough staff' (see Table 6.5). At Western, staffing levels were higher relative to activity and bed numbers, but CHI (2002b) still reported many critical comments about insufficient numbers of nursing staff. Managerial and ancillary staff also pointed to an increased workload that was not accompanied by higher staffing levels.

The advent of the Labour government in 1997 led to the adoption of restrictive Conservative plans for public expenditure for its first two years in office. Following this period of restraint, a gradual reappraisal of the expenditure requirements of the NHS has emerged that culminated in the unprecedented increases in health service expenditure unveiled in the April 2002 budget. Planned health service expenditure will increase by 7.4 per cent per annum after inflation over the five years to 2007–08. In expenditure terms planned NHS spending in the UK will increase from £65.4 billion in 2002–03 to £105.6 billion in 2007–08 (Treasury 2002). It is almost inconceivable that such large increases in expenditure will not have some beneficial impact on staffing and pay levels.

Although the fieldwork was concluded prior to the most recent expenditure increases, up to mid-2002 the majority of the workforce perceived that 'little had changed'. Among some staff these views stemmed from a concern that increased expenditure was to be channelled into the private sector via PFI contracts and an increased role for the private sector in service provision. Medical staff in particular expressed concern that resources were being used to achieve political objectives that didn't always accord with their own clinical priorities. For senior managers there was a 'reality gap' between increased expenditure and the ability of trusts to deliver. As one CEO commented:

> As targets are now linked to money we have got no excuses. In the past we could easily say, 'You haven't given us the money,' and also the public won't accept that any more [but] there's not been a reality check yet, in terms of the amount of money coming out and what's expected for it. Certainly there is much more money, but expectations about what we can deliver for that have not been matched together. This year no way can we meet all the cancer targets. We had an 8 per cent increase – a big increase – but we think we need 9–10 per cent to deliver everything that is expected of us. (Interview notes, August 2001)

All the trusts continued to confront severe financial pressures. For example, the newly merged Northern trust had accumulated a £6 million deficit by September 2002 (Northern Trust Board Update, September 2002). This was attributed to pressures relating to waiting list activity, and expenditure on bank nurses and locum doctors, as well as difficulties in delivering previously agreed savings plans.

The ratcheting-up of performance targets by the government and increased public expectations may outstrip the capacity of many trusts to meet their targets, especially when continuing staff and other capacity constraints (e.g. beds, operating theatres) are taken into account. The Labour government's short-term target-orientated approach appraises the NHS predominantly in quantitative rather than qualitative terms, but many of the medium-term investments in the NHS in terms of improved information management, enhanced pay and conditions for medical and other staff, and the continuing cost of new drug treatments, will only indirectly contribute to achieving these targets over the longer term (Thornton 2002: 4). For health service staff increased expenditure should ease staff shortages and ensure that they work in more modern infrastructure. Considerable uncertainty remains, however, as to whether increased NHS expenditure will reverse the process of work intensification that they have experienced over the last decade. Trust managers will continue to face budgetary pressures as they strive to achieve more stringent government targets, but in a context in which public sympathy for 'overstretched' health service staff can be expected to diminish.

Centralization

The second characteristic of the NHS, centralization, remained a pervasive feature of the trust context and had a major bearing on health service management and employment relations. It has become conventional wisdom that there was much greater scope for local innovation in employment practices during the mid-1990s, with the emphasis on trust freedoms, than since 1997, when a more centrally directed performance management framework has been established. The contrast has been overstated and remains a question of degree rather than a fundamental shift in policy.

Successive Conservative governments in the 1980s recognized the scope to develop much stronger central control and management of the health service. A crucial step was the establishment of general management that made possible the introduction of the internal market and the establishment of NHS trusts. In addition, however, as one senior health service manager noted, the emphasis on management autonomy was misplaced, because 'sometimes it feels that the main *raison d'être* of general management is not to manage local services but to make detailed ministerial accountability a constitutional reality' (Edwards 1993: 183). In the early 1990s a brief period ensued in which the first-wave trusts were granted considerable autonomy. Soon, however, the Conservative government became concerned about the political consequences of autonomy (e.g. high profile job losses) and their inability to monitor effectively developments in a proliferating number of trusts for which they were held responsible. The remedy was increased central direction of the health service and the development of hospital league tables and performance indicators, which has resulted in the current plethora of audit and inspection mechanisms.

During the Conservative government period managers in the case study trusts were required to achieve particular targets (e.g. management cost reductions) and there was great nervousness among senior managers about how much they could depart from national policy guidance on issues such as market-testing, as the experience at Western illustrated. Since the election of the Labour government, the audit culture has been extended by the development of the star rating system and increased inspection arrangements. The requirement to fulfil a range of contradictory targets has become the dominant preoccupation of managers. One consequence has been that the importance of centrally derived targets has increased senior management legitimacy to shape clinical practice. As one trust chief executive stated,

> We have a very clear policy that we don't interfere in clinical decisions, but we'll remind clinicians about their responsibilities in terms of long waiters – no-one waits over 18 months here. (Interview notes, August 2001)

For medical staff, performance targets risk distorting medical priorities, and this is an increasing source of tension between managers and doctors (National Audit Office, cited in Paton 2002: 134; Rosenthal 2002). Nationally the pressure on managers to achieve targets has led them to make inappropriate adjustments to waiting lists, a process that has been uncovered in nine trusts but is likely to be more common than this figure suggests (National Audit Office 2001). The risk of cheating not only reduces the credibility of the targets but paradoxically reinforces audit, but in a form based on compliance with bureaucratic procedures, further eroding management autonomy (Hood 2001: 308).

The fieldwork identified a series of additional problems associated with a top-down target orientated culture. First, staff resented the impositions of targets that they had not devised and that they argued had only a tenuous link with their primary job requirements. As one director of human resources commented:

> you see politicians exhorting CEOs to manage their organizations in a more involving way, the paradox for staff is what involvement have CEOs had [in shaping targets]? (Interview notes, April 2001)

Clinical staff suggested that the targets impeded their professional autonomy and increased their workload because not only had targets to be achieved but these outcomes had to be meticulously documented. The Audit Commission (2002: 22) has pinpointed targets and the paperwork associated with them as the most important reason why public sector workers leave their jobs, cited by half of former public sector workers. A related concern was that the target culture militated against staff involvement despite government exhortations to increase it. As one national trade union officer commented bluntly:

> why do you [managers] listen to your staff unless they have got something to say about how you are going to meet your waiting list target? That's why voice

is getting lost, it's not genuinely about innovation it's about delivery of political targets. (Interview notes, March 2002)

These sentiments were echoed by clinical staff who viewed the targets predominantly as political objectives to bolster support for the Labour government. This widely shared belief ensured that clinical staff had limited commitment to achieving the government's targets. Senior managers recognized that their continued job tenure, and the star ratings awarded to each trust, depended on the achievement of targets. They were anxious to persuade medical staff to undertake more work to reduce waiting lists, which often had to be undertaken at weekends. In a context in which consultants felt ill-disposed towards the government and chronically overworked, they were very reluctant to undertake additional work and demanded that trust managers pay them rates that they could command if operating at local private hospitals.

A further consequence of centralized control of the health service is that governments with large parliamentary majorities have faced few constraints in initiating plans for health service reorganization. Imprecise reform plans have been passed into legislation that managers have converted into operational management arrangements. The much repeated assertion that the health service is impervious to change is wide of the mark. The internal market is the archetypal example of this process, which, from the publication of the notoriously vague *Working for Patients* White Paper in January 1989 to the establishment of the internal market and the first trusts in April 1991, took little more than two years. This type of reform process, however, has led to a bias towards perpetual structural tinkering that distracts the workforce from service delivery. This bias towards structural reform has led to a neglect of operational processes and inhibits efforts to develop a more healthy workplace relations climate.

Professionalism in the workforce

The influence of professional staff and their representative organizations has been integral to the development of the health service. The Conservative government viewed professional staff as an impediment to reorganization. The establishment of general management, subsequent market-led reforms and tighter controls over performance has led to closer managerial control over professional staff.

Medical staff argued that their autonomy had diminished, but this did not relate to their direct control to treat patients as they saw fit. For many nurses their roles were more constrained; they had often expanded their roles, but this occurred within a more defined network of protocols and clinical pathways. Consequently, professional work has not in any straightforward sense become Taylorized as some of the literature reviewed in Chapter 1 suggested. Instead there has been a more complex redefinition of the role of professional staff that had a number of dimensions.

There was a strong sense among medical and nursing staff that all governments were imposing a low-trust model of management on professional staff, and they interpreted the audit explosion as a tangible expression of the loss of trust by governments in their performance. Alan Fox defined low-trust employment relations as a situation in which a variety of management controls were implemented that included tight supervision and formal rules of conduct to monitor and control opportunistic behaviour of staff. As one clinician stated to the CHI team at Western, 'Management are more concerned with meeting targets than treating patients.' It was acknowledged that these low-trust systems arose partly from failings of professional self-regulation, but systems based on distrust of professional actions are reinforcing changes in patient behaviour, undermining staff morale. One fieldwork respondent documented a catalogue of abusive behaviour that she had witnessed in her trust and asked plaintively, 'What has happened to people that they hold the health service and its staff in such low regard?' (Interview notes, July 2001).

Managers, however, recognized the contradictions of these low-trust approaches, not least because they shared some of the ambivalence of medical and nursing colleagues about the audit culture, and they continued to rely on nursing and medical staff to achieve government targets. While they exhorted staff to meet government targets, they continued to use more traditional forms of management that incorporated high-trust assumptions of professional discretion and autonomy. Managers therefore were able to draw on professional values of commitment to high service standards and employees' intrinsic interest in their job, to encourage staff to work beyond their contractual obligations. This managerial approach, which transmitted a government imposed performance culture to frontline staff alongside a continuing expectation that nursing and medical staff would maintain high professional standards of service, increased the pressure on the workforce.

Workload pressure has increased because professional roles continue to alter substantially. Health service reforms have placed obligations on professional staff to undertake more managerial work in additional to their professional duties. This has been evident in the attempts to involve medical staff in managerial roles and the shift in the role of ward sisters towards ward managers. In some cases senior managers acknowledged that the balance had swung too far and that professional staff needed to focus more on clinical care and relinquish some of their managerial duties. It was acknowledged also that staff had sometimes been ceded responsibility without control, which had a corrosive effect on staff morale. Because government targets pervade the working lives of professional staff, managers felt more confident in reorientating professional staff towards a more clinically orientated agenda. This has enabled the extension of clinical roles, including the development of nurse consultant and nurse practitioner roles, but these roles are shaped more forcibly by trust requirements than would have been the case in the past.

A final issue related to the extent that the professional character of the workforce shaped trade union practice. Long-standing rivalry between the RCN and Unison reflects different conceptions of union purpose and the well documented 'tribalism' in the health service (see Hunter 2002). In the case study trusts, however, there was little sense that this rivalry constituted a central issue in workplace relations. It was only at Western that some tensions emerged between Unison and the RCN over generic working, and these differences were not central to workplace relations.

The historical differences between the RCN and Unison remain very significant in terms of membership composition, affiliation to the TUC/Labour Party and distinctive approaches to trade union organization. Nevertheless the fieldwork indicated that these differences are narrowing as the material conditions and work experience of their members become more similar. In contrast to the 1980s when ancillary staff bore the brunt of restructuring initiatives, as the fieldwork indicated, nursing staff have been more directly affected by workplace reforms and have been confronted with increased workloads and challenges to their professional autonomy.

Government reforms have been designed to reduce status boundaries between separate occupational groups by encouraging training and development activities for all staff. The rapid expansion of health care assistants has ensured more interaction between previously separate occupational groups. These changes are reflected in the *Agenda for Change* proposals that will harmonize many conditions of service, widen the Nurses' Pay Review Body remit to include more non-nursing staff, and facilitate changes in working practices. This latter goal is being spearheaded by The Modernisation Agency's 'Changing Workforce Programme', which envisages radical alterations in professional boundaries and job roles in the NHS.

The RCN provides a good illustration of the impact of these developments. In the 1970s as income policies impacted on their membership, the RCN became a certified trade union, developed a shop stewards network and restructured its organization to enable greater membership participation. In 1995 the RCN abolished its rule prohibiting industrial action, and in autumn 2000 almost 80 per cent of members voted to admit level 3 health care assistants into associate membership (Royal College of Nursing 2001). This establishes a precedent for the RCN in terms of recruiting beyond its traditional base that could prove significant as the composition of the workforce continues to evolve. This shift of emphasis away from its primary pre-occupation with professional nursing issues has been uneven, and this was illustrated by its initially slow response to PFI, which the RCN viewed erroneously as having few implications for its membership (see Bach 2002: 330; Kessler and Heron 2001). The RCN has also proved reluctant to invest in developing its labour relations capacity, despite the importance of the *Agenda for Change* proposals. It remains to be seen whether the partial diminution of the differences between the RCN and Unison encourages greater inter-union co-operation or intensifies competition for members.

In summary there are strong grounds for suggesting that the central characteristics of the health sector outlined in Chapter 2 have a powerful impact on workplace developments. This was evident from the similarity in management approach towards a diverse range of organizational and employment issues, indicating that isomorphic pressures are very strong in the health service. Of the three characteristics identified, the fiscal context and the centralized structure of the health service remain intact and continue to shape strongly workplace practice. The role of professional staff, especially doctors and nurses, remains pivotal to understanding workplace employment relations, but the role of these occupational groups has altered markedly. This has arisen from: government reforms that have recast the role of professionals, ensuring that they are more responsive to managerial requirements; increased criticism of the professions, especially the medical profession, that has eroded its influence and undermined its ability to regulate its own affairs; and the changing composition of the workforce and altered occupational roles that are challenging the monopoly of expertise of the traditional professions. Not all changes were externally generated: there was some sense in the fieldwork, although it was not a primary focus of the research, that the values of professional staff were altering and that an ideology of altruism, sometimes termed the public sector ethos, was waning (see Allen 2001: 17; Public Administration Select Committee 2002: 15–16). Consequently, the traditional occupational identities and behaviours associated with professional staff are no longer as powerful an influence on workplace relations as has traditionally been the case in hospitals. The danger is that the baby of professional autonomy and staff commitment may be thrown out with the bathwater of restrictive professional practice.

Finding a cure?

This study has highlighted radical changes in the organization, management and practice of staff management in the health service over the last two decades. What are the policy implications that can be drawn from the research?

Health service reform

The root cause of many of the problems of low morale cited by fieldwork respondents related to the impact of a continuous process of restructuring in which the workforce had little sense that they could influence the process of reform at local or national level. These feelings of frustration held by managerial as well as other staff were exemplified by the disenchantment with the targets employees were expected to meet. The imposition of targets has improved the accountability of the health service and can assist the management process when targets are used as a guide to action. The shortcomings of the target culture were therefore less to do with the existence of targets in themselves, but rather the manner in which they were devised, the type of targets adopted, and the timescales involved. Because targets are established at national level for the whole of the health service, they are not tailored to local priorities. Each trust should be able to nominate a smaller number of targets that they view as reflecting local priorities for action, complementing a small number of national priorities.

These local targets should be drawn up in consultation with other local stakeholders, contributing to broadening the decision-making process within the health service. A more locally focused approach would avoid the danger that a trust performing effectively is given a target that penalizes its previous good performance, as may occur, for example, with targets geared to percentage reductions in absence or vacancy rates. It is much more logical to benchmark performance across trusts, rather than to establish an arbitrary national target. Overall the aim should be to highlight performance outliers rather than to enforce a punitive blame culture, as currently exists, in which managers are removed for failing to achieve targets. In addition, the timescale for the achievement of key targets should be extended to a five-year period with periodic monitoring to check progress. This would not only militate against the short-termism that pervades the health service and that inhibits more effective management but it would also prevent staff time being overly focused on the collection and reporting of information for central government purposes.

As with a number of other issues related to the balance between national requirements and local discretion, an immediate objection relates to the degree that any government is prepared to sanction some local variation in service mix or standards within an avowedly *national* health service. In practice more local priority-setting does not necessarily contradict the Labour government's approach. While it has been highly critical of variations between trusts in terms of service provision and outcomes, its star ratings system and proposals for foundation hospitals are premised on an assumption that not all trusts will perform to the same level, although it emphasizes that minimum standards have to be achieved. It remains to be seen whether a more diversified system of health provision arising from the proposed establishment of foundation hospitals and increased use of the private sector is compatible with national service standards. It may be that if the government seeks to establish a health service that is genuinely geared towards local needs then it will have to accept more diversity in practice. This approach would also fit in with the post-Fordist rhetoric that the Labour government espouses in terms of the importance of services being orientated to the diverse needs of individual consumers, rather than geared to the convenience of public sector producers.

It is probable that history will repeat itself with the development of foundation hospitals mirroring the evolution of trusts, with controversy giving way to acceptance as more foundation hospitals emerge. The strong isomorphic pressures that led to more than 500 NHS trusts being established between 1991 and 1995 can be expected to re-emerge, assuming that the financial incentives are sufficiently attractive to ensure trust managers seek foundation status. The development of foundation hospitals, an increased role for the private sector, and financial incentives for providers linked to performance, is the emerging political consensus on the future of the NHS. It would be a supreme irony if a Labour government, which established the NHS, presided over the creation of a mixed economy of health services to a degree that eluded the Conservative governments of 1979–97.

A second issue concerns the relationship between politics and management in the health service. The implementation of new public management reforms was intended to demarcate politics from management, with policy decisions taken by the government and implementation the responsibility of local managers. In addition to tiers of general managers the NHS Executive was established with responsibility for policy implementation. As this study has illustrated, the attempts to separate the responsibility for policy from the management of services has failed in the NHS, with constant central government intervention arising from the political sensitivity and fiscal consequences of health service expenditure. The Labour government has abandoned the attempt to demarcate politics and management. The roles of NHS chief executive and permanent secretary of the Department of Health have been combined, with the NHS Executive reabsorbed into the Department of Health.

This has led to an emerging orthodoxy that the health service has become too political and that this politicization has inhibited the effective management of the NHS. The solution that is frequently proposed is for the NHS to become semi-independent from government and reconstituted as a public corporation along the lines of the BBC or the Bank of England with its own constitution (Futures Group 2002: 8–10; Hutton 2000: 76–7). This solution is flawed in its own terms, because the formal separation of political and managerial spheres has not ensured the absence of political intervention. The experience of the nationalized industries and the executive agencies (e.g. events at the Child Support Agency and the Prison Service) indicate ministerial preferences for private and direct pressure on key individuals, rather than the use of formal arm's-length ministerial powers. Moreover, the problems of the health service arise not from too much politics but too little. Political debate is couched in narrow terms linked to the achievement of short-term waiting list targets and orientated to convincing the public of government achievements, rather than engaging in debate about potential alternative futures and wider public health issues that scarcely register in the current debate about the future of the health service (Iliffe 2002). Instead, a much wider debate is needed about the values and objectives of the health service that would allow more detailed scrutiny and greater clarity over the scope of NHS provision.

These issues are integrally linked to the fundamental lack of democratic control of the health service in which staff and the public feel disconnected from a centralized health service. There is little opportunity for public involvement in the NHS, with all trust board positions and higher tiers of the health service being appointed. Trust boards do not even offer the modicum of accountability that shareholders can exercise at annual general meetings. Although trusts conduct AGMs that are open to the public, unlike public companies in which shareholders can vote to sanction or remove directors, no such sanctions exist for trust boards (see Clatworthy *et al.* 2000: 168). The possibility of introducing some form of voting mechanism to enable the resident population served by a trust to endorse or censor management proposals at the AGM requires further exploration. In the absence of any local democratic control over health services the election of independent MPs such as Dr Richard Taylor in Kidderminster becomes the only way that local communities can express frustration at their lack of control over health service provision.

The constitution of trust boards requires reform. It was striking that in not one of the fieldwork interviews did any member of staff ever mention the role of the non-executive directors (with the important exception of the trust chair), suggesting that non-executive directors have little legitimacy and no clear constituency that they represent. This finding mirrors similar findings about health authority members in the 1980s (Ham 1986: 127). The membership of trust boards should include wider constituencies than at present, and these should be linked more explicitly to differing stakeholder interests. In particular, the election of staff members to trust boards would allow some of the lack of voice that staff currently perceive in trusts to be addressed.

The management of employment relations

Human resource management issues have become more central to the management agenda for NHS trusts since 1997, although this cannot be equated with a higher profile for the HR function within trusts. Staff shortages in particular have ensured that workforce issues have remained prominent; and even though recruitment for many occupational groups is likely to ease, issues of retention are paramount and the need to improve staff morale remains a key priority (Department of Health 2002a). Although the national HR strategy *Working Together* was an important signal that the low priority assigned to HR issues was changing, in practice this change has been primarily symbolic. *Working Together* encouraged a bureaucratic response in keeping with traditional HR practice in the NHS that focused on the production of management policies rather than altering staff and managerial behaviour. This type of response was influenced also by HR considerations remaining subservient to other trust requirements (waiting time and financial targets) and the uncertainties created by mergers and continuing reorganization.

The publication, in July 2002, of *HR in the NHS Plan* (Department of Health 2002a) represents a welcome departure from *Working Together*. It signifies an attempt to link the approach to HR to the overall NHS modernization agenda rather than being an adjunct to reform initiatives. Instead of focusing on bureaucratic outcomes in terms of developing policies, it is more concerned with addressing tangible problems and making the NHS a more attractive employer. It underlines the importance of HR for NHS performance and emphasizes that the HR function needs to become more central to NHS decision-making. These sentiments are timely.

Although nationally staff shortages were especially acute at the end of the 1990s, staff concerns are related not solely to the numbers of staff employed but also to the difficulties that staff confront in getting their concerns about staff shortages acknowledged and acted upon. The apparently haphazard manner in which staffing levels are decided, and the perception among employees that they have little influence over staffing levels and working hours, contribute to a sense that they have little power to alter working conditions and staffing levels. These findings echo national findings about staff management, with substantial unexplained differences between and within trusts in ward staffing levels (Audit Commission 2001b). The huge financial burden for the NHS of employing temporary nursing staff alongside the additional pressure that it places on ward staff have been widely noted (Audit Commission 2001c; Meadows *et al.* 2000: 38–9). The implications for individual nurses of poor workforce planning and a limited ability to influence their own working patterns was highlighted in an RCN survey of 6,000 members in which 43 per cent of nursing staff were not working their preferred shift patterns and relied on support from colleagues rather than managers to help them balance home and work commitments (Royal College of Nursing 2002: 22–5).

Staff concerns about perceptions of bullying and harassment, which surfaced at several of the trusts and was confirmed nationally by research among nurses (Royal College of Nursing 2002), raises more fundamental issues about the contradictions within the national HR agenda. Managers are required to improve the working lives of staff, increase flexibility and involve staff more fully. At the same time the pressure to reduce absence and improve performance encouraged a top-down management style and an HR approach that focused on increasing employee *output* but was less orientated to staff concerns.

The paradox is that the majority of staff interviewed retained a high level of commitment to their jobs, but their morale appeared to be low. This apparent paradox, noted a decade ago (Edwards and Whitston 1993: 166–72), stemmed from the inherent interest that many staff found within their jobs, and a strong public ethos that stemmed from both their professional socialization and their commitment to the values of the health service. Similar findings about the existence of a distinctive public ethos among health service staff and the importance that public sector workers attach to 'making a difference' have been noted in many studies (Audit Commission 2002; Steele 2000).

High levels of commitment, however, which have been a key strength for the NHS, are in danger of becoming its Achilles heel. First, because the majority of staff 'want to make a difference', they are genuinely concerned about the delivery of an effective service. When they perceive that they are unable to deliver such a service, they appear either to internalize many of these shortcomings, resulting in high levels of stress, or to engage in bullying and other forms of behaviour that undermine staff morale. This response is especially likely within a service industry in which the quality of service delivered and the individual person delivering that service are inseparable. Second, because the boundaries of many health service jobs are not easily delineated, it is relatively straightforward for the government and managers to increase workloads. Health service staff are more accepting of increased workloads than staff in other occupations that have more instrumental attitudes to work or where increased workloads are more transparent. There is little tradition of contesting or bargaining over work-effort levels in the health service, and many NHS staff remain reluctant to take industrial action. Shifting the burden of adjustment of increased workloads onto employees is a trend that has been noted in numerous studies in the UK and elsewhere (Allan 1998; Williams *et al.* 1998: 16–17).

Consequently the health service trades on the commitment of its staff. As such, over the last two decades the role of the state as a good employer has been undermined, despite the existence of a raft of progressive employment policies and a strong commitment to training and development activity (Audit Commission 2001a). The state remains a model employer, but the model that has been implemented within the health service over the last two decades stems directly from recent organizational and managerial reforms. This has channelled managers into a short-term approach towards staff management that has focused on tighter control of staff, more intensive working patterns and changes in the composition of the workforce. The limits of this approach as a route to improved performance are becoming apparent as evidence of low staff morale and problems of retention surface with increasing regularity (Finlayson 2002; Meadows *et al.* 2000; Royal College of Nursing 2002).

Improvements in human resource management are integrally linked with wider reforms that move away from the short-termism that has taken hold in the health service. Two HR issues require attention. First, the widespread assumption that the HR function has little to contribute to improving staff management in the NHS needs to be contested. Although effective staff management cannot be confined to the HR function, at present, within health service trusts and regional offices there is no top management role that is specifically charged with taking into account the implications for staff of organizational change. The establishment of PCTs with little if any HR expertise can only exacerbate this problem.

Of equal concern is the *Shared Services* initiative, which envisages a more centralized HR service for the health service arising from the development of a standardized electronic staff record (Department of Health 2002a: 33–4). This centralized technology-driven solution will hollow out much of the existing trust-based HR function, exacerbating the lack of visibility and influence of the HR function. It also has the potential to undermine context-specific HR knowledge that is integral to facilitating change at workplace level. Moreover, as with other recent national initiatives in the NHS, such as NHS Direct, it appears that substituting technology for labour is an increasingly important component of the Labour government's reform agenda (for related arguments see Leys 2001). The task of revitalizing the HR function has been recognized as an important component of the revamped national HR strategy, and this is an urgent task as the health service embarks on the most significant reforms of the pay system since its inception.

This task is related to the pressing requirement to increase employee voice within health service trusts and to consult staff more fully. The most important source of frustration noted in this and other studies is the perception among staff that they have little control over what happens at their workplace and that their voice is not heard and acted upon (Allen 2001; Meadows *et al.* 2001; Royal College of Nursing 2002: 69). Health service managers have developed an impressive array of top-down communication mechanisms, but these need to be matched by genuine scope for the expression of staff opinion. This lack of voice is being exacerbated by diminishing union influence, and by the difficulties that staff face in fulfilling their representative roles arising from a process of work intensification. Health service trade unions need to play a more central role within health service trusts, but this presents a major challenge in revitalizing workplace organization where few signs of renewal are evident.

Since its inception in 1948 the health service has frequently been perceived as being 'in crisis', and periods of heightened public concern have often been matched by structural reforms of the health service. Conservative governments left a contradictory legacy because of their inability to convert their ideological hostility towards the public sector into a coherent programe of reform. Managerial and market-style reforms fostered structural change and altered staff behaviour, but centralized systems of pay determination remained intact. The emphasis on greater management autonomy to reshape human resource management practices was constrained by fiscal restrictions, frequent political interventions and the resistance of highly organized professional groups.

The Labour government elected in 1997 intensified the process of managerial reform, but its ministers shared the predilection of their predecessors for constant intervention from the centre. The unrelenting stream of initiatives and targets has disorientated the workforce and distracted managers from longer-term policy development. This approach has inhibited the development of a more strategic conception of human resource management. The Labour government recognizes the problems that arise from the need to achieve visible improvements in health service performance linked to short-term electoral cycles and has tried to foster improvements in human resource management practice. The difficulty, however, is that the Labour government has continued with the managerialist assumptions of the previous Conservative governments and defined improved performance in largely quantitative terms that have reinforced the pressure on the workforce. If the Labour government is to find a cure to the problems that confront the NHS workforce, then a more radical break with the existing managerialist paradigm is required.

References

Abbott, P., and Meerabeau, L. (1998), 'Professionals, professionalization and the caring professions', in P. Abbott and L. Meerabeau, *The Sociology of the Caring Professions*, 2nd edn. London: UCL Press.

ACAS (1978), *Royal Commission on the Health Service: ACAS Evidence*, Report No. 12. London: ACAS.

Ackroyd, S., and Bolton, S. (1999), 'It is not Taylorism: mechanisms of work intensification in the provision of gynaecological services in an NHS hospital', *Work Employment and Society* 13(2), 369–87.

Ackroyd, S., Hughes, J., and Soothill, K. (1989), 'Public sector services and their management', *Journal of Management Studies* 26(6), 603–19.

Allan, C. (1998), 'The elasticity of endurance: work intensification and workplace flexibility in the Queensland public hospital system', *New Zealand Journal of Industrial Relations* 23(3), 131–51.

Allen, I. (2001), *Stress Among Ward Sisters and Charge Nurses*. London: Policy Studies Institute.

Appleby, J., Devlin, N., Deeming, C., and Harrison, T. (2002), 'Internal market: This little piggy . . .', *Health Service Journal* 112(5818), 24–9.

Arnold, J., Coombs, C., Loan-Clarke, J., Park, J., Preston, D., and Wilkinson, A. (2001), *Looking Good? The Attractiveness of the NHS as an Employer*. Loughborough: Loughborough University.

Arrowsmith, J., and Sisson, K. (1999), 'Pay and working-time: towards organisation based systems?', *British Journal of Industrial Relations* 37(1), 51–75.

Atkinson, J. (1984), 'Manpower strategies for flexible organizations', *Personnel Management* 16, 28–31.

Atkinson, P., and van den Noord, P. (2001), 'Managing public expenditure: some policy issues and a framework for analysis', OECD Economics Working Papers. Paris: OECD. Available at: *http://www.oecd.org/eco/eco*

Audit Commission (2001a), *Hidden Talents: Education, Training and Development for Healthcare Staff in NHS Trusts.* London: Audit Commission.

Audit Commission (2001b), *Ward Staffing: Review of National Findings.* London: Audit Commission.

Audit Commission (2001c), *Brief Encounters: Getting the Best from Temporary Nursing Staff.* London: Audit Commission.

Audit Commission (2002), *Recruitment and Retention: A Public Service Workforce for the Twenty-first Century.* London: Audit Commission.

Bach, S. (1989), *Too High a Price to Pay: Competitive Tendering for Domestic Services in the NHS?* Coventry: Industrial Relations Research Unit.

Bach, S. (1995), 'Restructuring the personnel function: the case of NHS trusts', *Human Resource Management Journal* 5(2), 99–115.

Bach, S. (1999a), 'From national pay determination to qualified market relations: NHS pay bargaining reform', *Historical Studies in Industrial Relations* 8 (Autumn), 99–115.

Bach, S. (1999b), 'Personnel managers: managing to change?' in S. Corby and G.White (eds), *Employee Relations in the Public Services.* London: Routledge.

Bach, S. (2001), 'Rolling back the state? Health sector reform and the restructuring of employment relations in Europe', *Competition and Change* 5(4), 335–54.

Bach. S. (2002), 'Muddling through on modernisation: public service employment relations under Labour', *British Journal of Industrial Relations* 40(2), 319–39.

Bach, S., and Della Rocca, G. (2000), 'The management strategies of public service employers in Europe', *Industrial Relations Journal* 31(2), 82–97.

Bach, S., and Sisson, K. (2000), 'Personnel management in perspective', in S. Bach and K. Sisson (eds), *Personnel Management: A Comprehensive Guide to Theory and Practice*, 3rd edn. Oxford: Blackwell.

Bach, S., and Winchester, D. (1994), 'Opting out of pay devolution? The prospects for local pay bargaining in UK public services', *British Journal of Industrial Relations* 32(2), 264–82.

Bach, S., and Winchester, D. (2003), 'Industrial relations in the public sector', in P. K. Edwards, (ed.), *Industrial Relations*, 2nd edn. Oxford: Blackwell.

Bach, S., Bordogna, L., Dell'Aringa, C., Della Rocca, G., and Winchester, D. (eds) (1999), *Public Service Employment Relations in Europe: Transformation, Modernisation or Inertia?* London: Routledge.

Bacon, N., and Storey, J. (2000), 'New employee strategies in Britain: towards individualism or partnership?', *British Journal of Industrial Relations* 38(3), 407–27.

Barley, S., and Kunda, G. (2001), 'Bringing work back in', *Organization Science* 12(1), 76–95.

Barnard, K., and Harrison, S. (1986), 'Labour relations in health service management', *Social Science and Medicine* 22(11), 1213–28.

Bartlett, W. (1991), 'Quasi-markets and contracts: a markets and hierarchies perspective on NHS reform', *Public Money and Management* 11(3), 53–60.

Barzelay, M. (2001), *The New Public Management: Improving Research and Policy Dialogue*. Berkeley: University of California Press.

Benson, L., Bruce, A., and Forbes, T. (2001), 'From competition to collaboration in the delivery of health care: England and Scotland compared', *Journal of Nursing Management* 9, 213–20.

Blackwell, N., and Kruger, D. (2002), *Better Healthcare For All: Replacing the NHS Monopoly*. London: Centre for Policy Studies.

Blair, T. (2002), *The Courage of Our Convictions: Why Reform of the Public Services is the Route to Social Justice*. London: Fabian Society.

Bosanquet, N. (1979), 'The search for a system', in N. Bosanquet (ed.), *Industrial Relations in the NHS: The Search for a System*. London: King's Fund.

Bottery, M. (1998), *Professionals and Policy*. London: Cassell.

Boyne, G. (2002), 'Public and private management: what's the difference?', *Journal of Management Studies* 39(1), 97–122.

British Medical Association (1989), *Special Report on the Government's White Paper 'Working for Patients'*. London: BMA.

Brown, W., and Rowthorne, B. (1990), *A Public Services Pay Policy*, Fabian Tract 542. London: Fabian Society.

Buchan, J. (1995), 'Patient-focus pocus', *Nursing Management* 2(7), 6–7.

Buchan, J. (1999), 'The greying of the UK nursing workforce: implications for employment policy and practice', *Journal of Advanced Nursing* 33(9), 818–26.

Buchan, J. (2000), 'Health sector reform and human resources: lessons from the United Kingdom', *Health Policy and Planning* 15(3), 319–25.

Buchan, J. (2002), 'Agenda for change: bitter pill', *Health Service Journal* 112(5816), 24–7.

Buchan, J., and Seccombe, I. (1994), 'The changing role of the NHS personnel function', in R. Robinson, and J. Le Grand, (eds), *Evaluating the NHS Reforms*. London: King's Fund.

Buchan, J., and Seccombe, I. (2002), *Behind the Headlines: A Review of the UK Labour Market in 2001*. London: RCN.

Buchan, J., Seccombe, I., and Smith, G. (1998), *Nurses Work: An Analysis of the UK Nursing Labour Market*. Aldershot: Ashgate.

Burawoy, M. (1979), *Manufacturing Consent: Changes in the Labour Process Under Monopoly Capitalism*. Chicago: University of Chicago Press.

Burchell, B., Lapido, D., and Wilkinson, F. (eds) (2002), *Job Insecurity and Work Intensification*. London: Routledge.

Burchill, F. (1995), 'Professional unions in the National Health Service: issues and membership trends', *Review of Employment Topics* 3(1), 13–42.

Burchill, F. (2000), 'The pay review body system: a comment and a consequence', *Historical Studies in Industrial Relations* 10, 141–57.

Burchill, F., and Casey, A. (1996), *Human Resource Management: The NHS: A Case Study*. London: Macmillan.

Butler, P. (1995), 'Walker wants a brave new world', *Health Service Journal* 105 (5471), 15.

Cabinet Office (1999), *Modernising Government*, Cm. 4310. London: The Stationery Office.

Caines, E. (1993), 'The impact of trusts in the management of the NHS', in E. Peck and P. Spurgeon, (eds), *NHS Trusts in Practice*. Harlow: Longman.

Calman, K., Hunter, D., and May, A. (2001), *Things Can Only Get Better: A Commentary on Implementing the NHS Plan*. Durham: University of Durham Business School.

Carpenter, M. (1988), *Working for Health: The History of COHSE*. London: Lawrence & Wishart.

Carr, F. (1999), 'Local bargaining in the National Health Service: new approaches to employee relations', *Industrial Relations Journal* 30(3), 197–212.

Carter, B., and Fairbrother, P. (1999), 'The transformation of British public-sector industrial relations: from model employer to marketized relations', *Historical Studies in Industrial Relations* 7, 119–46.

Carter, B., and Poynter, G. (1999), 'Unions in a changing climate: MSF and Unison experiences in the new public sector', *Industrial Relations Journal* 30(5), 499–513.

Certification Officer (2002), *Annual Report*. London: Certification Office for Trade Unions and Employers' Associations.

Chandler, A. (1962), *Strategy and Structure*. Cambridge, Mass.: MIT.

Child, J. (1997), 'Strategic choice in the analysis of action, structure, organizations and environment: retrospect and prospect', *Organizational Studies* 18(1), 43–76.

Clark, T., Elsby, M., and Love, S. (2001), *Twenty-Five Years of Falling Investment? Trends in Capital Spending on Public Services*, Briefing Note 20. London: Institute for Fiscal Studies.

Clarke, J., Gewirtz, S., and McLaughlin, E. (eds) (2000), *New Managerialism, New Welfare?* London: Sage.

Clatworthy, M., Mellett, H., and Peel, M. (2000), 'Corporate governance under "new public management": an exemplification', *Corporate Governance* 8(2), 166–77.

Clegg, H., and Chester, T. (1957), *Wage Policy and the Health Service*. Oxford: Blackwell.

Coker, N. (2001), *Racism in Medicine: An Agenda for Change*. London: King's Fund.

Cole, A. (2002), 'Chief executives: further to fall', *Health Service Journal* 112(5809), 28–31.

Colling, T. (1999), 'Tendering and outsourcing working in the contract state?', in S. Corby and G. White (eds), *Employee Relations in the Public Services*. London: Routledge.

Commission for Health Improvement (2001a), *Clinical Governance Review: Eastern Trust*. London: Commission for Health Improvement.

Commission for Health Improvement (2001b), *Annual Report 2000–01*. London: Commission for Health Improvement. *www.chi.nhs.uk*

Commission for Health Improvement (2002a), *Clinical Governance Review: Northern Trust*. London: Commission for Health Improvement.

Commission for Health Improvement (2002b), *Clinical Governance Review: Western Trust*. London: Commission for Health Improvement.

Cooper, A. (2002), 'Trust in health', in E. Vaizey, (ed.) *The Blue Book on Health: Radical Thinking on the NHS*. London: Politico's.

Cooper, D. J., Greenwood, R., Hinings, C. R., and Brown J. L. (1996), 'Sedimentation and transformation in organizational change: the case of Canadian law firms', *Organization Studies* 17(4), 623–47.

Cope, S., and Goodship, J. (1999), 'Regulating collaborative government: towards joined-up government?', *Public Policy and Administration* 14(2), 3–16

Corby, S. (1992), 'Industrial relations developments in NHS trusts', *Employee Relations* 14(6), 33–44.

Corby, S. (2000), 'Employee relations in the public services: a paradigm shift?', *Public Policy and Administration* 15(3) 60–74.

Corby, S., Millward, L., White, G., Drucker, J., and Meerabeau, E. (2001), *Innovations in Pay and Grading in NHS Trusts*. Greenwich: University of Greenwich.

Cousins, C. (1987), *Controlling Social Welfare: A Sociology of State Welfare Work and Organizations*. Brighton: Wheatsheaf.

Cully, M., O'Reilly, A., Millward, N., Forth, J., Woodland, S., Dix, G., and Bryson, A. (1998), *The 1998 Workplace Employee Relations Survey: First Findings*. London: DTI.

Cully, M., Woodland, S., O'Reilly, A., and Dix, G. (1999), *Britain at Work*. London: Routledge.

Currie, G., and Procter, S. (2001), 'Exploring the relationship between HR and middle managers', *Human Resource Management Journal* 11(3), 53–69.

Cutler, T., and Waine, B. (1997), *Managing the Welfare State*, 2nd edn. Oxford: Berg.

Day, P., and Klein, R. (2001), *Steering But Not Rowing?* Available at: *www.ncl.ac.uk/politics/whitehall/briefings/briefing4.html*

Dent, M., and Whitehead, S. (2002), *Managing Professional Identities: Knowledge, Performativity and the 'New' Professional*. London: Taylor & Francis.

Department of Health (1989), *Working for Patients*, Cm. 555. London: HMSO.

Department of Health (1997), *The New NHS: Modern, Dependable*, Cm. 3807. London: The Stationery Office.

Department of Health (1998), *Working Together: Securing a Quality Workforce for the NHS*. London: Department of Health.

Department of Health (1999a), *Agenda for Change: Modernising the NHS Pay System*. London: Department of Health.

Department of Health (1999b), *Making a Difference: Strengthening the Nursing, Midwifery and Health Visiting Contribution to Health and Healthcare*. London: Department of Health.

Department of Health (2000a), *The NHS Plan: A Plan for Investment, A Plan for Reform*. London: Department of Health.

Department of Health (2000b), *The Vital Connection: An Equalities Framework for the NHS*. Leeds: NHS Executive.

Department of Health (2001a), *Shifting the Balance of Power within the NHS: Securing Delivery*. Available at: *www.doh.gov.uk/shiftingthebalance/index.htm*

Department of Health (2001b), *Review Body for Nursing Staff, Midwives, Health Vistors and Professions Allied to Medicine: Review for 2002*. Written evidence from the Health Departments for Great Britain. London: Department of Health.

Department of Health (2001c), *Review Body on Doctors' and Dentists' Remuneration*. Written evidence from the Health Departments for Great Britain. London: Department of Health.

Department of Health (2002a), *HR in the NHS Plan*. London: Department of Health.

Department of Health (2002b), *Improvement, Expansion and Reform: The Next Three Years. Priorities and Planning Framework 2003–2006*. London: Department of Health.

Department of Health (2002c), *Delivering the NHS Plan: Next Steps on Investment, Next Steps on Reform*. London: The Stationery Office.

Department of Health (2002d), *NHS Hospital and Community Health Services Non-medical Staff in England: 1991–2001*. London: Department of Health.

Department of Health (2002e), *Chief Executive's Report to the NHS March 2001-April 2002*. London: Department of Health.

Department of Health (2002f), *Agenda for Change – Update*. Available at: *www.doh.gov.uk/agendaforchange/brief-syn.htm*

Department of Health (2002g), *Bulletin on Knowledge and Skills Framework* (issued 5 March). London: Department of Health.

Dillon, J. (2000), 'How New Labour blew £1bn on "expert" advice', *Independent on Sunday*, 28 May, 4.

DiMaggio, P., and Powell, W. (1983), 'The iron cage revisited: institutional isomorphism and collective rationality in organizational fields', *American Sociological Review* 48 (April), 147–60.

Dixon, J. (2001), 'Health care: modernising the leviathan', *Political Quarterly* 72(1), 30–8.

Dowling, B., Wilkin, D., and Coleman, A. (2002), 'Management in primary care groups and trusts', *British Journal of Health Care Management* 8(1), 12–15.

Dunleavy, P., and Hood, C. (1994), 'From old public administration to new public management', *Public Money and Management* (July–September), 9–16.

Dyson, R. (1979), 'Consultation and negotiation', in N. Bosanquet (ed.), *Industrial Relations in the NHS: The Search for a System*. London: King's Fund.

Edwards, B. (1993), *The National Health Service: A Manager's Tale 1946–1992*. London: Nuffield Provincial Hospitals Trust.

Edwards, C., and Robinson, O. (2001), ' "Better" part-time jobs? A study of part-time working in nursing and the police', *Employee Relations* 23(5), 438–53.

Edwards, P. K. (1986), *Conflict at Work*. Oxford: Blackwell.

Edwards, P. K. (2001), 'Industrial relations: from apparently anachronic to analeptic and anaclastic condition'. Paper presented at the 'Industrial Relations: An Anachronism' conference. University of Tubingen, June.

Edwards, P. K., and Scullion, H. (1982), *The Social Organisation of Workplace Conflict*. Oxford: Blackwell.

Edwards, P. K., and Whitston, C. (1993), *Attending to Work: The Management of Attendance and Shopfloor Order*. Oxford: Blackwell.

Ellwood, S. (1996), 'Full-cost pricing rules within the National Health Service internal market: accounting choices and the achievement of productive efficiency', *Management Accounting Research* 7(1), 25–51.

Escott, K., and Whitfield, D. (1995), *The Gender Impact of CCT in Local Government*, Equal Opportunities Commission Research Series, No. 12. Manchester: EOC.

Esping-Andersen, G. (1990), *The Three Worlds of Welfare Capitalism*. Cambridge: Polity Press.

Etzioni, A. (1969), *The Semi-Professions and their Organisation*. New York: Free Press.

Exworthy, M., and Halford, S. (eds) (1999), *Professionals and the New Managerialism in the Public Sector*. Buckingham: Open University Press.

Fairbrother, P. (2000), *Trade Unions at the Crossroads*. London: Mansell.

Fairbrother, P., and Poynter, G. (2001), 'State restructuring: managerialism marketisation and the implications for Labour', *Competition and Change* 5(3), 311–33.

Farnham, D., and Horton, S. (1996), 'Continuity and change in the public services', in D. Farnham and S. Horton (eds), *Managing People in the Public Services*. Basingstoke: Macmillan.

Ferlie, E., Ashburner, L., Fitzgerald, L., and Pettigrew, A. (1996), *The New Public Management in Action*. Oxford: Oxford University Press.

Ferner, A. (1988), *Governments, Managers and Industrial Relations*. Oxford: Blackwell.

Finlayson, B. (2002), *Counting the Smiles: Morale and Motivation in the NHS*. London: King's Fund.

Foster, A. (2002), 'Expressions of interest in early implementation of the new NHS pay system (Agenda for Change)', Letter to Chief Executives of NHS Trusts, 2 July. Available at *www.doh.gov.uk/agendaforchange*

Foster, D., and Scott, P. (1998), 'Competitive tendering of public services and industrial relations policy: the Conservative agenda under Thatcher and Major', *Historical Studies in Industrial Relations* 6 (Autumn), 101–32.

Foster, H., Smyth, J., and Hateley, W. (1985), 'Towards a more flexible pay bargaining system in the NHS', *Hospital and Health Services Review* 82(1), 23–6.

Fox, A. (1974), *Beyond Contract: Work, Power and Trust Relations*. London: Faber & Faber.

Fredman, S., and Morris G. (1989), *The State as Employer: Labour Law in the Public Services*. London: Mansell.

Freeman, R. (2000), *The Politics of Health In Europe*. Manchester: Manchester University Press.

Friedson, E.(1970), *Profession of Medicine: A Study in the Sociology of Applied Knowledge*. New York: Dodd, Mead.

Futures Group (2002), *The Future of the NHS: A Framework for Debate*. London: King's Fund.

Gallie, D., White, M., Cheng, Y., and Tomlinson, M. (1998), *Restructuring the Employment Relationship*. Oxford: Clarendon Press.

Gamble, A., and Kelly, G. (2001), 'New Labour's economics', in S. Ludlam and M. Smith (eds), *New Labour in Government.* London: Macmillan.

Giddens, A. (1990), *The Consequences of Modernity.* Cambridge: Cambridge University Press.

Glouberman, S. (1996), 'Some dimensions of restructuring', in S. Glouberman (ed.), *Beyond Restructuring.* London: King's Fund.

Gray, A., and Jenkins, B. (1995), 'From public administration to public management: reassessing a revolution?', *Public Administration* 73(1), 75–99.

Green, F. (2001), 'It's been a hard day's night: the concentration and intensification of work in late twentieth-century Britain', *British Journal of Industrial Relations* 39(1), 53–81.

Griffiths, R. (1983), *Report of the NHS Management Inquiry.* London: Department of Health and Social Security.

Grimshaw, D. (1999), 'Changes in skills-mix and pay determination among the nursing workforce in the UK', *Work, Employment and Society* 13(2), 295–329.

Grimshaw, D. (2000), 'The problem with pay flexibility: changing pay practices in the UK health sector', *International Journal of Human Resource Management* 11(5), 943–66.

Grimshaw, D., Kersholt, F., Lefevre, G., and Wilthagen, T. (2000), 'Working time transitions and employment statuses in the British, French and Dutch health-care sectors', in J. O'Reilly, I. Cebrian and M. Lallement (eds), *Working-Time Changes: Social Integration Through Transitional Labour Markets.* Cheltenham: Edward Elgar.

Guest, D. (1995), 'Human resource management, trade unions and industrial relations', in J. Storey) (ed.), *Human Resource Management: A Critical Text.* London: Routledge.

Guest, D. (2001), 'Industrial relations and human resource management', in J. Storey (ed.), *Human Resource Management: A Critical Text, 2nd edn.* London: Thomson Learning.

Guest, D., and Peccei, R. (1993), *The Effectiveness of Personnel Management in the NHS.* London: NHS Management Executive.

Guillebaud, C. (1956), *Report of the Committee of Enquiry into the Cost of the National Health Service,* Cmnd. 9663. London: HMSO.

Halpern, S. (1983), 'Manpower planning', *Health and Social Service Journal,* 17 February, 196–7.

Ham, C. (1986), *Managing Health Services: Health Authority Members in Search of a Role.* Bristol: University of Bristol.

Hancock, C. (1979), 'Special industrial relations problems in nursing', in N. Bosanquet (ed.), *Industrial Relations in the NHS: The Search for a System.* London: King's Fund.

Hancock, C. (1995), 'Is Local Pay Worth the Trouble?', *Health Service Journal* 105(5460), 19.

Hargadon, J. (1993), 'NHS trusts: two provider perspectives', in E. Peck and P. Spurgeon (eds), *NHS Trusts in Practice*. Harlow: Longman.

Harrison, A., and Dixon, J. (2000), *The NHS: Facing the Future*. London: King's Fund.

Harrison S. (2002), 'New Labour, modernisation and the medical labour process', *Journal of Social Policy* 31(2) 465–85.

Health Committee (1992), *NHS Trusts: Interim Conclusions and Proposals for Future Inquiries*. London: HMSO.

Health Committee (2002), *The Role of the Private Sector in the NHS*, First Report, London: The Stationery Office.

Heaton, N., Mason, B., and Morgan, J. (2001), 'Partnership and multi-unionism in the health service', *Industrial Relations Journal*, 33(2), 112–26.

Hood, C. (2000), *The Art of the State: Culture, Rhetoric and Public Management*. Oxford: Clarendon Press.

Hood, C. (2001), 'Public service managerialism: onwards and upwards or Trobriand cricket again?' *Political Quarterly* 72(3), 300–14.

Hood, C., James, O., and Scott, C. (2000), 'Regulation of government: has it increased, is it increasing, should it be diminished?', *Public Administration* 78(2), 283–304.

Hughes, D. (1991), 'The reorganisation of the National Health Service: the rhetoric and the reality of the internal market', *The Modern Law Review* 54(1), 88–103.

Hunter, D. (2002), 'A tale of two tribes: the tension between managerial and professional values', in B. New and J. Neuberger (eds), *Hidden Assets*. London: King's Fund.

Hurst, K. (1995), *Progress with Patient Focused Care in the United Kingdom*. Leeds: NHS Executive/Nuffield Institute for Health.

Hutton, W. (1996), 'Time-bomb ticks away on the wards', *The Guardian*, 20 March, 17.

Hutton, W. (2000), *New Life for Health: The Commission on the NHS Chaired by Will Hutton*. London: Vintage.

Iliffe, S. (2002), 'An alternative NHS reform', *Health Matters*, (Spring) 1–4. Available at *www.healthmatters.org.uk*

Incomes Data Services (2000a), 'Equal pay', *IDS Report* 805, 10–13.

Incomes Data Services (2000b), 'Pay in the public services review of 1999, prospects for 2000'.

Incomes Data Services (2001), 'Public sector pay in 2001', *IDS Report* 839, 8–15.

Industrial Relations Services (1993), 'Local bargaining in the NHS: a survey of first- and second-wave trusts', *Employment Trends* 537, 7–16. London: IRS.

Industrial Relations Services (1995), 'Annual review of pay and work practices: a survey of 180 NHS Trusts', *Health Service Report* 5, 6–11. London: IRS.

Industrial Relations Services (1997), 'Annual review of pay and employment practices part one: a survey of 137 NHS trusts, *Health Service Report* 16, 2–11.

Industrial Relations Services (1999), 'Working towards common HR goals: the state of play in 75 trusts', *Health Service Report* 24, 4–13.

Industrial Relations Services (2001a), 'Partners in care', *Health Service Report* 31 (Summer), 14–17.

Industrial Relations Services (2001b), 'HR in the health service: the story so far', *Employment Trends* 734 (August), 7–12.

Industrial Relations Services (2001c), 'Public sector pay in 2001–02', *Employment Trends* 742 (December), 16–25.

Institute of Personnel and Development (1997), *The IPD Guide on Broadbanding.* London: IPD.

Jarrold, K. (1995), Untitled letter to NHS trust chief executives, 11 April, EL (95) 49. Leeds: NHS Executive.

Johnston, P. (1994), *Success While Others Fail: Social Movement Unionism and the Public Workplace.* Ithaca: ILR Press.

Jolley, M., and Brykczyñska, G. (eds) (1993), *Nursing: Its Hidden Agendas.* London: Edward Arnold.

Jones, E. (1999), *Job Evaluation Comparison Project.* Report to the NHS job evaluation working party. Unpublished.

Kalleberg, A. (2001), 'Organising flexibility: the flexible firm in a new century', *British Journal of Industrial Relations* 39(4), 479–505.

Katz, H., and Darbishire, O. (2000), *Converging Divergences: Worldwide Changes in Employment Systems.* Ithaca: Cornell University Press.

Kelly, J. (1996), 'Union militancy and social partnership', in P. Ackers, C. Smith and P. Smith (eds), *The New Workplace and Trade Unionism.* London: Routledge.

Kelly, J. (1998), *Rethinking Industrial Relations: Mobilization, Collectivism and Long Waves.* London: Routledge.

Kennedy, I. (2001), *The Report of the Public Inquiry into Children's Heart Surgery at the Bristol Royal Infirmary 1984–1995: Learning from Bristol,* Cm. 5207(i). London: The Stationery Office. Available at: *www.bristol-inquiry.org.uk*

Kessler, I. (2000), 'Remuneration systems', in S. Bach and K. Sisson (eds), *Personnel Management: A Comprehensive Guide to Theory and Practice* 3rd edn. Oxford: Blackwell.

Kessler, I., and Heron, P. (2001), 'Steward organization in a professional union: the case of the Royal College of Nursing', *British Journal of Industrial Relations* 39(3), 367–91.

Kessler, I., and Purcell, J. (1996), 'Strategic choice and new forms of employment relations in the public service sector: developing an analytical framework', *International Journal of Human Resource Management* 7(1), 206–29.

Kessler, I., Purcell, J., and Coyle Shapiro, J. (2000), 'New forms of employment relations in the public services: the limits of strategic choice', *Industrial Relations Journal* 31(1), 17–34.

King's Fund/NAHA (1985), *NHS Pay: A Time for Change*. London: King's Fund.

Kitchener, M. (1999) 'All fur coat and no knickers', in D. Brock, M. Powell, and C. R. Hinings (eds), *Restructuring Professional Organization: Accounting, Health Care and Law*. London: Routledge.

Klaushofer, A. (2000), 'Homa's odyssey', *The Stakeholder* 4(2), 10–11.

Klein, R. (2001), *The New Politics of the National Health Service*, 4th edn. London: Prentice Hall.

Kochan, T., Katz, H., and McKersie, R. (1994), *The Transformation of American Industrial Relations*, 2nd edn. Ithaca: Cornell University Press.

Labour Party (2001), *New Ambitions for Our Country*, Election Manifesto. London: Labour Party.

Laffin, M. (1998), 'The professions in the contemporary public sector', in M. Laffin (ed.), *Beyond Bureaucracy*. Aldershot: Ashgate.

Lane, N. (1999), 'Inequality in the careers of NHS nurses: a regional case study of qualified nurses in NHS Wales', *Personnel Review* 28(4), 319–36.

Langlands, A. (1994), 'Local pay determination', letter to chief executives of NHS trusts, 6 June. Leeds: NHS Executive.

Lapsley, I., Llewellyn, S., and Burnett, G. (1998), *Inside Hospital Trusts: Management Styles, Accounting Regimes*. Edinburgh: Institute of Chartered Accountants of Scotland.

Lea, R. (2002), 'Healthcare in the UK: where do we go from here?', in E. Vaizey (ed.), *The Blue Book on Health: Radical Thinking on the Future of the NHS*. London: Politico's.

Lee-Potter, J. (1997), *A Damn Bad Business: The NHS Deformed*. London: Victor Gollancz.

Le Grand, J. (1994), 'Evaluating the NHS reforms', in R. Robinson and J. Le Grand (eds), *Evaluating the NHS Reforms*. London: King's Fund.

Le Grand, J. (1997), 'Knights, knaves or pawns? Human behaviour and social policy', *Journal of Social Policy* 26(2), 149–69.

Le Grand, J., Mays, N., and Dixon, J. (1998), 'The reforms: success or failure or neither?', in J. Le Grand, N. Mays and J. Mulligan (eds), *Learning from the NHS Internal Market: A Review of the Evidence*. London: King's Fund.

Le Grand, J., Mays, N., and Mulligan, J. (1998), *Learning from the NHS Internal Market: A Review of the Evidence*. London: King's Fund.

Leys, C. (2001), *Market-Driven Politics: Neoliberal Democracy and the Public Interest*. London: Verso.

Light, D. (2001), 'Managed competition, governmentality and institutional response in the United Kingdom', *Social Science and Medicine*, 52(8), 1167–81.

Lloyd, C. (1997), 'Decentralization in the NHS: prospects for workplace unionism', *British Journal of Industrial Relations* 35(3), 427–46.

Loveridge, R. (1971), *Collective Bargaining by National Employees in the United Kingdom*. Michigan: University of Michigan.

Lugsden, E. (2001), 'PFI and trade unions: a test of partnership?', paper presented at the BUIRA Annual conference, Manchester, Manchester Metropolitan University, 5–7 July.

Lupton, B., and Shaw, S. (2001), 'Are public sector personnel managers the profession's poor relations?', *Human Resource Management Journal* 11(3), 23–38.

Lyon, D. (1999), *Postmodernity*, 2nd edn. Buckingham: Open University Press.

Marginson, P., Edwards, P., Armstrong, P., and Purcell, J. (1995), 'Strategy, structure and control in the changing corporation: a survey-based investigation', *Human Resource Management Journal* 5(2), 3–27.

Marsden, D., and French, S. (1998), *What a Performance: Performance Related Pay in the Public Services*. London: Centre for Economic Performance, LSE.

Mather, G. (1991), *Government by Contract*. London: Institute of Economic Affairs.

McCarthy, W. (1976), *Making Whitley Work*. London: HMSO.

McCarthy, M. (1983a), 'Personnel management in the health service', *Personnel Management* (September), 31–3.

McCarthy, M. (1983b), *A New System of Pay Determination for the NHS: A Contribution to the Debate*. London: King's Fund.

McIlroy, J. (1995), *Trade Unions in Britain Today*. Manchester: Manchester University Press.

Meadows, S., Levenson, R., and Baeza, J. (2000) *The Last Straw: Explaining the NHS Shortage*. London: King's Fund.

Merrison, A. (1979), *Royal Commission on the National Health Service*, Cmnd. 7615. London: HMSO.

Milburn, A. (2001), *Speech to Chief Nursing Officers Annual Conference*, Harrogate, 14 November. London: Department of Health.

Millward, N., Bryson, A., and Forth, J. (2000), *All Change at Work?* London: Routledge.

Millward, N., Stevens, M., Smart, D., and Hawes, W. (1992), *Workplace Industrial Relations in Transition*. Aldershot: Dartmouth.

Mintzberg, H. (1979), *The Structuring of Organizations: A Synthesis of the Research*. Englewood Cliffs: Prentice Hall.

Mintzberg, H. (1996), 'Managing government, governing management', *Harvard Business Review* (May–June), 75–83.

Moran, M. (1999), *Governing the Health Care State: A Comparative Study of the United Kingdom, the United States and Germany*. Manchester: Manchester University Press.

Morgan, P. and Allington, N. (2002), 'Has the public sector retained its "model employer" status? *Public Money and Management* (January–March), 35–42.

Morris, G. (1999), 'Fragmenting the state: implications for accountability for employment practices in public service', *Public Law* (Spring), 64–84.

Morris, G. (2000), 'Employment in public services: the case for special treatment', *Oxford Journal of Legal Studies* 20(2), 167–83.

MSF (1992), *Skill Mix in Community Nursing*. London: MSF.

MSF (2000a), 'Equal pay – best therapy of all', *NHS News* 3 (July), 9–12.

MSF (2000b), *What's the Point? Discretionary Points or Discriminatory Points*. London: MSF/CPHVA.

Mullard, M. (1997), 'The politics of public expenditure control: a problem of politics or language games', *Political Quarterly* 68(3), 266–75.

Mullard, M. (2001), 'New Labour, new public expenditure: the case of cake tomorrow', *Political Quarterly* 72, 310–21.

Munro, A. (1999), *Work, Women and Trade Unions*. London: Mansell.

Munro, A. (2002), 'Working together – involving staff', *Employee Relations* 24(3), 277–89.

NAHAT (1994), *Approaches to Pay and Reward by NHS Trusts*. Birmingham: NAHAT.

NALGO (1984), *Two Steps Back: How NALGO Views the Introduction of the Griffiths Plans for NHS Management*. London: NALGO.

National Audit Office (2001), *Inappropriate Adjustments to NHS Waiting Lists*. London: National Audit Office.

National Audit Office (2002), *NHS Summarised Accounts 2000–01*. London: National Audit Office.

National Board for Prices and Income (1971), *The Pay and Conditions of Ancillary Workers in the National Health Service*, Report No. 166, Cmnd. 3230. London. HMSO.

NHS Executive (1995a), *Local Pay: Guidance for Purchasers*, EL (95) 34. Leeds: NHS Executive.

NHS Executive (1995b), *Management Costs in NHS Trusts: Financial Year 1994–95*. Leeds: NHS Executive.

NHS Executive (1997), *Managing Human Resources in the NHS: A Service Wide Approach*. Leeds: NHS Executive.

NHS Executive (1998), *Discretionary Points*, Advance Letter (NM) 2/98. Leeds: NHS Executive.

NHS Executive (1999a), *The NHS Performance Assessment Framework*. Leeds: NHSE.

NHS Executive (1999b), *Managers' Guide: Stopping Violence Against Staff Working in the NHS*. Available at: *www.doh.gov.uk/zero.htm*

NHS Management Executive (1992), *NHS Reforms: The First Six Months*. Leeds: NHSME.

Newman, J. (2001), *Modernising Governance: New Labour, Policy and Society*. London: Sage.

Niskanen, W. (1971), *Bureaucracy and Representative Government*. Chicago: Aldine Atherton.

Nurses' Pay Review Body (1992), *Ninth Report*, Cm. 1811. London: HMSO.

Nurses' Pay Review Body (1994), *Eleventh Report*, Cm. 2462. London: HMSO.

Nurses' Pay Review Body (1996), *Thirteenth Report*, Cm. 3092. London: The Stationery Office.

Nurses' Pay Review Body (1997), *Fourteenth Report*, Cm. 3538. London: The Staterionery Office.

Nurses' Pay Review Body (1998), *Fifteenth Report*, Cm. 3832. London: The Stationery Office.

Nurses' Pay Review Body (1999), *Sixteenth Report*, Cm. 4240. London: The Stationery Office.

Nurses' Pay Review Body (2000), *Seventeenth Report*, Cm. 4563. London: The Stationery Office.

Nurses' Pay Review Body (2001), *Eighteenth Report*, Cm. 4991. London: The Stationery Office.

Nurses' Pay Review Body (2002), *Nineteenth Report*, Cm. 5345. London: The Stationery Office.

Nursing and Midwifery Staffs Negotiating Council Staff Side (1998), *Guidance on Implementing Discretionary Points*. London: NMNC.

OECD (2000), Health Data. Paris: OECD. Available at: *www.oecd.org/els/health/software/fad16.htm*

OECD (2002), Health Data. Paris: OECD. Available at: *www.oecd.org*

Offe, C. (1985), *Disorganized Capitalism*. Cambridge: Polity Press.

Office of Public Services Reform (2002), *Reforming Our Public Services*. London: The Prime Minister's Office of Public Service Reform.

Osborne, D., and Gaebler, T. (1992), *Reinventing Government: How the Entrepreneurial Spirit is Transforming the Public Sector*. Reading, Mass.: Addison Wesley.

Paige, V. (1987), 'The development of general management within the NHS', *The Health Summary* (June), 6–8.

Paton, C. (1999), 'New Labour's health policy: the new healthcare state', in M. Powell, (ed.), *New Labour, New Welfare State? The 'Third Way' in British Social Policy*. Bristol: Polity Press.

Paton, C. (2002), 'Cheques and checks: New Labour's record on the NHS', in M. Powell (ed.), *Evaluating New Labour's Welfare Reforms*. Bristol: Polity Press.

Paton, C., with Hunt, K., Birch, K., and Jordan, K. (1998), *Competition and Planning in the NHS: The Consequences of the NHS Reforms*. Cheltenham: Stanley Thornes.

Perry, A. (1993), 'A sociologist's view: the handmaiden's theory', in M. Jolley and G. Brykczyñska (eds), *Nursing: Its Hidden Agendas*. London: Edward Arnold.

Pfeffer, J. (1998), *The Human Equation: Building Profits by Putting People First*. Boston, Mass. Harvard Business School Press.

Pollitt, C., and Bouckaert, G. (2000), *Public Management Reform: A Comparative Analysis*. Oxford: Oxford University Press.

Pollitt, C., Harrison, S., Hunter, D., and Marnoch, G. (1991), 'General management in the NHS: the initial impact 1983–1988', *Public Administration* 69(1), 61–83.

Potter, A. (2000), 'Current crisis is legacy of the managed market', *British Journal of Health Care Management* 6(2), 71–3.

Power, M. (1997), *The Audit Society: Rituals of Verification*. London: Oxford University Press.

Poynter, G. (2000), *Restructuring in the Service Industries: Management Reform and Workplace Relations in the UK Service Industry*. London: Mansell.

Pratchett, L., and Wingfield, M. (1996), 'The demise of the public service ethos', in L. Pratchett and D. Wilson (eds), *Local Democracy and Local Government*. London: Macmillan.

Procter, S., and Currie, G. (1999), 'The role of the personnel function: roles, processes and perceptions in an NHS trust', *International Journal of Human Resource Management* 10(6), 1077–91.

Public Administration Select Committee (2002), *The Public Service Ethos*, Seventh Report of Session 2001–02, vol. 1. London: The Stationery Office.

Purcell, J. (2001), 'The meaning of strategy in human resource management', in J. Storey (ed.), *Human Resource Management: A Critical Text*, 2nd edn. London: Thomson Learning.

Purcell, J., and Ahlstrand, B. (1994), *Human Resource Management in the Multi-Divisional Firm*. Oxford: Oxford University Press.

Ranson, S., and Stewart, J. (1994), *Management for the Public Domain: Enabling the Learning Society*. Basingstoke: Macmillan.

Rawlings, M. (1999), 'In pursuit of quality: the National Institute for Clinical Excellence', *The Lancet* 353(9158), 1079–82.

Review Body on Doctors' and Dentists' Remuneration (1999), *Twenty-Eighth Report*, Cm. 4243. London: The Stationery Office.

Rhodes, R. (1996), *Understanding Governance: Policy Networks, Governance, Reflexivity and Accountability*. Buckingham: Open University Press.

Robinson, R., and Le Grand, J. (1994), *Evaluating the NHS Reforms*. London: King's Fund.

Rosenthal, M. (2002), 'Medical professional autonomy in an era of accountability and regulation', in M. Dent and S. Whitehead (eds), *Managing Professional Identities: Knowledge, Performativity and the 'New' Professional*. London: Taylor & Francis.

Royal College of Nursing (2001), *Widening Membership to Health Care Assistants and Nurse Cadets*. London: RCN.

Royal College of Nursing (2002), *Working Well?* London: RCN.

Salmon, B. (1966), *Report of the Committee on Senior Nursing Staff Structure*. London: HMSO.

Salvage, J. (1985), *The Politics of Nursing*. London: Heinemann.

Scott, A. (1994), *Willing Slaves: British Workers Under Human Resource Management*. Cambridge: Cambridge University Press.

Seifert, R. (1992), *Industrial Relations in the NHS*. London: Chapman & Hall.

Self, P. (2000), *Rolling Back the Market: Economic Dogma and Political Choice*. Basingstoke: Macmillan.

Shaoul, J. (1996), *NHS Trusts: A Capital Way of Operating*, Department of Accounting and Finance Working Paper. Manchester: University of Manchester.

Shaoul, J. (1999), 'The economic and financial context: the shrinking state?', in S. Corby and G. White (eds), *Employee Relations in the Public Services: Themes and Issues*. London: Routledge.

Sisson, K. (1995), 'Change and continuity in British industrial relations: "strategic choice" or "muddling through"?' in R. Locke, T. Kochan, and M. Piore (eds), *Employment Relations in a Changing World Economy*. Cambridge, Mass: MIT.

Sisson, K. (2001), 'Human resource management and the personnel function: a case of partial impact?', in J. Storey (ed.), *Human Resource Management: A Critical Text*. London: Thomson Learning.

Small, N., and Baker, M. (1994), 'The first year: a view from a trust hospital management', in S. Harrison and N. Freemantle (eds), *Working for Patients: Early Research Findings*. Leeds: Nuffield Institute.

Social Services Committee (1984), *Griffiths NHS Management Inquiry Report. First Report from the Social Services Committee, Session 1983–4*. London: HMSO.

Steele, J. (2000), 'Public sector ethos still alive but undervalued', *British Journal of Health Care Management* 6(1), 15–17.

Stephens, P. (2001), 'The Treasury under Labour', in A. Seldon (ed.), *The Blair Effect: The Blair Government 1997–2001*. London: Little, Brown & Co.

Storey, J. (2001), 'Human resource management today: an assessment', in J. Storey (ed.), *Human Resource Management: A Critical Text*, 2nd edn. London: Thomson Learning.

Storey, J., and Quintas, P. (2001), 'Knowledge management and HRM', in J. Storey (ed.), *Human Resource Management: A Critical Text*, 2nd edn. London: Thomson Learning.

Stuart, M., and Martinez Lucio, M. (2000), 'Renewing the model employer: changing employment relations and "partnership" in the health and private sectors', *Journal of Management in Medicine* 14(5–6), 311–25.

Talbot, C. (1994), *Reinventing Public Management: A Survey of Public Sector Managers' Reaction to Change*. Corby: Institute of Management.

Terry, M. (1996), 'Negotiating the government of Unison: union democracy in theory and practice', *British Journal of Industrial Relations* 34(1), 87–110.

Terry, M. (2000), in M. Terry (ed.), *Redefining Public Sector Unionism: Unison and the Future of Trade Unions*. London: Routledge.

Thompson, M. (2001), 'Trust chief steps down days before CHI report', *Health Service Journal* 111(5768), 4–5.

Thornley, C. (1995), 'The model employer myth: the need for theoretical renewal in public sector industrial relations', paper to the 13th Labour Process Conference, Blackpool, April.

Thornley, C. (1998), 'Contesting local pay: the decentralization of collective bargaining in the NHS', *British Journal of Industrial Relations* 36(3), 413–34.

Thornley, C., and Winchester, D. (1994), 'The remuneration of nursing personnel in the United Kingdom', in D. Marsden (ed.), *The Remuneration of Nursing Personnel*. Geneva: International Labour Office.

Thornton, S. (2002), 'There are no quick fixes, so ministers must hold their nerve', *Financial Times*, 18 April, 5.

Timmins, N. (2001), 'Health funding boost used to clear deficits', *Financial Times*, 12 July, 5.

Tonkiss, F., and Passey, A. (1999), 'Trust, confidence and voluntary organisations: between values and institutions', *Sociology*, 33(2), 257–74.

Traynor, M. (1999), *Managerialism and Nursing: Beyond Oppression and Profession*. London: Routledge.

Treasury (2001), *Public Sector Pay in 2002–03: Pay Guidance*. Unpublished.

Treasury (2002), *Budget 2002: The Strength to Make Long-Term Decisions: Investing in an Enterprising, Fairer Britain*. London: The Stationery Office.

Trinder, C. (1990), *Pay Flexibility in the National Health Service*. London: Public Finance Foundation.

Truss, C., Gratton, L., Hope-Hailey, V., Stiles, P., and Zaleska, J. (2002), 'Paying the piper: choice and constraint in changing HR functional roles', *Human Resource Management Journal* 12(2), 39–63.

TUC (1981), *Improving Industrial Relations in the NHS*. London: TUC.

Unison (1996), 'Future pay bargaining arrangements for the NHS and the eradication of low pay', report to the health group conference. Unpublished.

Unison (2002), *Healthcare Service Group Executive Report 2001/02*. London: Unison.

Unison/King's Fund (1999), *Crafting a Workforce for the Twenty First Century*. London: Unison.

Waddington, J., and Kerr, A. (1999), 'Trying to stem the flow: union membership turnover in the public sector', *Industrial Relations Journal*, 30(3), 183–95.

Wall, A. (1993), 'Trusts the reasons to be cautious', in E. Peck and P. Spurgeon (eds), *NHS Trusts in Practice*. Harlow: Longman.

Wanless, D. (2001) *Securing Our Future Health: Taking a Long-Term View*, Interim Report. London: Treasury.

Wanless, D. (2002), *Securing Our Future Health: Taking a Long-Term View:*, Final Report. London: Treasury.

Waugh, P. (2001), '"Corporate" NHS tells hospitals to scrap their logos', *The Independent*, 6 August, 5.

Webb, J. (1999), 'Work and the new public service class', *Sociology* 33(4), 747–66.

Weber, M. (1978), *Economy and Society*. Berkeley: University of California Press.

Webster, C. (2002), *The National Health Service: A Political History*, 2nd edn. Oxford: Oxford University Press.

West, P. (1997), *Understanding the National Health Service Reforms: The Creation of Incentives*. Buckingham: Open University Press.

White, G. (2000), 'Determining pay', in G. White and J. Drucker (eds), *Reward Management: A Critical Text.* London: Routledge.

Whittington, R. (1993), *What is Strategy and Does it Matter?* London: Routledge.

Wildavsky, A. (1979), *The Art and Craft of Policy Analysis.* London: Macmillan.

Williams, S., Michie, S., and Pattani, S. (1998), *Improving the Health of the NHS Workforce.* London: Nuffield Trust.

Winchester, D. (1983), 'Industrial relations in the public sector', in G. Bain (ed.), *Industrial Relations in Britain.* Oxford: Blackwell.

Winchester, D., and Bach, S. (1995), 'The state: the public sector', in P. K. Edwards (ed.), *Industrial Relations: Theory and Practice in Britain.* Oxford: Blackwell.

Winchester, D., and Bach, S. (1999), 'Britain: the transformation of public service employment relations', in S. Bach, L. Bordogna, G. Della Rocca and D. Winchester (eds), *Public Service Employment Relations in Europe: Transformation, Modernisation or Inertia?* London: Routledge.

Yin, R. (1994), *Case Study Research: Design and Methods.* London: Sage.

INDEX